This book makes an important contribution to the ongoing dialogue between Buddhism and Christianity while holding firmly to a Trinitarian theology of religions. It represents a wonderful example of careful listening to another religious tradition in order to properly appreciate and learn from it. Boonyakiat's work is a genuine conversation where Christians discover what they can learn from Buddhism, in ways that not only contribute to deeper contextualization of the gospel, but that can even contribute to a deeper Christian spirituality. The many intersections between these traditions are deeply probed to discern points where mutual learning is possible, even when the destinations of these paths is radically different. Highly recommended.

William A. Dyrness, DrThéol, Doctorandus
Dean Emeritus and Senior Professor of Theology and Culture,
Fuller Theological Seminary, Pasadena, California, USA

A Christian Theology of Suffering in the Context of Theravada Buddhism in Thailand by Satanun Boonyakiat is a groundbreaking work. It is a comparative work that contributes to our understanding of our diverse religious world in a way that allows the reader to carefully hear the relevance of other faith traditions in a manner that at once upholds the fundamental teaching and truth of Christianity even as it is courageously willing to gain insight from other faith perspectives. This work in particular offers a rare opportunity for an informed dialogue between Christianity and Theravada Buddhism in light of their shared interest in suffering and its relationship to the divine. Indeed, this work is the very conversation that is needed in mission understanding and work in our modern world that avoids the reflexive dead-end of either a deaf fundamentalist exclusivism or a naïve inclusive pluralism that ends in relativism. Readers will not be disappointed by this fine work.

Thomas Alan Harvey, PhD
Academic Dean,
Oxford Centre for Mission Studies, Oxford, UK

The problem of suffering is the problem not only for Christian theology but also for Buddhism. Among Christian theologians, few have reflected more profoundly on suffering, human and divine, than the German, Jürgen Moltmann. In this extraordinary comparative theological study, Professor Satanun Boonyakiat of Thailand, the current "home" of Theravada, brings Moltmann's Christian interpretation in a critical-sympathetic dialogue with the foundational and authoritative Buddhist teachings as presented in the Scriptures and by some leading contemporary teachers. The end result is a fascinating theological, pastoral, and missiological reflection.

Veli-Matti Kärkkäinen, DrThéol, Habil
Professor of Systematic Theology,
Fuller Theological Seminary, Pasadena, California, USA
Docent of Ecumenics, Faculty of Theology, University of Helsinki, Finland

A Christian Theology of Suffering in the Context of Theravada Buddhism in Thailand

Satanun Boonyakiat

MONOGRAPHS

© 2020 Satanun Boonyakiat

Published 2020 by Langham Monographs
An imprint of Langham Publishing

www.langhampublishing.org

Langham Publishing and its imprints are a ministry of Langham Partnership

Langham Partnership
PO Box 296, Carlisle, Cumbria, CA3 9WZ, UK
www.langham.org

ISBNs:
978-1-78368-786-2 Print
978-1-83973-030-6 ePub
978-1-83973-031-3 Mobi
978-1-83973-302-0 PDF

Satanun Boonyakiat has asserted his right under the Copyright, Designs and Patents Act, 1988 to be identified as the Author of this work.

All rights reserved. No part of this publication may be reproduced, stored in a retrieval system or transmitted, in any form or by any means, electronic, mechanical, photocopying, recording or otherwise, without the prior written permission of the publisher or the Copyright Licensing Agency.

Requests to reuse content from Langham Publishing are processed through PLSclear. Please visit www.plsclear.com to complete your request.

Scriptures taken from the Holy Bible, New International Version®, NIV®. Copyright © 1973, 1978, 1984, 2011 by Biblica, Inc.™ Used by permission of Zondervan.

British Library Cataloguing-in-Publication Data
A catalogue record for this book is available from the British Library.

ISBN: 978-1-78368-786-2

Cover & Book Design: projectluz.com

Langham Partnership actively supports theological dialogue and an author's right to publish but does not necessarily endorse the views and opinions set forth here or in works referenced within this publication, nor can we guarantee technical and grammatical correctness. Langham Partnership does not accept any responsibility or liability to persons or property as a consequence of the reading, use or interpretation of its published content.

Contents

Acknowledgements vii

Abstract xi

Abbreviations xiii

Introduction 1

Chapter 1 9
   A Trinitarian Theology of Religions and Trinitarian Comparative Theology
      A Christian Theology of Religions 10
         A Traditional Typology 12
         A More Comprehensive Typology 14
      A Comparative Theology 26
         Francis X. Clooney 27
         James L. Fredericks 31
         Keith Ward 32
         Towards a Trinitarian Comparative Theology 37
      The Trinity and Human Suffering 45
      Conclusion 50

Chapter 2 53
   The Reality of Human Suffering
      The Basic Understanding of Suffering in Buddhism 54
         The Founder of Buddhism 54
         The First Noble Truth: The Truth of Suffering (*Dukkha*) 56
         The Three Characteristics of Existence 60
      Theological Understanding of the Reality of Suffering ... 63
         The Reality and Complexity of Suffering in the Biblical Perspective 64
         Reexamination of the Traditional Theological Understanding of Suffering 68
      Conclusion 79

Chapter 3 83
   The Causes of Suffering
      The Truth of the Cause of Suffering (*Samudaya*) 84
         Tanhā 85
         Avijjā 87

>   The Law of Kamma 89
>   Theological Understanding of the Causes of Suffering 92
>   Suffering Is the Result of Sin: The Message of
>   Retribution Theology 93
>   Suffering Is the Result of Oppression: The Message of
>   Liberation Theology 101
>   Suffering Is a Mystery: The Message of the Book of Job 107
>   Conclusion 119
>
> Chapter 4 123
>   *The Ways to the Extinction of Suffering*
>   The Buddhist Way to the Extinction of Suffering 124
>   Right Understanding (*Sammādiṭṭhi*) 129
>   Right Thought (*Sammāsankappa*) 129
>   Right Speech (*Sammāvācā*) 130
>   Right Action (*Sammākammanta*) 130
>   Right Livelihood (*Sammā-ājīva*) 131
>   Right Effort (*Sammāvāyāma*) 132
>   Right Mindfulness (*Sammāsati*) 132
>   Right Meditation (*Sammāsamādhi*) 133
>   The Theological Understanding of the Way to the Extinction
>   of Suffering 137
>   Martin Luther's Theology of the Cross 139
>   Kazoh Kitamori's *Theology of the Pain of God* 142
>   Jürgen Moltmann's *The Crucified God* 144
>   Kosuke Koyama 149
>   Conclusion 155
>
> Conclusion 159
>
> Bibliography 171

Acknowledgements

The completion of this dissertation truly reflects the grace of God and support from several people and institutions. Therefore, I would like to thank God and give him all the glory. At the same time, I would like to express my deepest appreciation to the following people and institutions:

My best friend, co-worker, and beloved wife, Dr Sirikanya Boonyakiat, who always stands beside me, sharing experiences of joy and sorrow, and who has helped me become a better servant of the Lord.

My dad, Mr Sompratana Boonyakiat, who went home to be with the Lord fourteen years ago, but whose legacy remains the source of my inspiration. My mother, Mrs Montha Boonyakiat, who always loves, cares for, and supports me. My wonderful siblings, Assistant Professor Dr Yingmanee (Boonyakiat) Tragoolpua, Mr Preechawut Boonyakiat, and Mrs Weerunya (Boonyakiat) Pattanapichian, who have never stopped loving me and taking care of me.

My father-in-law, Mr Gate Sujinda – who has gone home to be with the Lord – my mother-in-law, Mrs Chamnian Sujinda, and my brothers-in-law, Assistant Professor Dr Khajornsak Tragoolpua and Mr Chanok Pattanapichian, for their love, support, and encouragement.

Dr Chaiyun and Mrs Margaret Ukosakul. Their love, care, wise counsel, and support really made a difference in my life and family.

Dr William A. Dyrness, my primary mentor at Fuller Theological Seminary. It is my honor and privilege to be his student. His advice and insights are very valuable. Without his support and encouragement, this work would not have been completed.

Dr Veli-Matti Kärkkäinen, my secondary mentor at Fuller Theological Seminary. He introduced me to a Christian theology of religions and superbly helped me understand more about a Christian theology of suffering.

His teaching, encouragement, and understanding made a difference in my study at Fuller.

Dr Terry Muck, Dean of the E. Stanley Jones School of World Mission and Evangelism and Professor of World Religion and Mission at Asbury Theological Seminary. It is my honor and privilege to have him as an external examiner for my dissertation. His suggestions were very helpful, and his encouragement is deeply appreciated.

The faculty and staff of the Center for Advanced Theological Studies, School of Theology, Fuller Theological Seminary, particularly Dr Robert A. Hurteau (former Program Director), Dr Eugen Matei (Program Director), Lindsay Weldon (former Program Assistant), and Ericka P. Bettge (Program Assistant).

The staff of the International Student Services Office who wonderfully helped me and my wife with our US visas.

Professor Dr Siddhi Butr-Indr, associate member of the Royal Institute of Thailand, and Professor Saeng Chandngarm, former dean of the Faculty of Humanities, Chiang Mai University, professor emeritus of Chiang Mai University and lecturer at Mahamakut Buddhist University, Lanna Campus, Chiang Mai. Both of them kindly accepted the invitation to be my supervisors for Buddhism. They helped me better understand the Buddhist concept of suffering as well as the Four Noble Truths.

Trinity Theological College, Singapore, for allowing me to conduct research in the college's library.

Ms Kris Garis and Mrs Lori Rowe, together with Mr Bruce Rowe, for their kind help in editing my work.

Rev William J. Yoder, former Dean of the McGilvary College of Divinity (formerly the McGilvary Faculty of Theology) and Payap University, for encouraging me to further my studies and granting me a study leave.

The faculty, staff, and students at the McGilvary College of Divinity for their prayers and encouragement. A special thank you to all faculty members who carried my teaching load when I was on a study leave.

John Stott Ministries and Langham Partnership International for their financial and spiritual support. Without this wonderful support, it would not be possible for me to complete a PhD program at Fuller Theological Seminary.

Mr Peter Chao, Dr John Ng, Mr Michael Tan, and Eagles Communications, Singapore, for their generous support and sincere friendship.

Rev Robert Collins, Rev Dr Esther Wakeman, Rev Glen Hallead, Dr Ratsamee Dangsuwon, and Dara Academy for their kind support and encouragement.

My uncle and aunt, Mr Vinij and Mrs Salinee Vrasira, who provided accommodation for us when we first went to the US and assisted us in many ways.

Rev Boonyawat Manopan, Rev Prinda Manowong, and the staff and members of the First Church of Chiang Mai for their prayers and encouragement.

Dr Amnuay and Mrs Siree Tapingkae, Mr Chumsaeng and Dr Wannapa Reongjareonsook, Mr and Mrs Snitwongse, Mr and Mrs Oonpanyo, Mr Khempet Yungtonglang, Mr Chairach Kijkuokool, Mr Kamalakar Duvvur, Mrs Bharathi Nuthalapati, Mr Patrick Tan, and members of Thai Mission Church, Sila Church, and the First Thai Presbyterian Church in USA. Their friendship, love, care, advice, and support mean a lot to me and my wife.

All my friends who have been supporting and praying for me the past few years. Although I cannot mention all of them by name, they have played a very important role in the completion of this work.

Abstract

In Thailand, the Buddhist concept of suffering, especially the doctrine of the Four Noble Truths, governs the understanding of Buddhists and influences the responses of Christians to the reality of human suffering. This dissertation is an attempt to develop a Christian theology of suffering that is relevant to the context of Theravada Buddhism in Thailand.

This study consists of four chapters. The first chapter is intended to justify the methodology of this dissertation, namely a trinitarian comparative theology of religions. This chapter indicates that a Christian theology of suffering that is relevant to the context of Theravada Buddhism in Thailand, yet is faithful to Christian belief, must be grounded in both a trinitarian theology of religions and trinitarian comparative theology.

Chapter 2 compares and contrasts the basic Buddhist and Christian understanding of suffering. The purposes of this chapter are to demonstrate the complexity of human suffering and to critically assess the assumption that all forms of suffering are not part of the created order.

Chapter 3 is a comparative study of the Buddhist and Christian understanding of the causes of suffering. This chapter aims to develop a Christian theological understanding of the causes of suffering that is relevant to the context of Theravada Buddhism in Thailand.

The final chapter intentionally brings this comparative study to the heart of Buddhalogy and the Christian theology of suffering – the Buddhist and Christian answers to the problem of human suffering. This chapter gives a brief discussion of the Third and Fourth Noble Truths as well as an examination of the Christian understanding of God's response to the problem of human suffering as found in a theology of the cross. Moreover, this chapter highlights major similarities and differences between Buddhalogy and the Christian theology of suffering, and proposes how Thai Christians should respond to the reality of suffering.

Abbreviations

AN	Anguttara Nikāya
A.V.	Avadāna Kalpalatā
D.	Dīgha Nikāya
HDT	*Heidelberg Disputation*
JBL	*Journal of Biblical Literature*
LW	*Luther's Works*
MN	Majjhima Nikāya
SN	Samyutta Nikāya
Ven	The Venerable
Vin.	Vinaya Pitaka
Vis. M.	Visuddhi Magga
WA	*Martin Luthers Werke*

Introduction

This, O Monks, is the Noble Truth of Suffering: Birth is suffering; decay is suffering; death is suffering. Sorrow, lamentation, pain, grief and despair are suffering. Presence of objects we hate is suffering; separation from objects we love is suffering; not to obtain what we desire is suffering. Briefly, the five groups of existence connected with clinging are suffering.

This, O Monks, is the Noble Truth of the Cause of Suffering: Craving, which leads to rebirth, accompanied by pleasure and lust, finding its delight here and there. It is the craving for pleasure, the craving for existence, the craving for non-existence or self-annihilation.

This, O Monks, is the Noble Truth of the extinction of Suffering: It is the complete fading away and extinction of this craving, its forsaking and giving up, liberation and detachment from it.

This, O Monks, is the Noble Truth of the Path which leads to the extinction of suffering: It is the Noble Eightfold Middle Path, that is to say, Right View, Right Aspiration, Right Speech, Right Conduct, Right Means of Livelihood, Right Endeavor, Right Mindfulness, Right Meditation.

Dhammacakkappavattana Sutta 11 (SN LVI.11)

Suffering is the universal experience of humankind, but it is undesirable for people of all ages, races, colors, statuses, and religions. For Buddhism, suffering lies at the center of the Buddha's teachings as the fundamental problem of all forms of existence. In his first sermon of *Dhammacakkappavattana Sutta*, the Buddha proclaimed the Four Noble Truths (*Arriyasacca*), which consist of the truths of suffering (*dukkha*), the cause of suffering (*samudaya*), the extinction of suffering (*nirodha*) and the path leading to the extinction of suffering (*magga*). What the Buddha was saying is that suffering is inescapable. Everyone who is still in the circle of birth and death (*Samsara*) is subject to suffering. One must be aware that desire or craving is the real cause of suffering and one can be free from the circle of birth and death if one's desire is quenched. One can accomplish this by taking control of one's own nature through the Noble Eightfold Path.

The Four Noble Truths govern Buddhists' view on human life and suffering. In fact, it is generally regarded as the fundamental doctrine of Buddhism. Saeng Chandngarm, a Thai Buddhist scholar, indicates that this doctrine is the core of Buddhism as it summarizes all doctrines of the Buddha in the *Tipitaka*. In addition, it includes the theoretical and practical aspects of Buddhism as well as the results of the practical aspects.[1] While the doctrine of Dependent Origination (*Paticcasamuppāda*) is essential, it cannot be the heart of Buddhism because it does not include the Eightfold Middle Path leading to the extinction of suffering. Similarly, while the Threefold Training (*Sikkhāttaya*) – training in higher morality, mentality, and wisdom – as well as the Fundamental Teaching (*Ovādapātimokkha*) – not to do any evil, to do good, and to purify the mind – are important, they are simply practical aspects of Buddhism.[2]

Furthermore, the Four Noble Truths are not foreign to Christians who belong to Buddhist countries, particularly Thailand – a Buddhist country where the number of Christians is less than one percent of the population.[3] All Thai people can remember the thrust of this doctrine. It is taught in the Buddhism course that is compulsory in all Thai schools, both public and private. Interwoven with Thai culture, customs, traditions, ceremonies, and festivals, it is an underlying belief that guides Thai cultural artifacts in several

---

1. Chandngarm, *Arriyasatsee*, 9–14.
2. Chandngarm, 39–40.
3. In 2005, Buddhists constituted 94.8 percent of the population, Muslims constituted 4.5 percent of the population, and Christians (includes Roman Catholics and Protestants) constituted 0.7 percent of the population. See National Statistical Office, *Statistical Yearbook of Thailand 2006*, 119.

forms, for example, folklore, poetry, drama, novel, fiction, and narrative. Karuna Kusalasaya, a well-known Thai Buddhist writer, rightly observes:

> In their long history of existence the Thais seem to have been predominantly Buddhists, at least ever since they came to contact with the tenets of Buddhism. All the Thai kings in the recorded history of present-day Thailand have been followers of Buddhism. The country's constitution specifies that the King of Thailand must be a Buddhist and the Upholder of Buddhism... Indeed, to the Thai nation as a whole, Buddhism has been the main spring from which flow its culture and philosophy, its art and literature, its ethics and morality and many of its folkways and festivals.[4]

Consequently, the Buddhist concept of suffering certainly governs the understanding of Thai Buddhists, and, at the same time, it inevitably influences the responses of Thai Christians to the reality of human suffering.

Within this context, a Christian theology of suffering that is relevant to the Thai people must take into consideration the Buddhist concept of suffering, especially the doctrine of the Four Noble Truths. Unfortunately, current theological approaches to suffering, driven by the agenda of the people in the west, often focus on the problem of evil and theodicy rather than addressing the reality of human suffering per se. As a result, they make little, if any, sense to those who belong to other cultures and perceive suffering differently. An attempt to reconcile the existence of an omnipotent and loving God with the existence of evil and suffering in this world is undeniably essential and necessary, but the Thai people are still struggling with various questions that are more substantial for them. How can a Christian theology of suffering adequately address the severity of suffering raised by the Buddha? What are the similarities and differences between the Christian and Buddhist concepts of suffering? Do Christianity and Buddhism actually refer to the identical reality when they use the term suffering? Is desire in Buddhism equal to sin in Christianity, and is *nibbāna* (Pāli) – Sanskrit: *nirvāna* – equivalent to salvation? What is the relationship between the Buddha's Four Noble Truths and the gospel of Jesus Christ? How should Thai Christians \respond to the

---

4. Kusalasaya, *Buddhism in Thailand*, 22–23.

doctrine of the Four Noble Truths that is highly respected and firmly maintained by the majority of the Thais? It may not be possible to answer all these questions, but a Christian theology of suffering in the Thai context must attempt to address these issues.

Moreover, dealing with suffering in the broader framework of theodicy tends to provide theoretical answers that do not really help, but sometimes ironically add more pain for the afflicted. It deals with the problem of suffering in general, but fails to address this issue in its complexity and concrete situations. It focuses on famous questions, "*Why* does suffering happen?" or "*Why* does an omnipotent and loving God allow suffering?" but neglects more important questions, "*How* does God respond to human suffering?" and "*How* should one respond to the reality of suffering?" In the final analysis, a theology of suffering merely becomes an academic exercise that is disconnected from real life.

Therefore, the purpose of this dissertation is to develop a Christian theology of suffering that is relevant to the context of Theravada Buddhism in Thailand. Grounded in a trinitarian theology of religions and trinitarian comparative theology, this study is not just a comparison between the Buddhist and Christian concepts of suffering. Rather, it is an attempt to construct a theology of suffering that is firmly rooted in the biblical and theological concept of suffering, while critically engaging and learning from the Buddhist concept of suffering. In fact, the Four Noble Truths should be the starting point in doing a Christian theology of suffering in the context of Theravada Buddhism in Thailand because it demonstrates the fundamental Buddhist understanding of suffering. Hence, this study will begin by exploring each Noble Truth and the related Buddhist teachings. Then, the Buddhist understanding of suffering will be compared and contrasted with the corresponding biblical and theological concept of suffering. While the Christian view of suffering will be maintained, it will be reflected and enhanced by the insights gained from the Buddhist tradition. It is hoped that this study will provide a Christian theology of suffering that is relevant to the Thai people in particular and that is beneficial to a theology of suffering in general. Nevertheless, for the purpose of this dissertation, this is not a complete theological discussion of suffering, but it is a discussion of the Christian teachings on suffering in relationship to the Buddhist teachings on this topic.

It is significant to stress that this study will be limited to the context of *Theravada Buddhism in Thailand*. The phrase is used in order to distinguish the particular form of Buddhism in Thailand from *Mahayana Buddhism* and *Thai Buddhism*. First, Buddhism in Thailand belongs to Theravada tradition which is not identical with Mahayana tradition.[5] Theravada Buddhism, also known as Hinayana Buddhism or Southern Buddhism, is the oldest Buddhist school of thought. *Theravada* literally means "Doctrine of the Elders," indicating that it was formulated by the first council of the *Sangha*, or monks' community, soon after the Buddha's death.[6] It holds the Pāli Canon or *Tipitaka* as the most authoritative texts on the Buddha's teachings, and believes that its understanding of Buddhism represents the original teaching of the Buddha.[7]

For Mahayana Buddhism, its development can be traced back to the second and third council of the Sangha, around 383 BC and 247 BC respectively, but its official teachings were formulated only after the first century AD.[8] Mahayana means "Great Vehicle," in contrast to Hinayana, "Small Vehicle." This title was given by its adherents in order to convey the idea that Mahayana Buddhism is large enough to carry all humankind to salvation.[9] While Mahayana and Theravada schools share the fundamental teachings of Buddhism, particularly the Four Noble Truths, they differ in many ways, especially the understanding of *Bodhisattva*. Mahayanists holds that Bodhisattvas are future Buddhas who delayed their own attainment of Buddhahood in order to help others towards *nibbāna*. Thus, one can reach this highest goal through the intervention of Bodhisattvas. On the other hand, Theravadins believe in the historical Buddha and use the term Bodhisattva in referring the previous incarnations of Gautama Buddha. In order to attain *nibbāna*,

---

5. Buddhism is divided into two main schools: Theravada and Mahayana. At the present, Theravada School represents Buddhism in Cambodia, Laos, Myanmar, Sri Lanka, and Thailand. Mahayana School includes various forms of Buddhism in other Asian countries, particularly China, Japan, Korea, Tibet, Bhutan, Mongolia, and Nepal. For more information of different schools in Mahayana Buddhism, see Humphreys, *Buddhism*, chs. 13–15.

6. Nyanatiloka, *Buddhist Dictionary*, 331. According to the Theravada tradition, the first council of the *Sangha* was held in Rajagaha in 483 BC to settle the contents of the *Tipitaka*. See Burnett, *The Spirit of Buddhism*, 69.

7. Coomaraswamy, *Buddha and the Gospel of Buddhism*, 222.

8. Rahula, "Theravada - Mahayana Buddhism," 455–457.

9. Humphreys, *Buddhism*, 47–48.

one must depend on oneself in following the path of the Buddha.[10] From this understanding, it can be said that the Theravada Buddhist concept of suffering clearly rejects the idea of God or Savior who can help humankind from suffering. Humankind must solely depend on their efforts in the quest for freedom from suffering.

Second, *Theravada Buddhism in Thailand* indicates the conservative school of Buddhism that is found in the country whereas *Thai Buddhism* is normally used to refer to the Thai Buddhist tradition which is strongly influenced by Brahmanism and animism.[11] Even though Thai Buddhism is more popular among the Thai people, this dissertation will focus on the teachings of Theravada Buddhism in Thailand without discussing the beliefs of Thai Buddhism because of two main reasons. First, Thai Buddhism is closely related with animism, occultism, magic, and superstition, but its official doctrines are still taken from *Tipitaka*. Moreover, many Thai Buddhist leaders, for example, two renowned scholars, Ven Phra Buddhadāsa Bhikkhu and Ven Phra Dhammapitaka, have been trying to purify Buddhism in Thailand from doctrinal contamination and bring it back to the pristine teachings of the Buddha as found in *Tipitaka* in the recent years.[12] Second, since this study engages the teachings of Theravada Buddhism, it will also be beneficial for those who live in Theravada Buddhist countries and anyone who interacts with Theravadins. Moreover, since the Four Noble Truths are also adopted by Mahayana Buddhism, this study can serve as a starting point in doing a theology of suffering in the context Mahayana Buddhism as well.

This dissertation consists of four chapters. The first chapter is intended to justify the methodology of this dissertation. I will argue that a theology of suffering that is relevant to the context of Theravada Buddhism in Thailand, yet is faithful to Christian belief, must be grounded in both a trinitarian theology of religions and trinitarian comparative theology, namely *a trinitarian comparative theology of religions*. It will begin by introducing the discipline

---

10. Dhammanada, *What Buddhists Believe*, 93–94. For more information about similarities and differences between Theravada and Mahayana Buddhism, see Rahula, "Bodhisattva Ideal in Buddhism," 461–471; Rahula, "Theravada - Mahayana Buddhism," 453–360; Dhammanada, *What Buddhists Believe*, 93–97.

11. However, it is important to note that this distinction is not absolute. While it is possible to differentiate between Theravada Buddhism in Thailand and Thai Buddhism in academia, it is difficult to make a distinction between them in the real world.

12. Kusalasaya, *Buddhism in Thailand*, 24.

of a theology of religions and by exploring its biblical foundations. After a discussion of different approaches to a theology of religions and drawing attention to a trinitarian theology of religions, it will introduce the discipline of comparative theology and propose that a *Christian* comparative theology must be a *trinitarian* comparative theology – a comparative theology which is firmly rooted in the sound doctrine of the Trinity. Subsequently, a trinitarian comparative theology of religions will become a foundation for the discussions in the remaining chapters. Moreover, the first chapter will give an overview of how the doctrine of the Trinity can help Christians develop a deeper theological understanding of suffering. Special attention will be given to a theology of the cross, which clearly reveals that the Triune God – Father, Son, and Holy Spirit – is a suffering God who actively participates in human suffering.

As mentioned, the Four Noble Truths should be the starting point in doing a Christian theology of suffering in the context of Theravada Buddhism in Thailand. The discussion in chapters 2–4 will follow the order of the Four Noble Truths. Chapter 2 is the study of the basic Buddhist and Christian understanding of suffering. First, an examination of the First Noble Truth, the truth of suffering (*dukkha*), and other major Buddhist teachings about the reality of suffering, especially the doctrine of the Three Characteristics of Existence (*Ti-lakkhana*) – Impermanence (*Aniccatā*), Suffering (*Dukkhatā*), and Soullessness (*Anattatā*) – will be covered. Then, it will compare and contrast these concepts with the biblical and theological understanding of human suffering. Special attention will be given to the possibility of suffering in the ontology of creation. The purposes of this chapter are to demonstrate the complexity of human suffering and to critically assess the assumption that suffering is not part of the created order.

The third chapter aims to develop a Christian theological understanding of the causes of suffering that is relevant to the context of Theravada Buddhism in Thailand. The focus will first be on the Second Noble Truth, the Truth of the Cause of Suffering (*Samudaya*) as well as the Buddhist concepts of *tanhā* (craving or desire), *avijjā* (ignorance), and the law of *kamma* (the law of cause and effect). Then, it will examine some of the causes of suffering that Christian theology makes in comparison with the Buddhist concept of the cause of suffering. While there are many interpretations of the causes of suffering in Christianity, this chapter will focus on three interpretations that relate to the

Buddhist teachings and are relevant to the Thai context: suffering is the result of sin; suffering is caused by oppression; and suffering is a mystery.

The final chapter intentionally brings this comparative study to the heart of Buddhalogy and the Christian theology of suffering – the Buddhist and Christian answers to the problem of human suffering. It will begin with a brief discussion of the Third Noble Truth, the extinction of suffering, and then summarize the Fourth Noble Truth, the way to the extinction of suffering. Next, an examination of the Christian understanding of God's response to the problem of human suffering as found in a theology of the cross proposed by Martin Luther, Kazoh Kitamori, Jürgen Moltmann, and Kosuke Koyama will be covered. Finally, it will highlight major similarities and differences between Buddhalogy and the Christian theology of suffering, and propose how Thai Christians should respond to this inescapable reality.

Written from a Christian perspective, I acknowledge my Christian worldview may influence my reading of Buddhism. Therefore, though it will inevitably be influenced by my Christian convictions, I will attempt to explain the Buddhist concept of suffering as accurately as possible. The exploration of the Buddhist concept of suffering in this paper is not comprehensive. Instead, it simply provides the basic Buddhist understanding of suffering that is the context in which a Thai Christian theology of suffering is developed. It is important to emphasize that while I certainly maintain my Christian position, the comparison between the Buddhist and Christian concepts of suffering is to be viewed as an academic attempt to highlight the similarities and differences between both traditions, not as an endeavor to reveal the superiority of any tradition. Furthermore, the example of authentic Buddhist-Christian dialogue that results does not ignore the uniqueness of Buddhism and Christianity but rather encourages both traditions to take their differences and distinctions seriously. Both of them should humbly and genuinely contribute from their point of views, while at the same time sincerely listen to each other. The outcome of this dialogue would be a mutual enrichment for each participant as well as a better understanding of each other. In the final analysis, it is hoped that this study will enable the Thai people, both Buddhists and Christians, to better understand and experience the way to overcome the misery of life that we all share.

CHAPTER 1

A Trinitarian Theology of Religions and Trinitarian Comparative Theology

Before comparing the Buddhist and Christian concepts of suffering and developing a Christian theology of suffering in the context of Theravada Buddhism in Thailand, it is useful to discuss the disciplines that provide the basis for this study. This chapter aims to introduce a theology of religions and comparative theology, and highlight a *trinitarian* theology of religions and *trinitarian* comparative theology as the foundations for this study. An understanding of these disciplines will help the reader better comprehend the scope and direction of this study. An emphasis on a trinitarian framework will clearly define a guiding vision and conviction of this theological endeavor. Moreover, this chapter will give an overview of a relationship between Trinitarian theology and a theology of suffering by exploring the basic concept of a theology of the cross proposed by Martin Luther, Kazoh Kitamori, and Jürgen Moltmann. This general survey will prepare the reader for a detailed discussion of a theology of the cross in chapter 4. In the final analysis, Trinitarian theology will serve as the criterion for assessing whether this study offers a theology of suffering that is genuinely Christian, and, at the same time, truly relevant to the context of Theravada Buddhism in Thailand.

As relatively new branches of theology, a theology of religions and comparative theology are still seeking their formations and nomenclatures. Several approaches to a theology of religions and experiments in comparative theology have been offered in recent years. These options excitingly open the door for contemporary theologians to develop theologies that are more suitable for the pluralistic era. Among these alternatives, I believe that a theology of religions and comparative theology that are entrenched in the sound doctrine of the Trinity are the best available options at the present time because they enable Christians to engage with other faiths fruitfully, yet remain faithful to the Christian faith. Therefore, a Christian theology of suffering in the context of Theravada Buddhism in Thailand should be developed within the framework of a trinitarian theology of religions and trinitarian comparative theology.

This chapter consists of three sections: a Christian theology of religions, a comparative theology, and the Trinity and human suffering. For a Christian theology of religions, contemporary approaches will be explored and evaluated. Special attention will be given to a trinitarian approach to a theology of religions. For comparative theology, its definition and examples will be given and assessed. Following the trinitarian approach to the former discipline, I will propose that a comparative theology that is genuinely Christian must be a *trinitarian* comparative theology. Moreover, different from comparative theologians that attempt to replace a theology of religions with a comparative theology, I will argue that both disciplines are needed for a productive Christian response to today's pluralistic ideal. For a relationship between the Trinity and suffering, I will give an overview of how the Triune God responds to human suffering and draw attention to a theology of the cross, which clearly bridges Trinitarian theology and theology of suffering. Subsequently, a trinitarian theology of religions, trinitarian comparative theology, and the doctrine of the Trinity will provide directions and guidelines for a quest for a Christian theology of suffering in the context of Theravada Buddhism in Thailand.

A Christian Theology of Religions

Religious pluralism is a much greater challenge today than it was in the past. In the West, an awareness of religious diversity has increased significantly. The reality of other religions is no longer confined to third world nations, but can be found easily in western society. In the East, the challenge of religious pluralism is even greater. Contrary to the western scene, Christianity in the eastern world often finds itself wandering in the shadow of other great and long-established religious traditions. Within this context, the intensity of the questions raised by pluralism is greatly magnified. Furthermore, what makes religious pluralism the great challenge to Christianity is its new meaning. Religious pluralism is not merely the plurality of religions, but it is the position that maintains equality among world religions with none having ultimate authority.[1] Consequently, this religiously pluralistic world calls for a Christian theology that can respond to the questions and challenges of pluralism, not just a theology that is limited to a Christian sphere.

A Christian theology of religions was born in this pluralistic context. It is generally agreed that this new discipline in theology began in the Catholic circles around the period surrounding the Second Vatican Council (1962). Afterwards, it extended to Protestant circles. The World Council of Churches, for example, published materials concerning this discipline: *The Living Faiths and Ultimate Goals* (1974) and *Towards World Community: Resources and Responsibilities for Living Together* (1975). Currently, the theology of religions is one of the most rapidly growing disciplines of theological studies.[2] Veli-Matti Kärkkäinen indicates the definition and nature of this discipline:

> Theology of religions is that discipline of theological studies which attempts to account theologically for the meaning and value of other religions. Christian theology of religions attempts to think theologically about what it means for Christians to live with people of other faiths and about the relationship of Christianity to other religions.[3]

There are three points that must be noted. In the first place, this branch of theology differs from various disciplines of religion, for example, the history of religions, religious sociology, and philosophy of religion. This is true because the theology of religions interprets data within a faith perspective and claims the right to assert a value judgment, but the sciences of religion observe, evaluate, and compare religions from without.[4] In the second place, a Christian theology of religions must be done from a Christian perspective. It is possible for other religious traditions to have their own theology of religions, or, as Dupuis puts it, faith-interpretation of religions. However, each tradition must reflect on the meaning of other religions on the basis of

---

1. Netland, *Encountering Religious Pluralism*, 21.
2. Kärkkäinen, *An Introduction to the Theology of Religions*, 22.
3. Kärkkäinen, 20.
4. Dupuis, *Toward a Christian Theology of Religious Pluralism*, 5.

its own convictions and foundations.[5] For this reason, a Christian theology of religions must hold fast to faith in Jesus Christ as traditionally affirmed by the Christian tradition, and, at the same time, be open to the positive role and importance of other religions in the overall plan of God for humankind.[6] Finally, theology of religions (plural) and theology of religion (singular) are different, but inseparable. While the theology of religions is a general study about the relationship between Christianity and various religions as a whole, the theology of religion focuses on one specific tradition. Indeed, theology of *religions* must precede the theology of *religion*. It asks the general questions which apply to all religions before specific questions for each tradition can be considered.[7]

As a recent theological discipline, a Christian theology of religions is still searching for its canons. Several typologies have been proposed to categorize and make sense of various approaches to a theology of religions. These typologies can be organized into two groups: a traditional typology and more comprehensive typology. This section will survey these categories and approaches, and it will assess their suitability and capability in responding to the immense challenge of pluralism. Finally, it will draw attention to a trinitarian theology of religions as the preferred option at the moment.

A Traditional Typology

Currently, the most well-known typology is a threefold division of exclusivism, inclusivism, and pluralism. This classification is determined primarily by the question of salvation. As many scholars have indicated, this traditional typology falls short of categorizing diverse positions of contemporary theologians; nevertheless, it is important to understand it because it provides general positions of Christians on other religions.

Exclusivism

More conservative views relating to a Christian theology of religions are usually grouped in a category called exclusivism. This exclusivist approach maintains that salvation can be found only in the Gospel of Jesus Christ, and

---

5. Kärkkäinen, *Trinity and Religious Pluralism*, 3.
6. Dupuis, *Toward a Christian Theology of Religious Pluralism*, 1.
7. Dupuis, 9.

it sees little or no truth in other religious traditions. For this reason, those who do not hear and respond positively to the gospel are excluded from its salvific benefits. This approach has been the major approach of the Christian church until the Enlightenment, and it is still held in the more conservative circles of the Christian church. It is apparent that this approach received its title not from its adherents, but by those who rejected this view and aimed to cast it in a negative light.[8] Consequently, some scholars suggest that we should entitle this category "particularism" in order to erase negative connotations associated with the term exclusivism.[9]

Inclusivism

The main tenet of inclusivism is the desire to uphold the uniqueness of Jesus Christ while also maintaining that salvation can be found in other religions. Inclusivists hold that while salvation is ontologically founded on the person of Jesus Christ, it is available and efficacious through other religious traditions as well. Accordingly, the religions have a positive role in God's redemptive purpose for humankind. However, the followers of other traditions are not saved through their religions, but through the redemptive work of Christ. This approach to a theology of religions is the official teaching of the Roman Catholic Church after the Second Vatican Council and it is the most common view of contemporary theologians.

Pluralism

A pluralistic approach to a theology of religions rejects the finality and normativity of Jesus Christ, but affirms the validity and value of all religions. According to the pluralists, no religion is superior to others because all of them are historically and culturally conditioned human responses to the one Ultimate Reality. As a result, each religion can be a valid means for salvation. They are different paths that lead to the same goal, Ultimate Reality – however that is named in each tradition. Jesus Christ is simply one savior among other savior figures in the world. He is the savior for Christians, but he is not the one savior for all people. This pluralistic approach is supported by

---

8. Netland, *Encountering Religious Pluralism*, 46.
9. See Okholm and Phillips, *Christians and Religious Pluralism*.

several influential theologians, for example John Hick and Paul Knitter, and it is significantly embraced by the more liberal wing of the Christian church.

An evaluation of this traditional typology reveals that even though it is widely recognized and almost becomes *the* typology of theology of religions, many writers criticize it as inadequate, over-simplified, and even misleading. Intently focusing on the question of salvation, this category does not adequately respond to other challenges of pluralism such as the questions of truth and revelation in other religions, the relationship between other religions and Christianity, and the role of other religions in the divine purpose for humankind.[10] While this category highlights three general approaches towards the religions, it fails to address the complexity of each approach.[11] For instance, the inclusivist positions of the Roman Catholic Church, mainline Protestants, and evangelicals are significantly different from one another. Furthermore, several contemporary views of religions cannot be limited within the boundaries of this category. A particular view may contain certain aspect of these approaches. Some evangelicals, for example Clark Pinnock and Amos Yong, affirm a positive role of other religions in God's redemptive plan, yet uphold that salvation is to be found only in Christ. For this reason, a more comprehensive typology is needed for categorizing and making sense of the current approaches to a theology of religions.

A More Comprehensive Typology

Contemporary theologians propose a typology for a Christian theology of religions that addresses the challenge of pluralism in a more comprehensive way. The current typology can be categorized into four paradigms:

---

10. An example of the attempt to account for the relationship between Christianity and world religions in various aspects can be found in Corduan, *A Tapestry of Faiths*. He proposes that the relationship between Christianity and world religions is a very complex one. It should be examined in six dimensions: soteriological, content, revelatory, apologetic, moral, and communication.

11. Examples of the attempt to specify various approaches to a theology of religions can be found in Knitter, *Introducing Theologies of Religions* and Copeland, "Christian Theology and World Religions." Knitter proposes four models for a theology of religions: replacement, fulfillment, mutuality, and acceptance. Moreover, he divides the replacement model into total and partial replacement. Copeland argues that an appropriate category should be more specific and should be perceived as a non-exclusive classification. He suggests ten approaches for a theology of religions: negativism, semi-negativism, dialecticism, semi-dialecticism, confessionalism, christocentric pluralism, theocentric pluralism, kingdomcentric pluralism, paradoxical pluralism, and pre-eschatological agnosticism.

ecclesiocentrism, Christocentrism, theocentrism, and pneumatocentrism/trinitarianism.[12] Each approach consists of several positions that are not necessary identical, but which share similar convictions, for example, ecclesiocentric theologians may have different opinions concerning revelation in other religions, but they unanimously maintain that salvation is accessible only by the gospel of Jesus Christ proclaimed by the Christian church. Moreover, these approaches can overlap each other in a particular matter, for example, Christocentric and pneumatocentrism/trinitarianism share the conviction that other religions are not salvific, but they can have positive roles in God's plan of salvation. Therefore, the current approaches should not be understood as clear-cut categories, but as paradigms that reveal major orientations towards the meaning and value of other religions and their relationship with Christianity. Understanding these paradigms, as well as their strengths and weaknesses, will help us better comprehend different frameworks for a Christian theology of religions. At the same time, it will reveal that the trinitarian approach can effectively respond to the challenge of pluralism, and, as a result, it could be a basis for a Christian theology of suffering in the context of Theravada Buddhism in Thailand.

Ecclesiocentrism

Ecclesiocentrism is similar to exclusivism, or particularism, but it does not merely emphasize a soteriological concern. The core of an ecclesiocentric approach can be stated in terms of three principles: (1) The Bible is God's distinctive revelation and it is able to reveal divine revelation. (2) Jesus Christ is the center of Scripture and Christian faith. He is fully God and fully human. Salvation and revelation are available to humankind only through him. (3) God's saving grace is accessible and effective only in the Christian church and its proclamation of the gospel.[13] Accordingly, ecclesiocentrism denies a possibility of salvation beyond the boundaries of the Christian church and the positive role of other religions in God's purpose. It affirms the traditional rule *extra ecclesiam nulla salus*: "Outside the church, no salvation."

---

12. See Kärkkäinen, *An Introduction to the Theology of Religions*; and Kärkkäinen, *Trinity and Religious Pluralism*.

13. Kärkkäinen, *An Introduction to the Theology of Religions*, 167.

Currently, the major attitude to other religions in the academic arena has shifted from this position, but it is still largely held by many Christians, particularly evangelical, Pentecostal, Charismatic, and other independent churches. Nevertheless, many contemporary evangelical scholars represent a more open-minded ecclesiocentrism. While they deny the possibility of salvation outside the gospel of Jesus Christ proclaimed by the Christian church, they affirm the possibility that other religions may contain revelation and play a positive role in God's plan. Among these scholars are Timothy Tennent and Gerald McDermott. In his *Christianity at the Religious Roundtable: Evangelicalism in Conversation with Hinduism, Buddhism, and Islam*, Tennent regards his position as an "engaged exclusivist" that "affirms the faith that was once for all entrusted to the saints," but also includes "a more open stance regarding general revelation as a *preparatio evangelica*."[14] Therefore, he encourages evangelicals to participate more in an interreligious dialogue. In *Can Evangelicals Learn From World Religions? Jesus, Revelation, and Religious Traditions*, McDermott opens the door for God's truths in other religions without sacrificing the finality of Christ. Based on Jonathan Edward's idea of covenant and typology, he argues that there is revelation called "reveal type" that is planted in non-Christian religions by the triune God. This revelation, he claims, "may be shadowy rather than clear and incomplete rather than full, but it can be divine revelation nonetheless."[15] God might use this revelation to save those who have not heard about Christ, to bless all humankind during this earthly life, or, more importantly, to help Christians better understand God's truths.[16]

The strength of an ecclesiocentric approach is that it affirms the authority of Scripture, the supremacy of Christ, and the need for an explicit faith in Christ. Therefore, this view can be seen as the most secure approach to world religions. It is truly a *Christian* theology of religions, not just a philosophy of religions. However, the weaknesses of this position can be found in two main areas. First, it often overlooks God's work in the life and tradition of people of other faiths. Second, it cannot adequately respond to the challenges and questions of pluralism. The followers of ecclesiocentrism, driven by a negative

---

14. Tennent, *Christianity at the Religious Roundtable*, 26.
15. McDermott, *Can Evangelicals Learn from World Religions?*, 107.
16. McDermott, 114–117.

attitude towards other religions, often condemn other faiths and withdraw from engaging with non-Christians. As a result, they are marginalized in this pluralistic society and unable to make much impact on people of other faiths. Thus, the urgent task of this approach is to account for the theological meaning and role of world religions in God's economy.[17]

Christocentrism

Christocentrism is the inclusive approach of a Christian theology of religions. It is Christocentric in the sense that it focuses on the saving work of Christ and its benefits without restricting them to the Christian community. The paradigm shift from ecclesiocentrism to Christocentrism implies a drastic "decentering" of the church. Indeed, Jesus Christ, not the church, stands at the center of the Christian mystery.[18] Christocentrism can be generally defined in terms of the following principles: (1) Jesus Christ is unique, normative, and superior to other religious figures, and so salvation only comes in and through Christ. (2) God's grace and salvation are not limited to the Christian church, but the church is the main instrument of salvation. (3) Other religions are regarded positively as part of God's plan of salvation, but they are not the ordinary means of salvation.[19] Consequently, the followers of other faiths can also be saved through Christ, not through their religions.

Due to the fact that the Christocentric perspective has the largest number of adherents as well as a great variety of different ecclesiastical settings, this approach has been divided into three subcategories: Catholic, mainline Protestants, and evangelical. In the Roman Catholic circle, the change from ecclesiocentrism to Christocentrism began during the period of the Second Vatican Council (1962-1965). The affirmation of Christocentrism is found in three main texts: *Lumen Gentium*, the document on the doctrine of the church (16–17), *Nostra Aetate*, the document on the theology of religions (2), and *Ad Gentes*, the document on the missionary task of the church (3, 9, 11).[20] *Lumen Gentium* 16 declares that salvation is available to people in different religions and to those who, "without any fault of theirs, have not yet arrived

---

17. Kärkkäinen, *An Introduction to the Theology of Religions*, 344.
18. Dupuis, *Toward a Christian Theology of Religious Pluralism*, 185.
19. Kärkkäinen, *An Introduction to the Theology of Religions*, 169.
20. Flannery, *Vatican Council II*.

at an explicit knowledge of God and who, not without grace, strive to lead a good life."[21] *Nostra Aetate* places the encounter between the church and world religions in the broad context of the same origin and destiny of humankind in God and the search to answer the ultimate questions that overwhelm the human spirit.[22] In *Ad Gentes*, the council explains that the function of the church's missionary activities is to purify, raise, and bring whatever goodness found in people and religions to perfection in Christ.[23] Besides the council, the influential adherents of this view in the Roman Catholic circle are Karl Rahner, Hans Küng, Jacques Dupuis, and Gavin D'Costa.[24]

Similar to the Roman Catholic camp, most mainline Protestants embrace a Christocentric approach. This position can be seen in the affirmations of the World Council of Churches (WCC) as well as the writings of several mainline Protestant theologians. The Commission on World Mission and Evangelism of the WCC declares, "It is important to recognize that a follower of another religion has his reason for believing in it. . . . These reasons may be part of the preparation for his understanding of the Gospel."[25] The 1996 Salvador World Mission Conference indicates, "We cannot point to any other way of salvation than Jesus Christ; at the same time, we cannot set limits to the saving power of God."[26] This approach is supported by Wolfhart Pannenberg, Lesslie Newbigin, Paul Tillich, and M. M. Thomas, yet their positions are quite varied. Pannenberg and Newbigin support Christocentrism, but still defend an orthodox Christian faith; Tillich and Thomas move closer to the border of pluralism as they emphasize social concern and unity among religions rather than question about truth.[27]

Christocentric evangelicalism is significantly different from the first two subcategories because it does not deny the possibility of salvation in other

---

21. Lumen Gentium 16. Flannery, *Vatican Council II*, 36–368.
22. Nostra Aetate 2.
23. Ad Gentes 9.
24. This study will not discuss their positions in detail. However, the positions of these theologians are closely related with the conciliar documents. In fact, Rahner and Küng were drafters of the document of Vatican Council II.
25. Orchard, *Witness in Six Continents*, 15.
26. Quoted in Kärkkäinen, *An Introduction to the Theology of Religions*, 159.
27. Kärkkäinen, 348. See also Newbigin, *The Gospel in a Pluralist Society*; Pannenberg, *Systematic Theology*; Thomas, "Christology and Pluralistic Consciousness"; and Tillich, *Christianity and the Encounter of World Religions*.

faiths, but, at the same time, it does not completely affirm salvation of non-believers or the value of other religions. The major advocates of this view are Sir Norman Anderson and Clark Pinnock. In his *Christianity and World Religions: The Challenge of Pluralism*, Anderson compares the Old Testament saints who never heard of Christ with the followers of others religions who have never heard the gospel, but are sincerely seeking God in their own traditions. He proposes that in same way that the Jews in the Old Testament were saved through Christ's redemptive work on the cross, today's non-believers can be saved without an explicit faith in Christ. However, none of them receives salvation by their own works, but by what Christ did for them.[28] Pinnock insists that a high Christology that upholds the uniqueness of Jesus Christ does not necessarily lead to pessimism of salvation or an exclusivist attitude towards non-Christians. In contrast, he believes in an optimism of salvation. He is convinced that God's redemptive work in Jesus Christ was intended to benefit the whole world because the Gospel of Christ reveals that the outcome of salvation will be great and generous.[29] This does not lead to universalism because all people must respond to God by faith. However, Pinnock clearly states that it is through faith, not the content of their theology, that people are saved.[30]

There are three main advantages of a Christocentric approach. First, it still maintains the centrality of Christ, that he is unique, normative, and superior to other saving figures, and so salvation only comes in and through him. Second, it recognizes that truth and grace are present in world religions through the work of the Spirit.[31] Third, it rightly emphasizes the essential role of an interreligious dialogue. However, this approach contains at least two critical drawbacks. First, this understanding is rather unclear and ambiguous. This problem can be seen in the great variety among the advocates of this approach as well as the statements of faith that can be interpreted in various ways, for example, some declarations of Vatican II and affirmations of the WCC. Second, the notion that salvation can be achieved without an explicit faith in Christ, along with the emphasis on dialogue, will inevitably stand

---

28. Anderson, *Christianity and World Religions*.
29. Pinnock, *A Wideness in God's Mercy*, 17.
30. Pinnock, 157.
31. Knitter, *Introducing Theologies of Religions*, 100–101.

against the Great Commission's command that Christians are to proclaim the gospel of Jesus Christ to all nations. Though the advocates of this view argue that this is not the case, it is hard to accept that the evangelistic effort of the church will not be affected by this position.

Theocentrism

The term theocentrism literally means "God-centered." It demonstrates the main idea of a pluralistic approach that rejects the uniqueness and normativeness of Christ, or any other saving figure, but emphasizes God, or the one Ultimate Reality, as the source of revelation and salvation.[32] Theocentrism holds that salvation must be acknowledged as present and effective in its own way in each religious tradition. Accordingly, no religion can claim to be normative and superior to others. The influential adherents of this position are John Hick, Paul Knitter, Stanley J. Samartha, and Raimundo Panikkar.[33] Among these theologians, John Hick and Paul Knitter have exercised the greatest influence on the current scene of a Christian theology of religions.

For Hick, the essence of pluralism is the notion that there is "both the one unlimited transcendent divine Reality and also a plurality of varying human concepts, images, and experiences of and responses to that Reality."[34] Therefore, all religions are merely different ways to salvation. Knitter points out that the salvation or well-being of humans and earth must be the starting point and common ground for an interreligious dialogue because all religions share the common context, the earth, which is being threatened by the reality of suffering. Dialogue among religions is necessary in order that all partners will be able to discover Truth and cooperate more effectively in saving the planet and its inhabitants. However, everyone must enter a conversation with firm conviction about his or her truth, but no one can claim that his or her religion has the "final word" or "absolute revelation" of all truth.[35] Consequently, he proposes that the traditional understanding of the uniqueness of Jesus needs to be revised and reaffirmed. He suggests that one-and-only declarations about Jesus should not be understood as creedal

---

32. Kärkkäinen, *An Introduction to the Theology of Religions*, 170.

33. See Hick, *A Christian Theology of Religions*; Knitter, *No Other Name?*; Panikkar, *The Unknown Christ of Hinduism*; and Samartha, *One Christ, Many Religions*.

34. Hick, *The Second Christianity*, 83.

35. Knitter, *One Earth, Many Religions*.

or orthodox statements, but as the "love language" that his disciples used to describe their personal experience with Jesus. Thus, pluralist Christology affirms that Jesus is *truly* divine and savior, without insisting that he is the *only* divine and savior. Nevertheless, Knitter maintains that the uniqueness of Jesus can be reaffirmed through his differences from others, not his superiority over all others.[36]

The strength of the theocentric position is its ability to address the concrete problems of today's society in various ways. In the situation of the heartbreaking events caused by religious conflicts around the world, the pluralists call all religious traditions to forsake claims of absolute truth and instead strive for the common good of all people. In the context of a suffering humanity and earth, pluralists rightly proclaim the need for unity among world religions. They also warn Christians against focusing on themselves while neglecting the suffering Other and longing for a glorious world after death but forgetting about this finite world. All religions must take global responsibility with concrete actions if they want to be relevant to the contemporary world.

Nevertheless, the pluralists' deep concern for the current crisis of the world brings about three serious mistakes in their approach. First, it is not faithful to biblical and theological foundations. While this position claims that its basis is orthopraxis rather than orthodoxy, it fails to realize that the foundation and validation of orthopraxis is based on the coherence of the praxis of God in Scripture and in the present situation.[37] As a result, it blindly affirms the possibility and probability of other true, saving religions, which obviously contradicts what God has revealed in Scripture. Second, this approach denies the fundamental belief of Christianity. For example, both Hick and Knitter need to revise Christology to fit their paradigm. Instead of reflecting on the pluralistic world on the basis of Christopraxis – the work of Jesus Christ in Scripture and the work of the Spirit in the world today – they reflect on Christology, particularly the incarnation and uniqueness of Christ, on the basis of the current situation. Finally, a pluralistic approach has a conflicting nature. As many scholars have indicated, while the pluralists proclaim a theology that refuses any absolute truth claim, they are ironically and inevitably

---

36. Knitter, *Jesus and the Other Names*.

37. For a more comprehensive discussion on praxis see Anderson, *The Shape of Practical Theology*.

making an absolute truth claim about their theology. Consequently, we can say that no one can be the real pluralist. We are all exclusive or inclusive to some degree.

Pneumatocentrism and Trinitarianism

In this section, pneumatocentrism and trinitarianism will be discussed together because of two reasons. First, these positions are closely related and they do not contradict each other. Second, most scholars agree that the genuine pneumatocentric approach must be grounded in a trinitarian position. The pneumatocentric approach focuses on the presence and work of the Holy Spirit in the life and tradition of people of other faiths. In fact, many theologians who represent the previous approaches to the theology of religions have already discerned the role of the Holy Spirit in world religions. Unfortunately, earlier pneumatocentric approaches tended to separate the Spirit from other Trinitarian members. It is often mentioned that the Spirit represents universality whereas Christ represents particularity. As a result, the work of the Spirit is misunderstood as working against the work of Christ. Dupuis responds to this error: "One needs to affirm clearly the universal action of the Sprit throughout human history, either before or after the historical event Jesus Christ. But Christian faith has it that the action of the Spirit and that of Jesus, though distinct, are nevertheless complementary and inseparable."[38]

It was only recently that a pneumatocentric approach to the theology of religions was coherently constructed. In his *Discerning the Spirit(s): A Pentecostal-Charismatic Contribution to Christian Theology of Religions*, Amos Yong tries to relate Charismatic theology to the challenge of pluralism. He describes a Charismatic theology of religions as "the effort to understand both the immensely differentiated experiences of faith and the multifaceted phenomena of religious traditions and systems that is informed by experiences of the Spirit in the light of Scripture, and vice versa."[39] Yong's most recent contribution to a pneumatological theology of religions that stresses the importance of the Trinity can be found in his *Beyond Impasse: Toward a Pneumatological Theology of Religions*.[40] He affirms that a pneumatological

---

38. Dupuis, *Toward a Christian Theology of Religious Pluralism*, 197.
39. Yong, *Discerning the Spirit(s)*, 24.
40. Yong, *Beyond the Impasse*.

theology is a trinitarian theology. Furthermore, he proposes three axioms for the pneumatological theology of religions in a Trinitarian framework: (1) God is universally present and active in the Spirit; (2) God's Spirit is the life-breath of the imago Dei in every human being and the presupposition of all human relationships and communities; (3) The religions of the world, like everything else that exists, are providentially sustained by the Spirit of God for divine purposes.[41]

Since the pneumacentric approach must be grounded in the trinitarian understanding, contemporary theologians are moving to a trinitarian theology of religions. Besides Jacques Dupuis and Amos Yong, there are two significant adherents of the trinitarian approach: Gavin D' Costa and Veli-Matti Kärkkäinen. Though D' Costa faithfully follows the inclusivist theology of Vatican II, he clearly approaches the theology of religions from a trinitarian perspective. He insists on the integral relationship between the three persons of the trinity, which then translates into the relationship between triune God and the church.[42] Kärkkäinen indicates in *Trinity and Religious Pluralism* that Christian trinitarian theology, which maintains that the only possible way to talk about the God of the Bible is to refer to the Father, Son, and Spirit, has enormous implications for the theology of religions. It prevents theologians from mythologizing or generalizing the concept of God and the incarnation of Christ. It rejects the pneumatocentric approach that separates the Spirit from the Father and Son.[43] Furthermore, he explains that a trinitarian approach helps us avoid the mistake of putting Christ and God as opponents as if one could choose between a Christocentric and theocentric position.[44] Finally, grounded in "Augustinian rule of thumb," which regards the inner works of the Trinity as separable and the outer works as inseparable, Kärkkäinen proposes a principle for discerning the presence of the Spirit in the world:

> In order to refer to the presence of the Spirit, whether as the divine breath of all living creatures, as a salvific gift in the life of believers and of the church, or as the agent of the eschatological consummation in the coming of the kingdom, one needs to

---

41. Yong, 44–46.
42. See D'Costa, *The Meeting of Religions and the Trinity*.
43. Kärkkäinen, *Trinity and Religious Pluralism*, 169.
44. Kärkkäinen, "How to Speak of the Spirit among Religions," 123.

speak of the Spirit of Yahweh, the Spirit of the Father of Jesus Christ. Pneumatological discourse unrelated to the Father and the Son may seem to promise more, yet it begins to lose its contours and often ends up being nothing other than a way to affirm a typically modernist idea of "rough parity" of all religions.[45]

The New Testament also teaches that Son and Spirit presuppose each other. The Spirit is at work in the life and ministry of Christ, and after the resurrection the Spirit is the Spirit of Christ. Consequently, Kärkkäinen concludes that the work of the Spirit "cannot be set in opposition to the person and ministry of Jesus Christ, any more than the person and ministry of the Son can be opposed to the work of the Father," and "wherever the Spirit inspires the knowledge of God, whether within the sphere of the church or outside it, salvation brought about by the Spirit is referred to as the saving work of Christ, namely, his incarnation, death, and resurrection."[46]

From the various approaches to a theology of religions discussed above, I believe that this approach is the most appropriate approach because it remains faithful to the traditional Christian tradition, yet it is able to respond to the challenge of pluralism effectively. Different from Christocentric and theocentric approaches (and some forms of pneumatocentrism) that tend to create a false conflict between the persons of the Trinity in the theology of religions, the trinitarian position accounts for the meaning and value of world religions on the basis of biblical and trinitarian theology. In contrast to ecclesiocentrism that fails to discern the work of the Triune God outside the Christian community, the trinitarian perspective enables us to see the wider scope of God's work in his created world. Even though other religions are not salvific, they can help us better comprehend the mystery of God. This is not to deny differences among religions, but it is to encounter the religious Other in an atmosphere where each participant can be challenged and learn, which can help us deepen our own faith.[47]

However, we must be aware that the trinitarian approach is not free from limitations. It seems that the greatest difficulty of the trinitarian paradigm is discerning the presence and work of the Triune God outside the Christian

---

45. Kärkkäinen, 123.
46. Kärkkäinen, 123.
47. Kärkkäinen, *Trinity and Religious Pluralism*, 179.

church. Since the whole created order is now distorted by sin, and religions contain a mixture of good and evil, discerning the work of God in religions is not a simple task. Furthermore, the Holy Spirit is not the only agent in the spiritual realm since demonic presence and activity is also revealed in world religions. Therefore, one must carefully and prayerfully examine a particular teaching or phenomenon of world religions in order not to misunderstand the reality behind it.

Another advantage of a trinitarian approach to a Christian theology of religions is its ability to promote an authentic interfaith dialogue that does not require participants to give up their absolute truth claims. While the pluralists argue for the misguided idea of tolerance, which means not saying anything negative about other religions, the trinitarian theologians hold that tolerance does not mean putting away differences or distinctions, but taking seriously the challenge of differences. Kärkkäinen explains that "those who work within the trinitarian unity-in-diversity paradigm need to listen patiently to the Other, discern where they are right and where they err, as well as their own truth and errors, and still affirm the Other even with their differences."[48]

In the context of the immense challenge of pluralism in Thailand, Thai Christians should neither remain silent in the Christian community nor give up their Christian absolute truth claim in order to relate to the Buddhist community. Unfortunately, most Thai churches polarize to these two extremes, which prevent them from adequately responding to pluralism and making a difference in the Thai society. The more conservative wing of the Thai Church usually maintains an exclusive position towards Buddhism and other religions and has little connection with them. The more open-minded group of the Thai Church embraces both inclusive and pluralistic approaches, and often dialogues with other religions. Sadly, Christians who are participating in an interfaith dialogue with these approaches often give up absolute truth claims and the uniqueness of Christian faith in order to be compliant with a pluralistic agenda. As a result, Thai Buddhists are unable to hear the authentic message of the gospel within Buddhist-Christian dialogue. On the contrary, a trinitarian approach to a Christian theology of religions will enable Thai Christians to affirm the meaning and value of their national religion without

---

48. Kärkkäinen, 179.

compromising biblical truth. It encourages them to enter the conversation with humility and respect, yet it requires them to boldly declare that Jesus Christ is the one and only Savior of the world.

Grounded in a trinitarian Christian theology of religions, this study can be viewed as a Buddhist-Christian dialogue on the subject matter of suffering. It will engage and learn from Buddhism with humility and respect, and, at the same time, it will boldly proclaim that Jesus Christ is the one and only Savior who can save humankind from suffering. As a result, it offers an atmosphere where each participant will learn and be challenged, which makes possible a better understanding of each other as well as mutual enrichment for each participant. For Christians, it opens the door for them to comprehend another approach to the problem of human suffering. In addition, similarities and differences found in a comparison between the Buddhist and Christian concepts of suffering will help both sides develop a better understanding of the Christian faith. Similarities and differences between the Buddhist and Christian concepts of suffering may reinforce what both sides believe, or they may revise and revitalize their understanding of suffering.

In order to foster a productive Buddhist-Christian dialogue, this study needs to incorporate the methods of a trinitarian comparative methodology. Hence, the next section will introduce comparative theology and highlight trinitarian comparative theology as the foundation for this study.

A Comparative Theology

Notwithstanding several insights gained from a theology of religions, some theologians point out that this discipline has reached an impasse which restricts its productivity in engaging with other religions.[49] Hence, a small but growing number of Christian theologians are beginning to move from a

---

49. See, for example, Fredericks, *Faith among Faiths*, and Richard Schebera, "Comparative Theology." For Fredericks, a theology of religions is at an impasse because the proponents of each approach to non-Christian religions have been successful in exposing the inadequacies of the others. Therefore, it is obvious that the current approaches are inadequate and a fully systematized theology of religions is not possible at the present time. Schebera points out that a theology of religions revolves around the three models and their variations. The books and journals in this field repeatedly attempt to show the superiority of one model over the other. There is little room for creativity or alternate arguments. Within this situation, interreligious dialogue becomes pointless because the answers to the questions raised by religious pluralism have been already given. There is nothing left to discuss because each model had a preconceived

theology of religions to a new sub-discipline of theology called comparative theology in recent decades. The term "comparative theology" has been used since the nineteenth century in contrast to "theoretic theology" or to signify the study of religious doctrines. Nevertheless, David Tracy indicates it is currently understood in two ways: (1) a branch of the history of religions that attempts to compare theologies from different religious traditions, and (2) a theological enterprise that studies two or more religious traditions and compares them on theological grounds.[50] Grounded in the latter definition, comparative theologians no longer seek a fully systematized theology of religions, but they are doing theology comparatively. Among these theologians, Francis X. Clooney, James L. Fredericks, and Keith Ward have exercised the greatest influence on the current scene of comparative theology. Considering their positions will help one better understand this appealing discipline. Furthermore, examining the advantages and shortcomings of comparative theology will point to the necessity of constructing a comparative theology on the basis of the sound doctrine of the Trinity.

Francis X. Clooney

Francis X. Clooney, professor at Harvard Divinity School, is known as an outstanding indologist and creative Catholic theologian. Viewing himself as a comparative theologian, he intends to "inscribe within the Christian theological tradition theological texts from outside it, and to (begin to) write Christian theology only out of that newly composed context."[51] He explains that a comparative theology is distinguished by "its commitment to the detailed consideration of religious traditions other than one's own. It is detailed, deeply reflexive, self-corrective in the course of its own investigation, even in regard to its basic questions, methods, and vocabulary." Therefore, it is "a theology deeply changed by its attention to the details of multiple religious and theological traditions; it is a theology that occurs truly only after comparison."[52] Complaining that theologies of religions are basically abstract enterprises, developed solely on the Christian tradition without reference

---

answer. Therefore, a theology of religions may give some self-understanding to Christians, but it is irrelevant to non-Christians.

50. Tracy, "Comparative Theology," 446.
51. Clooney, *Theology after Vedānta*, 7.
52. Clooney, "Comparative Theology," 521–522.

to any other religion, Clooney suggests that they must be constructed only after comparative theological studies, they are to be rewritten with a greater commitment to details and examples.[53] However, he indicates that a comparative theology is not simply heir to a theology of religions but is a unique theological discipline that seeks to rethink every theological issue and reread every theological text. In contrast to theologians of religions who are committed to a particular approach to other religions, comparative theologians are willing to learn from other traditions by understanding them on their own terms and in a way that is not predicated on the presuppositions of their tradition. Moreover, comparativists resist generalizations about religions, but they are committed to the demands of religious traditions as well as the goal of a reflective retrieval of their own beliefs in order to restate them more effectively.[54] Clooney says:

> Comparative theologians operate within boundaries marked by the tension between a necessary vulnerability to truth as one might find it and be affected by it in the materials studied, and loyalty to truth as one has already found it, lives it, and hopes according to it. Comparative theologians do not wish to reduce the studied traditions to mere, disposable information to be used as they see fit; this reduction would fundamentally distort the other, by depriving it of its imposing structures, its transformative power and its claims to universality – the very features which should most interest the theologian.[55]

Clooney's contributions to the development of a comparative theology can be seen in his three masterworks: *Theology after Vedānta: An Experiment in Comparative Theology*, *Seeing Through Texts: Doing Theology among the Śrīvaiṣṇavas of South India*, and *Hindu God, Christian God*. Among these publications, *Theology after Vedānta* is a central focus of Clooney's scholarship. As its subtitle suggests, *Theology after Vedānta* is intended as an experiment in the practice of comparative theology that is comprised of three activities. First, it is a study of Advaita (Non-Dualist) Vedānta, the school of Indian

---

53. Clooney, *Theology after Vedānta*, 193–194.
54. Clooney, 6–9.
55. Clooney, 5–6.

thought developed from the upaniṣads. Second, it is an exercise in Christian comparative theology – a theology that is rethought and rewritten after a careful reading of Advaita Vedānta. Third, it is an exploration of the tension between the study of Advaita Vedānta and the construction of a Christian comparative theology. Dedicating three full chapters to the discussion of Advaita Vedānta Text – Advaita Vedānta in its wholeness which includes the upaniṣads, Uttara Mīmāṃsā Sūtras, and later commentaries, Clooney presents a careful reading of the Text, explores Advaita Vedānta truth that flows from the Text, and explains the proper manner of reading the Text. Finally, he put the *Summa Theologiae* of Thomas Aquinas in comparison with Advaita Vedānta. To be precise, he rereads and rewrites the *Summa Theologiae* after Advaita Vedānta. He concludes that this endeavor brings about a retrieval of the manner that Aquinas read and used the Bible to constitute the *Summa Theologiae* as well as a recovery of the nature and role of commentaries on the *Summa Theologiae*.[56]

In the process of reading the *Summa Theologiae* and Advaita Vedānta together, Clooney suggests five strategies that move a comparison beyond simply specifying similarities and differences between two texts to discovering the truth of comparison arising from the encounter of the texts: coordination, superimposition, conversation, metaphor, and collage. The first two strategies are borrowed from the Advaita tradition. Coordination is a practical strategy that allows the Advaitins to use texts from different upaniṣads together in meditation, taking advantage of their common terms, parallel structures, and conclusions, yet preserving the distinctiveness of each text. Applying this method to Christian and Advaita theological texts, it is possible to compare similar terms and themes as well as comparable structures without a requirement for a theoretical position on the truth or status of the compared texts.[57] Superimposition is "a form of meditation in which the meditator deliberately imposes one reality upon another for the sake of an enhanced meditation."[58] Clooney, therefore, superimposes Advaita Vedānta upon the *Summa Theologiae* with an awareness of the differences between them, the temporary nature of the superimposition process, and the goal of an enhanced

---

56. See Clooney, *Theology after Vedānta*.
57. Clooney, 168–169.
58. Clooney, 169.

meditation on the latter. Here, the familiar *Summa Theologiae* is seen anew, read differently because it is superimposed by something radically different from it.[59] Conversation is referred to as "the imaginative process of reading back-and-forth in the conversation of one's own tradition with another," and "a reading which must be reflectively performed.... One comes to the comparison with something to contribute, while yet remaining vulnerable to the implications of what one might hear."[60] Metaphor is a strategy that involves a creative act of juxtaposition and imagination. It enables the comparativists to continue the practice of comparison even when the compared texts are seemingly incomparable, and it allows them to extend the meaning of each text and to recognize the new meanings produced by reading both texts together.[61] Collage is a method of taking the texts out of their original contexts and juxtaposing them so that the readers will interact with the texts in a new way that is not limited to the traditional interpretations but is open to new possibilities.[62]

It is important to underline that, for Clooney, these strategies represent different ways to read texts from different theological traditions together, but the choice of a particular method (or methods) remains open for the comparativists. In the conclusion of *Theology after Vedānta*, Clooney says:

> In any case, the singleminded devotion of this book to a single experiment precludes large generalizations.... We must end tentatively: at this early stage in the articulation of comparative theology it is important to accept patiently the richness of the variety of comparative models which can be generated out of specific exercises, and to resist the urge to draw attractive conclusions for which there is neither a basis nor a need.[63]

---

59. Clooney, 170. For the Advaitins, a proper superimposition has three characteristics. First, the higher reality is to be superimposed on a lower reality. Second, each reality must be recognized in the process of superimposition. Finally, this process is temporary. It is used in a particular meditation and for a set purpose. Clooney, however, argues that this method should be used without identifying one tradition as superior to the other because it is more advantageous to compare the texts from a more neutral position.

60. Clooney, 170.

61. Clooney, 172–173.

62. Clooney, 174.

63. Clooney, 208.

James L. Fredericks

Another influential comparative theologian is James L. Fredericks, professor at Loyola Marymount University. His campaign for a comparative theology can be seen in "A Universal Religious Experience? Comparative Theology as an Alternative to a Theology of Religions" and *Faith Among Faiths: Christian Theology and Non-Christian Religions*. Based on his conviction that a fully systematized theology of religions is not possible today, Fredericks proposes in "A Universal Religious Experience?" that this discipline should be replaced by a comparative theology. He points out that the theologies of religions are often articulated in ignorance of the religions they claim to interpret, and the theological presuppositions about religions tend to undermine the necessity of studying these religions in their concrete specificity. In contrast, comparative theology engages with other religions and focuses on limited comparisons or case studies. The results of this encounter can be varied, ranging from the possibility of seeing oneself in the Other to the description of utter differences. Moreover, it brings about a transformation in Christian theological interpretations through the power of the Other. Therefore, comparative theologians operate within a tension between vulnerability to the transformative power of other religions and loyalty to the Christian tradition.[64]

In *Faith Among Faiths*, Fredericks says that a theology of religions has reached an impasse in its quest for adequate approaches and productive responses to religious diversity, and he insists that a comparative theology is a way to get beyond this impasse. Viewing theologies of religions as theoretical approaches to religious pluralism, Fredericks indicates that comparative theology is a process or practice in which Christians learn *about* other religions and then learn *from* them in order to understand themselves more fully.[65] Here, his vision of comparative theology is not limited to being an alternative to a theology of religions but as a more effective way of doing a Christian theology.[66] He says that comparative theology is "the attempt to understand the meaning of Christian faith by exploring it in the light of the teachings of other religious traditions. The purpose of comparative theology is to assist Christians in coming to a deeper understanding of their own religious

---

64. See Fredericks, "A Universal Religious Experience?"
65. Fredericks, *Faith among Faiths*, 8–9.
66. Knitter, *Introducing Theologies of Religions*, 205.

tradition."[67] Clooney concurs with Fredericks on this point. In *Hindu God, Christian God*, Clooney expands his ambition for a comparative theology as he claims that theology in today's pluralistic context must be viewed as an interreligious, comparative, dialogical, and confessional enterprise.[68]

Based on Fredericks' vision for comparative theology, one may expect him to engage in an extensive comparison with other religions in the same fashion as Clooney; unfortunately, this is not the case. Fredericks devotes most of *Faith Among Faiths* to the discussion of a superiority of this new discipline over a theology of religions, but he offers only one chapter with two examples of doing theology comparatively. In chapter 7, he compares Jesus' parable of the Prodigal Son with a story about Krishna and the milkmaids, and he reads this familiar Christian story in the light of the image of divine love portrayed in the Hindu story. Then, at greater length, he examines the teaching of Dogen, one of the founders of Zen Buddhism in Japan, on the non-duality of life and death, then reads the Christian doctrine of resurrection in its light. In both examples, he demonstrates that allowing the story of other religions to stir and sharpen our minds and imaginations will help us perceive our own stories and images with new eyes and ears. As a result, Christians can have a deeper understanding of the parable of the Prodigal Son, or discover aspects which have been overlooked, and they can more clearly see a tension between the resurrection as a present reality and the resurrection as a future event.[69]

Keith Ward

Perhaps the clearest exercises in comparative theology are those of Keith Ward, a British philosopher and theologian who is the Regius Professor of Divinity at the University of Oxford. His ambitious project of a comparative theology consists of four books: *Religion and Revelation: A Theology of Revelation in the World's Religions*, *Religion and Creation*, *Religion and Human Nature*, and *Religion and Community*. In these books, Ward develops theologies of revelation, creation, human nature, and community using a comparative methodology. For him, this series is "a systematic Christian

---

67. Fredericks, *Faith among Faiths*, 139–140.
68. Clooney, *Hindu God, Christian God*, ch. 1.
69. Clooney, ch. 7.

A Trinitarian Theology of Religions and Trinitarian Comparative Theology

theology, undertaken in a comparative context."[70] It clearly demonstrates his understanding of the nature and method of a comparative theology.

In the first book, *Religion and Revelation*, Ward intends to articulate a concept of revelation which is true to the Christian tradition, yet is open to interaction with other traditions. For him, this is an "open orthodoxy" – a faithful, open-minded, and developing understanding of Christian faith.[71] While he affirms that theologians should commit to their religious tradition, he declares that "it is wrong to limit theology proper to one's own group and make it simply an exploration of what is officially believed by that group or even of what is contained in the Scripture and tradition of that group."[72] He says:

> I am suggesting that theology is a pluralistic discipline. In it, people of differing beliefs can co-operate, discuss, argue, and converse. Even within one Church, discussion and argument is an obvious feature of a lively religious practice. Understanding grows by debate, by hearing others and by hearing how others hear one's own views; by opposition as well as by consensus. . . . Unless one characterizes others as irredeemably sinful, ignorant or stupid, there may always be something to learn from them. Unless one is sure that one's own view is irrevisably correct, there is always a possibility of error or at least of restricted vision. There is a danger in unrestrictedly free thinking; but it is a lesser and preferable danger to that of compulsory intellectual conformity.[73]

Based on this concept, Ward argues that theology should not be limited to a specific group, using terms like "Catholic theology," "Anglican theology," or even "Christian theology," but it should be viewed as the discipline of reflection upon ideas of the ultimate reality and goal of human life, which can be carried out by people of different beliefs. For such a view, "one may well find oneself defending a particular view of God and of revelation, which may involve one in obedience to the authority of some religious group, but

---

70. Ward, *Religion and Community*, 339.
71. Ward, *Religion and Revelation*, 1–2.
72. Ward, 46.
73. Ward, 45.

one can pursue the discipline without advocating the views of such a group. One may even wish to ally oneself with a group while actively disputing some of its beliefs, even those which some members of the group hold to be essential."[74] According to Ward, this is a full and proper theologian who is a revisionist within his or her own tradition. A revisionist theologian, however, does not discard his or her own tradition. Rather, he or she sees it not as an unchangeable set of beliefs, but seeks to enlarge it as it encounters new understandings and situations.[75]

Seen from this perspective, comparative theology is "an intellectual discipline which enquires into ideas of the ultimate value and goal of human life, as they have been perceived and expressed in a variety of religious traditions."[76] Ward explains further:

> Comparative theology must be a self-critical discipline, aware of the historical roots of its own beliefs; a pluralistic discipline, prepared to engage in conversation with a number of living traditions; and an open-ended discipline, being prepared to revise beliefs if and when it comes to seem necessary.... For some, it will be possible to assert that commitment to the unrevisable authority itself is in principle revisable, even if one cannot foresee any real possibility of revising it without loss of faith.[77]

In *Religion and Creation*, Ward develops a comparative theology of creation and God.[78] Since this is the second part of his comparative theology project, Ward does not give an extensive discussion about a comparative method. Instead, he practices it by comparing the doctrines of creation and God in Judaism, Islam, Hinduism, and Christianity. His endeavor, however, explicates the purpose and nature of a comparative theology. The ultimate goal of comparative theology is exemplified when Ward says that he is writing from a Christian perspective, but he locates it within a global context which will broaden and deepen it. His purpose, therefore, is to articulate and reconceptualize his Christian understanding of creation and God through a

---

74. Ward, 46.
75. Ward, 47.
76. Ward, 40.
77. Ward, 48.
78. See Ward, *Religion and Creation*.

positive interaction with the non-Christian concepts.[79] A comparative theology's commitment to the detailed consideration of religious traditions is also affirmed by the fact that Ward focuses on a detailed study of a small number of contemporary thinkers rather than exploring a wide range of information about the doctrines of creation and God. Moreover, I believe that his exposition of the concept of the Trinitarian God of Christianity implicitly reveals that this doctrine can be used as a framework for an authentic Christian comparative theology. Despite the fact that Ward resists the attempt to limit theology for a specific group or even religion, his findings about the concept of the Trinity point to the opposite direction. While he admits that the doctrine of God as Trinity has a resemblance to the concepts of God in other religions, he affirms that it remains distinctive.[80] He says:

> The Christian idea of the Trinity is thus not wholly at odds with the sorts of reflection that take place in other religious traditions. But it does articulate the concept of God in a way which is most unlikely to have taken the exact form it has without a dependence upon what is taken to be a decisive divine self-disclosure in the person of Jesus.[81]

Consequently, it can be said that while the understanding of God as Trinity is widened and deepened by a comparative theological study, this unique doctrine of Christianity stands as a criterion for a comparative theology that is truly constructed from a Christian perspective. I will resume this argument at the end of this chapter.

In the third book of the series, *Religion and Human Nature*, Ward engages in a detailed comparative study of the concepts of human nature and destiny.[82] Similar to the previous volume, this study makes clearer the characteristics of a comparative theology. Ward maintains that he is writing from a Christian standpoint, but he locates Christian ideas of human nature and the ultimate destiny of humanity in the context of diverse religions with the purpose of developing a Christian understanding that is sensitive and responsive to the teachings of other religious traditions. However, these teachings are not to

---

79. Ward, 3–4.
80. Ward, 337.
81. Ward, 338.
82. See Ward, *Religion and Human Nature*.

be viewed as a mere foil for Christian teaching. Ward says, "My interest is to formulate a Christian view about human nature, informed by other religious views which both contrast with it and, at many points, converge with it. Thereby I hope to extend Christian horizons and understand some of the limitations or distortions which others have perceived in the Christian tradition."[83] In this process, he interacts with the Hindu, Buddhist, Jewish, and Muslim representatives in order to make sure that he accurately understands their positions. In addition, he takes into consideration the different concepts of various Christian traditions concerning the concept of human nature.[84] In the conclusion to this volume, Ward admits that "the differences between religious traditions are nowhere clearer than in their views of human nature."[85] Therefore, the conclusions of comparative theology in this topic must remain tentative. He says:

> One should neither insist that one's own beliefs are obviously the only or unrevisably true ones, nor pretend that all differences of belief are unimportant, nor that one can live comfortably without having any beliefs in this area at all. This requires the resolute pursuit of truth from whatever standpoint one finds oneself beginning from, together with a preparedness to understand as sympathetically as possible alternative views, and learn from them as far as possible.[86]

From this study, it is apparent that comparative Christian theologians must be open and willing to learn from others, and they must ensure that they have an adequate understanding of a particular topic of other faiths as well as that of the various strands of Christianity. Even though they may not be able to grasp the final truth, they must pursue it as comprehensively as possible.

In the final book of Ward's tetralogy, *Religion and Community*, Ward explores the ways in which religion and society interact and the ways in which world religions need to adapt themselves to the pluralistic world.[87] He also aims to develop a concept of the Christian community, the church, which is

---

83. Ward, 8–9.
84. Ward, 8.
85. Ward, 324.
86. Ward, 327.
87. See Ward, *Religion and Community*.

enriched by the insights of other faiths, and, at the same time, to investigate the possibilities of the church's misunderstanding of itself.[88] In the final chapter, he summarizes the thrust of each volume, and brings the readers back to the essence of his project – a comparative theological discipline.[89] He says that the religious pluralism of the world requires an attempt to interpret traditional beliefs in the light of ever-growing scientific knowledge and awareness of many different religious interpretations of human existence in the world. A comparative theology, therefore, is a "co-operative enterprise." As Ward says, "It is a way of doing theology in which scholars holding different world-views share together in the investigation of concepts of ultimate reality, the final human goal, and the way to achieve it."[90]

Towards a Trinitarian Comparative Theology

From the above discussion, we can see several advantages of comparative theology. However, a closer look at this promising discipline reveals some crucial shortcomings. This section will highlight major strengths and weaknesses of a comparative theological study, and it will propose that a comparative theology that is authentically Christian must be a trinitarian comparative theology.

There are three main advantages of comparative theology. First, it widens the methodology of Christian theological studies. Comparative theologians rightly point out that Christian theology in today's pluralistic world can no longer be developed exclusively on the basis of Christian Scripture and tradition. An awareness of different religious interpretations of human existence in the world obviously challenges prevailing Christian teachings that operate only within a Christian worldview. The pluralistic ideal, which champions equality among world religions and denies any absolute truth claim, calls for a theology that can respond to its questions and challenges. In addition, a dominant status of non-Christian religions in the eastern world forcefully demands a Christian theology that can make sense of other faiths. Consequently, current theologians must take into consideration the teachings of other religions in their attempt to develop a theology that is truly relevant to the pluralistic context.

---

88. Ward, 4.
89. Ward, ch. 14.
90. Ward, 339.

A vision to expand a theological methodology is also shared by theologians who do not belong to a comparative camp. At the present, theologians across the Christian spectrum generally agree that the resources for doing theology are not only the Bible and Christian tradition, but also insights from other traditions and disciplines. In *The Analogical Imagination*, David Tracy suggests that theologians must genuinely expose themselves to the interpreters of other traditions, e.g. followers of other religions, philosophers, social scientists, and artists. They must enter the conversation with a willingness to converse with others and reformulate fundamental questions that are worth asking in the radically pluralistic present.[91] Practical theologians maintain that theology is to be carried out in the light of Christian Scripture and tradition, and in critical dialogue with other sources of knowledge, e.g. anthropology, psychology, sociology, economics, and ecology.[92] A great number of theologians of religions also make use of non-Christian doctrines in constructing a Christian theology, for example, Timothy Tennent, Gerald McDermott, Harold Netland, Stanley J. Samartha, Raimundo Panikkar, Amos Yong, and Veli-Matti Kärkkäinen, among others.

More importantly, theologians around the globe such as Kazoh Kitamori, Kosuke Koyama, Choan-Seng Song, and Aloysius Pieris have been developing indigenous theologies that are noticeably beyond the boundary of the Christian tradition. Interestingly, they construct theologies that integrate with non-Christian doctrines as well as Asian worldviews. These indigenous Christian theologies, as Terry Muck comments, should be viewed as part of the wider, global theology that takes into consideration the teachings of other religions. The twenty-first century theologians, he says, "must do theology with and among the teachers and practitioners of Buddhist, Hindu, and Muslim theologies," and they are demanded "to do theology in a way that takes as its starting point the worldview of discrete cultures, and the questions such a worldview and cultural context creates. Only then, once we discern the specific questions, can we hope to use the gospel story as the resource for providing the needed answers."[93] This understanding clearly supports the

---

91. Tracy, *The Analogical Imagination*, 351–352.

92. See, for example, Anderson, *The Shape of Practical Theology*, and Browning, *A Fundamental Practical Theology*.

93. Muck, "Theology of Religions after Knitter and Hick," 16–17.

assumption of this study that the Buddhist understanding of suffering should be the starting point in doing a Christian theology of suffering in the context of Theravada Buddhism in Thailand.

Second, comparative theology brings about development in Christian theological understanding. This strength of comparative theology is grounded on its commitment to the Christian tradition, reflexive nature, and openness to other religions. As mentioned previously, comparative theologians uphold the Christian faith, but they are not content with theology that is confined to a Christian worldview, or simply affirms a traditional Christian understanding of the particular matters. Perceiving religious diversity as fertile soil for the growth of Christian theology, they take into consideration the non-Christian teachings in their reflective retrieval of Christian doctrines. As a result, comparativists are able to obtain positive contributions from religious pluralism, and they can move beyond conventional Christian theology towards a wider and deeper theological understanding that is more sensitive and responsive to the context of diverse religions. Theologies of Francis X. Clooney, James L. Fredericks, and Keith Ward clearly show that comparative theology bestows profundity and breadth to current Christian theological understanding.

In view of this understanding, it is hoped that this study, as a comparative theological study of the Christian and Buddhist concepts of suffering, will make a contribution to a Christian theology of suffering. While it unashamedly upholds the Christian understanding of suffering, it is courageously open for insights from the Buddha's teachings. Moreover, it will rethink and reformulate the traditional Christian concept of suffering in light of the encounter with a Buddhist view of human predicament. Hence, this study aims to develop a Christian theology of suffering that is relevant to the Buddhist context, and, at the same time, it seeks to enrich a Christian theology of suffering in the global context. In other words, to borrow Fredericks' definition of a comparative theology, this study is the attempt to understand the meaning of the Christian concept of suffering by exploring it in the light of the Buddhist teachings of suffering, and its purpose is to assist Christians in coming to a better understanding of the Christian concept of suffering.[94]

Third, a comparative theology enables Christians to engage with the followers of other faiths in a non-threatening and more constructive manner.

---

94. Fredericks, *Faith among Faiths*, 139–140.

This strength of comparative theology is based on its dialogical nature and commitment to detailed study. From the above discussion, it is obvious that an interreligious dialogue lies at the core of comparative theology. Different from exclusivists who often disregard interfaith dialogue and pluralists who promote dialogue, but require the participants to forsake their absolute truth claim, comparativists emphasize the significance of dialogue that allows religious practitioners to maintain their uniqueness yet be open to truth they might find in other religions. Moreover, comparativists reject generalizations about religions and are committed to the necessity of studying other religions in their concrete specificity. Instead of generalized comparisons between religious traditions, comparativists compare particular points between religions, for example teachings, symbols, and personalities, in order to find out whether the understanding of that particular point might enhance the understanding of its parallel in the other religion.[95] Consequently, a comparative method makes possible a non-hostile yet authentic interreligious dialogue in which Christians can genuinely share their faith with the religious others, and respectfully listen to them. The outcome of this dialogue is not only mutual understanding between religions but also mutual enrichment for each participant.

It is interesting that a comparative approach to interfaith dialogue is very similar to that of a trinitarian theology of religions in the sense that both of them take the challenge of differences between religions seriously. They neither surrender to the exclusivists' notion of incompatibility between religions nor suppress the differences under the rough parity of pluralism. On the contrary, they address the different religious concepts on their own terms, allowing religious practitioners to make known their positions, yet they encourage them to listen to one another and attempt to discern the truth arising from the conversation. This approach to an interfaith dialogue is greatly beneficial for Thai Christians who are in the midst of a Buddhist majority. It enables Thai Christians to uphold the Christian faith, but listen to Buddhist teachings, and it helps them appreciate Buddhist insights, yet come to a deeper understanding of Christian belief.

In spite of several advantages of comparative theology, there are two critical drawbacks that demand a more careful development of comparative

---

95. Schebera, "Comparative Theology," 10.

methods and framework. First, a comparative theology does not have a clear methodology. Though comparativists agree with a general model of comparative theology, they do not have a standard comparative methodology. Perhaps, at this moment, it is more appropriate to speak of several *comparative theologies* rather than a comparative theology. Take, for example, the comparative theologies of Clooney and Ward. While both of them agree that a comparative theology is distinguished by its commitment to the detailed comparison of religious traditions, the scope of Clooney's work is undoubtedly much narrower than that of Ward. While both of them compare the Christian faith with other religious traditions, Clooney's comparative strategies are much more complex than Ward's method. Clooney uses five strategies that enable him to compare the texts in different levels, such as their meanings, functions, and structures, but Ward mainly compares different religious understanding of the particular topics. While both of them are willing to learn from other religions, it seems that Clooney gives much more weight to the non-Christian teachings than Ward does. In *Theology after Vedānta*, Clooney devotes three full chapters to the study of Advaita Vedānta Text before he briefly discusses the *Summa Theologiae*, and rereads and rewrites it *after* Advaita Vedānta. Different from Clooney, Ward prioritizes a Christian understanding which is true to the Christian tradition, yet is sensitive and responsive to the teachings of other religions. Consequently, comparative theology is still in its early stages, and much more development is needed to provide a more standard comparative methodology. This does not mean that an identical comparative methodology is required for all comparativists, but it suggests that a mature comparative theology should be characterized by the more congruent comparative methods. Perhaps a comparative study of different comparative approaches should be conducted so that theologians in the comparative camp can develop more coherent methods that provide a clearer direction for a comparative theological study.

Second, comparative theology does not have a clear criterion in managing the tension between its faithfulness to the Christian tradition and vulnerability to other religions. As mentioned, comparativists admit that a comparative study entails a crisis between being loyal to the Christian faith and being open to other faiths as well as being ready to change. On the one hand, this is a preferable tension that brings about self-examination and growth. On the other hand, as Ward says, it can lead to a danger of unrestrictedly free thinking or even a loss of faith.[96] It is clear that the outcome depends on comparativists' ability to deal with this inevitable tension. Unfortunately, the current form of comparative theology does not include any guidelines for this critical endeavor. Those who are engaged with a comparative study are solely dependent on their own judgment and preference, which may or may not lead to a constructive result. Therefore, comparative theologians need a point of reference that assists them in determining whether they are truly fulfilling the vision of a comparative theology, or if they are, in fact, falling into a pitfall of syncretism that does not enhance but degrade a Christian theology.

In view of the uniqueness of the Christian concept of the Trinity and its enormous implications for a theology of religions, as proposed by Kärkkäinen, I would argue that this doctrine can be used as a criterion for assessing a constructive Christian comparative theology. In other words, a trinitarian framework enables theologians to discern if their comparative theological findings are truly faithful to the Christian faith while being open to and enriched by other faiths. Contemporary theologians agree that the affirmation that the one God is Father, Son, and Spirit is a distinguishing mark of Christianity.[97] Moreover, this doctrine lies at the center of Christian theology; as Emil Brunner says, "It is a theological doctrine which defends the central faith of the Bible and of the Church."[98] It is not the result of philosophical speculation, but it is a product of a Christian reflection on the biblical narratives. For this reason, Stanley J. Grenz and John R. Franke suggest:

> A truly Christian theology must be trinitarian because the biblical narrative, which speaks about the history of God, focuses on the triune God. Not only does the Trinity as theology's structural motif emerge out of the biblical narrative, however; it also arises from the theological heritage of the church. The doctrine of the Trinity has stood at the heart of theology throughout church history, providing impetus to the theological task and giving shape to the theological deposit that has continually arisen from that enterprise.[99]

---

96. See Ward, *Religion and Revelation*, 45, 48.
97. Kärkkäinen, *The Doctrine of God*, xiii.
98. Brunner, *The Christian Doctrine of God*, 206.
99. Grenz and Franke, *Beyond Foundationalism*, 177.

As a consequence, a comparative theology that is genuinely Christian must be a trinitarian comparative theology that is steadfastly anchored in the narratives of Scripture as well as salvation history, at the center of which stands the coming of the Son to establish the kingdom of the Father in the power of the Spirit. While it welcomes insights from other religious traditions, it will reread and rewrite a traditional Christian understanding in the light of the trinitarian relation and actions of God the Father, the Son, and the Holy Spirit. Hence, new understanding arising from a trinitarian comparative theological study will not, and cannot, be contradictory to the praxis of Christ, but it will reflect the nature and purpose of God's ongoing mission to the world. Ray S. Anderson says:

> Theological reflection does not lead to new revelation, for God has spoken once and for all in the revelation of Jesus Christ, and holy Scripture is the normative and infallible truth of that revelation. However, theological reflection takes note of the presence of the One who is revealed in his continuing ministry of reconciliation through the Holy Spirit. The same Jesus who inspired the true account of his own life and ministry through the Holy Spirit in the form of Scripture continues to be present in the act of reading, hearing and interpreting the Scriptures.[100]

Nevertheless, it would be mistaken to view the Trinity as a mere safeguard of the Christian tradition. Indeed, the doctrine of the Trinity provides a solid theological ground for an openness to learn from other religions. A trinitarian theology indicates that God is relational. The one true God's intratrinitarian relationships between the Father, Son, and Spirit and his relationship with human beings serve as a paradigm for relating to the religious Other. It opens the door for Christians to understand more about other religions, and it also helps them gain a deeper knowledge of Christianity through the encounter with the religious Other.[101] An intratrinitarian relationship between the Son and Spirit, which indicates the continuity of the present work of the Holy Spirit with the finished work of Jesus of Nazareth, also affirms the Spirit's presence in the world and points to the possibility of the Spirit's activity in

---

100. Anderson, *The Shape of Practical Theology*, 55.
101. Kärkkäinen, *Trinity and Religious Pluralism*, 179.

other religions. Seen from this perspective, a comparative methodology is no longer driven by the pluralistic agenda, but it is guided by a trinitarian theology. As a result, a trinitarian comparative theology will be able to uphold the Christian faith, yet enhance it through the encounter with other faiths.

Grounded in a trinitarian comparative theology, this study can be perceived as a Christian comparative theology of suffering in the context of Theravada Buddhism in Thailand. It is not just a comparison between the Christian and Buddhist understanding of suffering, but it is a Christian theology of suffering that is developed from a comparative theology. To be more precise, it is a theology of suffering that is firmly rooted in the Christian concept of suffering, yet it critically engages and learns from the Buddhist concept of suffering.

However, different from comparative theologians who propose that a theology of religions should be replaced with a comparative theology, I will argue that both disciplines are indispensable for constructing a Christian theology that can effectively respond to the challenge of religious pluralism. While a theology of religions provides a framework for theologians who engage with other religious traditions, a comparative theology gives the specific methods and direction for their comparative studies. As Stephen J. Duffy says:

> There is a need for both a theology of the religions and comparative analysis and synthesis because the two are the distinct but inseparable and integral *a priori* and *a posteriori* moments of a single theological project which aims at bringing Christianity into fruitful engagement with the non-Christian traditions.[102]

Therefore, it can be said that a methodology of this dissertation is drawn from *a trinitarian comparative theology of religions*. It is a Christian theological discipline that attempts to account theologically for the meaning and value of other religions through a comparative study of the particular subject matters with the purpose of developing a Christian understanding that is more sensitive and responsive to the teachings of other religions, yet is firmly anchored in the sound doctrine of the Trinity.[103]

---

102. Duffy, "A Theology of Religions and/or Comparative Theology?," 105. Emphasis in the original.

103. Examples of recent works that are grounded in the same methodology are: McDermott and Netland, *A Trinitarian Theology of Religions*; Kärkkäinen's constructive

As a consequence, this study is an exercise in a trinitarian comparative theology of religions. It maintains that the Christian God is none other than the Father, Son, and Spirit. It acknowledges the presence of the Triune God outside the Christian community, yet it insists that the work of the Spirit that may be found in other religions cannot be contrary to the persons and works of the Father and Jesus Christ. Nevertheless, the discussion in this study will be limited to the topic of suffering. It begins with an exploration of the Buddhist concept of suffering that governs the understanding of Thai Buddhists and influences the responses of Thai Christians to the reality of human suffering. Then it will compare and contrast this understanding with the Christian concept of suffering in order to develop a Christian theology of suffering that is more relevant to the context of Theravada Buddhism in Thailand and more beneficial to the global context.

The Trinity and Human Suffering

In the previous sections, I have argued that the doctrine of the Trinity provides a solid theological ground for a theology of religions and comparative theology. It enables both disciplines to be genuine Christian theologies that are faithful to the Christian tradition yet also open to learning from other faiths. In this section, I will give a general survey of how the doctrine of the Trinity can help Christians develop a deeper theological understanding of suffering. Special attention will be given to a theology of the cross proposed by Martin Luther, Kazoh Kitamori, and Jürgen Moltmann. While their proposals will be studied more thoroughly in the final chapter, a brief discussion in this section will help the reader grasp a clearer picture of the relationship between Trinitarian theology and a theology of suffering. Nevertheless, it is important to stress that this dissertation does not aim to offer a full-scale Trinitarian theology of suffering. Its purpose is to develop a Thai theology of suffering using the methodology of a theology of religions and comparative theology that are entrenched in the sound doctrine of the Trinity. Further

---

Christian theology for the pluralistic world series that consist of *Christ and Reconciliation, Trinity and Revelation, Creation and Humanity, Spirit and Salvation,* and *Hope and Community*; and Kärkkäinen, *Doing the Work of Comparative Theology*. These are important works that help Christians deepen theological understanding by engaging with other religions and disciplines.

study needs to be done in order to construct a comprehensive Trinitarian theology of suffering.

As mentioned, the doctrine of the Trinity stands at the heart of Christian theology. A theological endeavor that is genuinely Christian must be rooted in biblical narratives and salvation history, at the center of which stands the coming of the Son to establish the kingdom of the Father in the power of the Spirit. In order to develop a solid theology of suffering, one must approach it from a trinitarian perspective. As I shall examine in later chapters, much human suffering is the result of sin, and only God can free humankind from sin and, in turn, suffering. Therefore, God's response to human suffering – specifically his sustaining and redemptive work – must be interpreted as a trinitarian act of the Father, Son, and Holy Spirit.

An examination of biblical evidences reveals that God has responded to the reality of suffering through his sustaining and redemptive work for humanity and the whole creation. In spite of human rebellion which leads to distorted creation and human affliction, the Creator God continues to uphold creation through his sustaining work (Ps 104; Col 1:17; Heb 1:3). It is through his sovereignty and providence that the world continues to exist. In the silence of God, he is still at work in and through his creation.[104] However, the Creator God is not only the Father, but the Triune God. While the Father has the primary role in the act of creation, other members of the Trinity also have important roles in it. The involvement of the Son, the Word, in the act of creating and sustaining the universe is clearly affirmed in several biblical passages – for example, John 1:1–3, 10; Colossians 1:16–17; Hebrews 11:3; Revelation 4:11. The role of the Holy Spirit as God's power in the creative act and God's provision of life for creatures, especially for human beings, is evidently stated in Genesis 1:2; 2:7; 6:3, 17; 7:22; Job 26:13; 33:4.[105]

Besides his sustaining work, God responds to the reality of suffering by taking the initiative in redeeming the created order. The offspring of the woman mentioned in Genesis 3:15 is understood as referring to Christ who would crush the head of Satan. God's redemptive work for Noah and his family during the flood (Gen 6-9), his election of Abraham (Gen 12) and his

---

104. See chapter 3 of this work.
105. Grenz, *Theology for the Community of God*, 101-106. See also Gunton, *The Triune Creator*, 14–24.

liberation of the Israelites from slavery in Egypt (Ex 3-14) obviously reveal his redemptive plan for all humankind. Numerous accounts of God's deliverance and answers to the cries of believers also affirm that he is the God who actively responds to human misery. Several Old Testament passages point to the new world in which evil and suffering will be abolished, and peace and justice will be achieved (e.g. Isa 2:2–4; 11:6–9; 24–27; Ezek 38–39; Mic 4:1–4). The New Testament also makes clear that God will finally end the reign of sin, evil, and suffering in this world (e.g. Matt 24; Mark 13; Luke 21; Rev 21:1–5).

The center of God's redemptive work is in Jesus Christ, particularly his passion and death on the cross. Through Christ, God intervened in creation in order to participate in human suffering as well as to save human beings and the whole created order. First of all, he placed himself alongside humankind as he "became flesh and lived among us" (John 1:14). As human, Jesus fully shared limitations and pains that are parts of human life yet he is without sin (Matt 4:2; John 11:33–35; Heb 4:15). During his earthly ministry, Jesus always responded to the afflicted. He healed the blind, the sick, the paralytic and those who suffered from other diseases or demon-possession (e.g. Matt 8:14–17; 9:27–34; 12:9–13). He often touched the lepers, who would never be touched by anyone, and healed them (e.g. Matt 8:1–4; Mark 1:40–41; Luke 5:12–13). He called those who were regarded as "sinners" to follow him and he dwelt among them (Matt 9:9–11; Mark 2:13–17; Luke 19:1–10). At the cross, God, through Christ, shares the affliction of humankind in order to redeem us from sin and its consequences. This is the new meaning of suffering! The resurrection and glorification of Christ after he has suffered and died also reveals that justice will eventually be done. In the midst of inexplicable pain and unjust suffering, believers can be assured that they will finally be raised from the dead and share Christ's glory (1 Thess 4:13–18).

However, God's redemptive work on the cross is not exclusively achieved through the Son, but it belongs to all there persons of the Trinity. In *The Triune Creator*, Colin E. Gunton argues that God's sustaining and redemptive work should be perceived as an action of the Triune Creator, who continues to be involved with the creation. God's work of creation is not limited to the beginning and the end, but it is in and towards the world through the Son and Spirit. There are christological and pneumatological dimensions to a trinitarian theology of creation that make it possible to understand that the Triune God is upholding the order of creation and enabling it to achieve its final perfection that was intended for it from the beginning.[106] God is at work through the Son and the Spirit. The Son upholds the creation's movement, and redirects it to its original goal through his death and resurrection. The Holy Spirit maintains the order of creation, and restores it to perfection. At the same time, the Spirit is the one who upholds Jesus of Nazareth and mediates the Father's action in raising him from the dead.[107] Therefore, it is clear that God's sustaining and redemptive work is a trinitarian action that aims to bring the whole created order back from suffering to perfection.

The trinitarian understanding of God's redemptive work can be clearly seen in a theology of the cross. While a theology of the cross is supported by many theologians, the most prominent theologians who shape it are Martin Luther, Kazoh Kitamori, and Jürgen Moltmann. Luther first introduced the *theologia crucis*, theology of the cross, in the Heidelberg Disputation in April 1518. The most important statements concerning this theology can be found in Thesis 19 and 20:

> That person does not deserve to be called a theologian who looks upon the invisible things of God as though they were clearly perceptible in those things which have actually happened [Rom 1:20]. He deserves to be called a theologian, however, who comprehends the visible and manifest things of God seen through suffering and the cross.[108]

Here, it is important to note that many scholars, for example, McGrath and Kärkkäinen, have pointed out that the English translation of Thesis 20 is seriously inaccurate and misleading. It connotes nearly the opposite concept from the original. Whereas *posteriora Dei* literally means "rearward part of God," it is mistakenly translated as "manifest things of God."[109]

For Luther, the cross must be the foundation and criterion for Christian thinking about God, and the crucified God is the key to a proper understanding of the nature of God.[110] Luther's theology of the cross consists of three basic aspects. First, it is a theology of revelation, which is indirect and hidden

---

106. Gunton, *The Triune Creator*, 10.
107. Gunton, 176–178.
108. *LW*, 31:52.
109. Kärkkäinen, "Evil, Love and the Left Hand of God," 148.
110. McGrath, *Luther's Theology of the Cross*, 1.

in the suffering and the cross of Christ. Second, it maintains that God makes himself known through suffering. Third, it is a theology of faith and of faith alone.[111]

Luther's *theologia crucis* was taken further by Japanese theologian Kazoh Kitamori. Over and against a traditional Christian theology that maintains divine immutability and impassibility, Kitamori argues that God himself experienced pain on the cross. For Kitamori, the pain of God is not based on his empathy with human suffering or involvement in history, but it arises from an internal conflict within his own nature regarding his love and wrath. He says, "God who must sentence sinners to death fought with God who wishes to love them. The fact that this fighting God is not two different gods but the same God causes his pain. Here heart is opposed to heart with God."[112] The clearest manifestation of God in pain is the cross of Christ because it describes God's love as having conquered his wrath. Therefore, Kitamori argues that the pain of God is the heart of the gospel. He says, "God in pain is the God who resolves our human pain by his own. Jesus Christ is the Lord who heals our human wounds by his own (1 Pet 2:24)."[113] More precisely, Kitamori proposes that a theology of the cross is actually a description of the pain of God.[114]

Following Luther and Kitamori, Jürgen Moltmann suggests that the cross of Christ is the center of Christian theology.[115] Moreover, he argues that the cross is not just an event between God and humankind, but it is a trinitarian event between the Father, Son, and Holy Spirit.[116] He says, "What happened on the cross was an event between God and God. It was a deep division in God himself, in so far as God abandoned God and contradicted himself, and at the same time a unity in God, in so far as God was at one with God and corresponded to himself."[117] Therefore, the cross belongs to the inner life of

---

111. I will return to Luther's argument in chapter 4.
112. Kitamori, *Theology of the Pain of God*, 21.
113. Kitamori, 20.
114. Kitamori, 110.
115. Moltmann, *The Crucified God*, x.
116. Moltmann, 245.
117. Moltmann, 244.

God. It is an event of the love of the Son, the grief of the Father, and the Spirit of life, love, and election to salvation.[118]

Based on this understanding, Moltmann says that the cross must be understood in trinitarian terms: the Father surrenders his own Son to death; the Son offers himself as a sacrifice; and the sacrifice of the Father and the Son is done through the Holy Spirit, who is the link between the Father and the Son in their separation.[119] In addition, the Spirit of life proceeds from the cross of Christ, enabling it to contain within itself all the depths of human history. All suffering and death has been included on the cross, and life and joy has been integrated into eternal life and the eternal joy of God.[120] Therefore, a theology of the cross incorporates not only the justification but also the regeneration of human beings. It is the acceptance of men and women to become God's children, heirs of God's kingdom. For Paul, this is the experience of the Spirit that allows believers to cry like Jesus, "Abba! Father! (Rom 8:14–15), and it eschatologically points to the hope of righteousness (Gal 5:5), which is the foundation for the new creation of all things.[121]

A brief discussion of the relationship between the Trinity and suffering reveals that a theology of the cross is indispensable in developing a Christian theology of suffering. It helps Christians better understand the Triune God's response to human suffering. It can assist Christians to respond to the problem of suffering in a more appropriate manner. Therefore, a theology of the cross will be studied in more detail in the final chapter, which will focus on the Buddhist and Christian answers to the problem of human suffering.

Conclusion

In summary, a Christian theology of religions and comparative theology provide the foundations for a Christian theology of suffering in the context of Theravada Buddhism in Thailand. Both disciplines are necessary for constructing a Christian theology that can effectively respond to the challenge of religious pluralism. A theology of religions provides a framework for engaging

---

118. Moltmann, 246–249.
119. Moltmann, *The Trinity and the Kingdom*, 82–83.
120. Moltmann, *The Crucified God*, 246.
121. Moltmann, *The Spirit of Life*, 149.

with other religious traditions. A comparative theology gives the specific methods and direction for their comparative studies.

While there are several theologies of religions and comparative theologies, I believe that a trinitarian theology of religions and trinitarian comparative theology are the most appropriate approaches at the present time. Both of them enable theologians to engage with other faiths fruitfully yet remain faithful to the Christian faith. They make possible a Thai Christian theology of suffering that is more relevant to the Buddhist context, as well as a global Christian theology of suffering that is more applicable to the radically pluralistic world. Hence, the methodology of this study is characterized as a trinitarian comparative theology of religions.

Besides providing a framework for a Christian theology of suffering, the doctrine of the Trinity is a key to understand God's response to the problem of human suffering. In this study, I take my clue to a relationship between the Trinity and suffering from Martin Luther, Kazoh Kitamori, and Jürgen Moltmann, who argue that the cross of Christ reveals that the triune God of Christianity is a suffering God who actively participates in human suffering. The basic concept of a theology of the cross is given in this chapter, and it will be elaborated in the final chapter of this work.

For this reason, this study is an exercise in a trinitarian comparative theology of religions on the subject matter of suffering. It maintains that the God of Christianity must be understood in terms of the Father, Son, and Holy Spirit. It affirms the presence of the Triune God outside the Christian community, yet it insists that the work of the Spirit that may be found in other faiths must be in agreement with the persons and works of the Father and Jesus Christ. Moreover, it seeks to interpret God's response to human suffering from a trinitarian perspective. It is hoped that this framework and guiding vision will enable this study to achieve its purpose of developing a more profound Christian theology of suffering that is enriched by the Buddhist concept of suffering, but remains faithful to the Christian tradition. To this end, this paper will begin an exercise of a trinitarian comparative theology of religions.

CHAPTER 2

The Reality of Human Suffering

As the beginning of an attempt to developing a Christian theology of suffering in the context of Theravada Buddhism in Thailand, this chapter will scrutinize the basic understanding of suffering in the Buddhist and Christian traditions. Grounded in a methodology of a trinitarian comparative theology of religions, it will focus on the First Noble Truth, the Truth of Suffering (*Dukkha*), and the related teachings of Buddha, as found in the Pāli Canon, which strongly shape the worldview of the Thai people concerning affliction. Furthermore, it will study the Theravada interpretation of these doctrines, especially that of the distinguished Thai Buddhist scholars, for example, Ven Phra Buddhadāsa Bhikkhu, Ven Phra Dhammapitaka, Pin Muthukan, and Saeng Chandngarm. This basic Buddhist concept of suffering, in turn, provides a context for reflection on and reexamination of a traditional Christian theology of suffering.

I will argue that the First Noble Truth enables Christians to better comprehend the reality and complexity of suffering as well as to accept that some forms of suffering can be part of human nature. Different from the traditional Christian approach to suffering, which often prioritizes its intellectual dimension – and, therefore, minimizes it under the shadow of the problem of evil and theodicy that requires a logical explanation – Buddhism emphasizes the concrete human experiences of suffering and seeks to respond to them appropriately. While Christianity tends to generalize suffering and attributes it to sin, Buddhism observes the sophistication of human predicament and points to various reasons behind it. Moreover, Buddhism teaches that some types of suffering are unavoidable because they are naturally connected to finitude and mortality. Viewing these differences in the light of a trinitarian comparative theology of religions, I would propose that Christians are called to discern the general revelation of God in this seemingly opposite approach to suffering. This chapter will show that the Buddhist wisdom has much to teach Christians about the complex reality of suffering. Furthermore, paradoxically as it may sound, the First Noble Truth helps Christians develop a clearer understanding of God's revelation in Scripture concerning suffering. It reminds us that suffering cannot be naively attributed to sin, and some forms of suffering may actually belong to and have a positive role in God's good creation. In the final analysis, this understanding enables Christians to be more open to the reality of human suffering and to move beyond solving a logical problem of suffering to solving the actual problem of suffering.

The Basic Understanding of Suffering in Buddhism

In order to comprehend the fundamental concept of suffering in Buddhism, it is crucial to study its founder – the Buddha – the First Noble Truth, and the Three Characteristics of Existence. However, for the purpose of this dissertation, this section will provide neither a complete historical background of Buddhism nor extensive discussion of the above doctrines.[1] In contrast, it will give an introductory knowledge on the Buddha and explore the essence of his primary view on suffering, which is preliminary to other aspects of the Four Noble Truths.

The Founder of Buddhism

The historical founder of Buddhism was the Buddha, the Enlighten One, whose name was Siddhattha (Siddhartha in Sanskrit) and family name was Gotama. He was born in 563 BC in the Indian city of Kapilavatthu, now in Nepal, in which his father, Suddhodana, was the ruler. His mother was Siri Maha-Maya. She died seven days after the young prince was born. When Siddhattha was sixteen, he married a beautiful princess named Yasodhara, who bore him a son, Rahula, thirteen years later. Even though Prince Siddhattha was living in his father's palace, protected by his father from seeing

---

1. For a more comprehensive study on a historical background and doctrines of Buddhism, see Butr-Indr, *The Social Philosophy of Buddhism*; Grimm, *The Doctrine of the Buddha*; and Oldenberg, *Buddha*.

sorrow, frustration, perplexities, and ultimately the suffering of life, he was somehow exposed to the reality of life. He saw four unpleasant scenes: an old man with gray hair tottering out of a hut, an ill man lying on the ground, a corpse being carried by people, and a wise ascetic clothed in orange robes. This humane experience stimulated him to find the way to the cessation of universal suffering. Eventually, he decided to renounce his worldly life and undertook the lifestyle of the ascetic.

After renouncing all bondages in his life, Siddhattha began to pursue his goal. He first placed himself under Alara and Uddaka, two outstanding Hindu teachers at that time. He studied and followed their system and methods of ascetic practices. He learned a great deal about meditation from them, but he found no resolution to the problem of human suffering. Consequently, he withdrew from them and tried extreme bodily asceticism. Unfortunately, it was still not the path to the Enlightenment.

After six years of seeking, Siddhattha gained the insight of *Dhamma* after meditating alone under a Bodhi tree. He ultimately realized the knowledge and the experience of the Four Noble Truths (*Arriyasacca*) that could set humankind free from the endless circle of birth and rebirth, which, in turn, would save them from suffering.[2] After his Enlightenment, he became known as the Buddha, which means "The Enlightened One" or "The Awakened One."[3] Through his compassion, he taught Dhamma to others in order that they might also be enlightened. He wandered along the roads of India for forty-five years to teach people about this truth until the day he passed away at Kusinara at the age of eighty.

Since that time, the Buddha's story and teachings had been orally transmitted for centuries until the Pāli Canon was first written in about 80 BC when King Vattagamani reigned in Ceylon.[4] The Pāli Canon, which is called *Tipitaka* (three baskets), consists of three collections of texts: *Vinaya Pitaka* (the Text of Discipline), *Sutta Pitaka* (the Text of Discourse), and *Abhidhamma Pitaka* (the Text of Metaphysics). The Four Noble Truths are recorded in *Sutta Pitaka*;

---

2. The term *Arriyasacca*, coming from two Pāli words – *arriya* (noble) and *sacca* (truth) – literally means "the noble truth" or "the most excellent truth." It can also be rendered "the truth that enables one to become a noble person who can quench one's own craving or longing." See Chandngarm, *Arriyasatsee*, 30–31.

3. Humphreys, *Buddhism*, 25.

4. Coomaraswamy, *Buddha and the Gospel of Buddhism*, 261.

however, these truths are explained with greater details, and in different ways, throughout the Pāli Canon.⁵

The First Noble Truth: The Truth of Suffering (*Dukkha*)

The Four Noble Truths begin with the truth of suffering (*Dukkha*). The Buddha declares:

> This, O Monks, is the Noble Truth of Suffering: Birth is suffering; decay is suffering; death is suffering. Sorrow, lamentation, pain, grief and despair are suffering. Presence of objects we hate is suffering; separation from objects we love is suffering; not to obtain what we desire is suffering. Briefly, the five groups of existence connected with clinging are suffering.⁶

From these statements, most people misunderstood that Buddhism is pessimistic since it views life as nothing, but suffering. Nevertheless, many Buddhist scholars have pointed out that Buddhism should no longer be perceived as pessimism, or even optimism, but it must be understood as realism. Venerable Walpola Rahula, a renowned Buddhist scholar, says:

> Buddhism is neither pessimistic nor optimistic. If anything at all, it is realistic, for it takes a realistic view of life and of the world. It looks at things objectively (*yathābhūtaṃ*). . . . It tells you exactly and objectively what you are and what the world around you is, and shows you the way to perfect freedom, peace, tranquility and happiness.⁷

This objection is based on the fact that the Pāli word *Dukkha* has a much broader sense than its English equivalent, "suffering."⁸ It is correct that, in ordinary usage, it can be translated as "suffering, pain, sorrow, or misery," but, in Buddhism, it has a more profound philosophical meaning, and conveys wider concepts, such as "imperfection, impermanence, emptiness,

---

5. Rahula, *What the Buddha Taught*, 16.

6. Dhammacakkappavattana Sutta 11 (SN LVI.11).

7. Rahula, *What the Buddha Taught*, 17. See also Dhammapitaka, *Arriyasat*, 6; Chandngarm, *Arriyasatsee*, 52–53; and Humphreys, *Buddhism*, 76.

8. In English, "suffering" is defined as "physical or mental pain, the state or experience of one who suffers, and a pain endured or a distress, loss, or injury incurred." See Cove, *Webster's Dictionary*, 2284; and Wehmeier, *Oxford Dictionary of Current English*, 1300.

and insubstantiality."[9] For the Buddha, suffering has three basic meanings: *Dukkha-dukkhatā*, *Viparināma-dukkhatā*, and *Sankhāra dukkhatā*.[10]

First, *Dukkha-dukkhatā* is the state of suffering in terms of feeling and sensation. This term is close to the English word "suffering." It includes both physical and emotional suffering – hurt, pain, sorrow, grief, and so on. This type of suffering corresponds to the Pāli word "*Dukkhavedanā*"; the feeling of suffering, caused by a disagreeable sensation, is experienced.[11]

Second, *Viparināma-dukkhatā* is the state of suffering that is inherent in the change or the state of suffering which concealed within the infidelity of happiness. This kind of suffering is caused by the changes within and the cessation of happiness. Venerable Phra Dhammapitaka explains:

> In the normal condition, the person feels alright. There is no suffering. But after the person experiences some kind of pleasant feeling and that feeling faded or ended, the same condition becomes suffering. It's almost as if the suffering is hidden, only to reveal itself when the pleasant feeling fades. The more intense the pleasant feeling is, the more intensely does it change into suffering, and the suffering seems to expand in proportion to the intensity of the pleasant feeling. If the pleasant feeling had not arisen, the suffering dependent on it would likewise not have arisen.[12]

Third, *Sankhāra dukkhatā* is the state of suffering due to formations. All things are under the conflictual state caused by birth and decay. They are not constant or perfect within themselves, but they exist as part of the cause and effect continuum. Thus, they will cause suffering, i.e. the feeling of suffering (*Dukkha-dukkhatā*), whenever they become the objects of craving or clinging. This kind of suffering is the essence of the Three Characteristics of Existence

---

9. Rahula, *What the Buddha Taught*, 16–17. In fact, Rahula insists that this term should be left untranslated because the current translation is superficial, inadequate, and misleading.

10. See D. III.216; SN IV.259; and SN V.56.

11. Dhammapitaka, *Buddhadhamma*, 87.

12. Dhammapitaka.

(*Ti-lakkhana*).[13] It is the most important kind of all root-caused suffering since it describes the inherent nature of all existence.[14]

From this understanding, the First Noble Truth does not merely address physical and emotional pain, but it also includes other meanings of suffering. Consequently, a careful examination of the First Noble Truth is needed in order to accurately understand the Buddha's view of human life and the world. This section will consider the meaning of the First Noble Truth, and explore several kinds of suffering mentioned in the *Tipitaka*.

In the first place, the Buddha says, "Birth is suffering; decay is suffering; death is suffering."[15] The Buddha does not deny happiness in life, but he is pointing out that everything is impermanent, and it brings about the feeling of suffering.[16] Birth is suffering because it is the starting point of all forms of suffering. The person who is born will be compelled to decay, death, and all forms of suffering.[17] Decay is suffering because it reduces human strength, potency, and power, and it brings about diseases. It is important to note that decay does not begin when people are old, but it has started when humans are born. In other words, as Muthukan puts it, "we move nearer to death, in every single breath."[18] Death is suffering simply because it exists in humanity, physically as well as mentally, in every single breath too, and it forces humans to die, and, at the same time, it destroys and ends all happiness in life.[19] Suffering associated with birth, old age, and death can also be described as the natural state of suffering or the built-in suffering (*Sabhāvadukkha*). This kind of suffering is unavoidable because it is the true basis of all human life. All people must encounter it.[20]

---

13. The details of the Three Characteristics of Existence (*Ti-lakkhana*) will be discussed below.

14. Dhammapitaka, *Buddhadhamma*, 87–88.

15. SN LVI.11.

16. Elsewhere, the Buddha admits different forms of happiness. For example, in Anguttaranikāya, the Buddha acknowledges four types of happiness: happiness resulting from economic security – enjoyment of wealth – happiness on account of freedom from debt, and happiness on account of living a faultless life. See AN II, 69

17. Muthukan, *Buddha-Sart*, 2:19.

18. Muthukan, *Golwitee Gae Tuk*, 169.

19. Muthukan, 188; and Muthukan, *Buddha-Sart*, 2:28.

20. Muthukan, *Golwitee Gae Tuk*, 157–160.

In the second place, the Buddha says, "Sorrow, lamentation, pain, grief and despair are suffering. Presence of objects we hate is suffering; separation from objects we love is suffering; not to obtain what we desire is suffering."[21] Besides the built-in suffering, the Buddha points out that human beings must encounter various types of suffering, which are grouped under the miscellaneous suffering (*Pakiṇṇakadukkha*). Whereas all human beings equally encounter the same built-in suffering of birth, decay, and death, each person faces many kinds of miscellaneous suffering of different factors and conditions and in different degrees of intensity. The built-in suffering can be compared with the fixed members of the family, and miscellaneous suffering is like different guests that visit our home.[22] The Buddha does not specifically mention the forms of miscellaneous suffering. He simply describes the results of this sort of suffering. Therefore, miscellaneous suffering consists of many types of suffering, and it should not be limited.[23]

Finally, the Buddha concludes the First Noble Truth by saying that "briefly, the five groups of existence connected with clinging are suffering."[24] This statement reveals the Buddha's understanding of the true nature of humanity and the fundamental cause of human suffering. The Buddha believes that the world and all living creatures, human beings in particular, are the combination of the five groups of existence or five aggregates. The physical body is the material aggregate (*rupa*), and the mental aspect is divided into four aggregates of feeling (*vedana*), perception (*sanna*), mental formations (*sankhara*), and consciousness (*vinnana*).[25] Besides these five aggregates, there is nothing left to be the permanent self of what is called "the individual." Hence, everything that exists has no permanent self. These aggregates also have no permanent self. They are to be understood as classificatory groupings that have no real existence. As Ven Phra Buddhadāsa Bhikkhu says, a key point in

---

21. SN LVI.11.
22. Muthukan, *Buddha-Sart*, 2:16–17.
23. Muthukan, *Golwitee Gae Tuk*, 203.
24. SN LVI.11.
25. While the material and feeling aggregates are straightforward, the last three aggregates require an elaboration. Perception aggregate refers to an awareness or recognition of sense impressions. Mental formations aggregate is the actively thinking component in an individual. Consciousness aggregate means knowing the objects by way of eye, ear, nose, tongue, body, and mind. It is the basis for other aggregates of the mental aspect. See Bhikkhu, *Koomeu Manut*, 101–105; and Dhammapitaka, *Buddhadhamma*, 15–11.

Buddhism can be summarized as, "The five aggregates are *anattatā* (no self)."[26] Nevertheless, humans do not comprehend this reality. They misunderstand that all things, including human beings, have no permanent selves. They mistakenly and unconsciously attach or cling to the selfhood. Consequently, human beings are subjected to suffering.[27]

The Three Characteristics of Existence

Another fundamental teaching of Buddhism, particularly on the topic of suffering, is taken root in "the Three Characteristics of Existence" (*Ti-Lakkhana*), which consists of the State of Impermanence (*Aniccatā*), the State of Suffering (*Dukkhatā*), and the State of Soullessness or Non-self (*Anattatā*). The Buddha proclaimed:

> Whether Perfect Ones appear in the world, or whether Perfect Ones do not appear in the world, it still remains a firm condition, an immutable fact and fixed law: that all formations are impermanent, that all formations are subject to suffering, that everything is without a self.[28]
>
> What do you think, O monks: Is corporeality (*rupa*) permanent or impermanent? Impermanent, O Venerable One. Are feeling (*vedana*), perception (*sanna*), mental formations (*sankhara*) and consciousness (*vinnana*), permanent or impermanent? Impermanent, O Venerable One.
>
> But that which is impermanent, is it something pleasant or painful? It is painful, O Venerable One.
>
> But, of what is impermanent, painful and subject to change, could it be rightly said, "This belongs to me, this am I, this is my ego?" No, Venerable One.
>
> Therefore, whatever there is of corporeality, feeling, perception, mental formations and consciousness, whether past, present or future, one's own or external, gross or subtle, lofty or low, far or

---

26. Bhikkhu, *Koomeu Manut*, 115.

27. The Buddhist understanding of the cause of suffering will be discussed in detail in the next chapter.

28. AN III.134.

near, of all these things one should understand, according to reality and true wisdom: "This does not belong to me, this am I not, this is not my ego."[29]

In one who understands eye, ear, nose, tongue, body and all the remaining formations as impermanent, painful and not-self, in him the fetters are dissolved.[30]

First, the Buddha realizes that all things are impermanent, non-static, instable, in a state of decay and decomposition.[31] He points out that nothing is static, but it changes without beginning or end. Nothing is the same as this moment as it was a moment ago and nothing will remain the same in the future. Even the hills are slowly being worn away. Every part of a human body has been changed from yesterday. Second, the Buddha teaches that all things are in the tense and contradictive state caused by impermanence. As a result, nothing is perfect or constant. It cannot provide complete fulfillment to those who desire enjoyment, but it would cause suffering for those who attach to it.[32] Hence, in the three characteristics of existence, suffering does not refer to painful or frustrating experiences (*Dukkhavedanā*), but it refers to the stressful and conflictual state resulting from impermanence (*Dukkhalakkhana*). In other words, it connotes the fact that all things cannot remain the same, and then this truth goes contradictory to human attachment.[33] This is suffering in the broadest sense.

Finally, the Buddha teaches that all things have no permanent self. Under the Law of Cause and Effect, the state of non-self results from the two former characteristics. Different from the Brahmanic concept of the eternal soul or unchanging self, *Ātaman*, the Buddha believed that everything that exists has no permanent self (*Anattatā*). Since all things are impermanent, all things are inevitably under suffering – they cannot remain the same. They can stop neither impermanence nor the contrary forces of birth and dissolution because they have no permanent self. Thus, the concept of non-self primarily means, "no authority or not under power." In the final analysis, all of existence does

---

29. SN XXII.59.
30. SN XXXV.53.
31. Dhammapitaka, *Tri-Luk*, 4.
32. Dhammapitaka, 4–5.
33. See Muthukan, *Buddha-Sart*, 3:197–199; and Dhammapitaka, *Tri-Luk*, 4–5.

not actually exist as it seems to be, but it is just a process of formations and motions that different components combine with one another without the centrality or control of the so-called self.[34] Therefore, while Attā cries out, "This belongs to me, this am I, this is my ego," Anattatā proclaims, "This does not belong to me, this am I not, this is not my self."[35]

Even though impermanence, suffering, and non-self are the common characteristics of existence that commonly and constantly reveal themselves, most common people are unable to notice them. This is because they are concealed by three things: continuity (*Santati*), movement (*Iriyapatha*), and wholeness (*Ghana*). First, impermanence is obscured by continuity. Birth and death occur within existence all the time, but the circle of birth and death happens in a very fast continuous process. As a result, people misunderstand that it is permanent. For example, the person close to us every day and night may seem to be the same, but when the time passes we will notice the changes in that person. In fact, those changes always happen, gradually and imperceptibly.[36]

Second, suffering (i.e. conflictual state resulting from impermanence) is concealed by movement. The state of impermanence resulting from the contrary forces within different components may take some time to appear. During that time, if there is any movement, suffering may not be noticed. For instance, after remaining in the same gesture for a long time, a person usually makes a move to ease his or her ache. As a result, suffering is ended and the person may overlook the reality of suffering in his or her life.[37]

Finally, non-self is covered up by wholeness. Actually, a particular thing consists of many components. When all elements and conditions are taken away, that thing will no longer remain. However, human beings cannot see this truth because they, under their ignorance, are misled by wholeness. For a common example, we can see a shirt, but not cloth. We can see a toy, but not plastic. This is true to life. If we view life through a correct perspective, we will be able to distinguish different components of life and realize the no-self.[38]

---

34. Dhammapitaka, *Tri-Luk*, 50–51, 56.
35. SN XXII.59.
36. Dhammapitaka, *Tri-Luk*, 23–24.
37. Dhammapitaka, 24–26.
38. Dhammapitaka, 26–27.

In summary, the term "suffering" in Buddhism has a complex meaning. On the one hand, it simply means physical and emotional pain. On the other hands, it refers to the state of suffering that is inherent in the change and conflictual state resulted from impermanence. The Buddha points out that human beings must encounter various kinds of suffering. Physical and emotional suffering associated with birth, old age, and death is unavoidable because it is the true basis of human nature. The feeling of suffering is the result of craving or clinging to someone or something. Moreover, the Buddha teaches that suffering is the stressful and conflictual nature of all things caused by their impermanence. Therefore, nothing can provide complete fulfillment to those who attach to it. The Buddha proclaims this truth not to add a burden to human misery, but to help people recognize it and to start the process of solving suffering. The Buddha believes that suffering is resolvable. He pointed out that overcoming suffering is not accomplished by avoiding problems or neglecting suffering but by confronting the reality of suffering and learning how to respond to it correctly. Therefore, the essence of the first truth is rightly accepting the reality of suffering as it is, and perceiving life and the world as they are.[39] This basic Buddhist concept of suffering is a context for reflection on and reexamination of a traditional Christian theology of suffering in the following section.

Theological Understanding of the Reality of Suffering

As mentioned earlier, this dissertation is not an extensive theological study of suffering, but it is an exercise in a trinitarian comparative theology of religions on this topic. It does not attempt to explore and evaluate several theologies of suffering that are available in the present, but it seeks a Christian theology of suffering that is developed from a comparative theology in the context of Theravada Buddhism in Thailand. This section will not discuss different theological positions concerning suffering, but it will study the basic Christian understanding of suffering in comparison with the First Noble Truth.[40] The

---

39. Dhammapitaka, *Buddhadhamma*, 906.

40. For a thorough discussion of several approaches to the problem of evil and suffering, see Inbody, *The Transforming God: An Interpretation of Suffering and Evil*; Richard, *What Are*

exposition of the fundamental Buddhist understanding of suffering indicates that Buddhism sees suffering as an inescapable part of the human experience, not something from which one could seek escape. Suffering is a complex reality ranging from simple physical and emotional pain to sophisticated concepts of the stressful and conflictual state caused by impermanence. However, Buddhism holds that this miserable experience is solvable. Humankind can overcome it by perceiving life and the world as they are and responding to them in a correct manner. Consequently, this section will try to answer two crucial questions arising from the study of the basic Buddhist concept of suffering. The first question is "Does the Christian Scripture also affirm the reality and complication of human suffering?" The second question is "Does the traditional Christian understanding of suffering portray an accurate picture of this reality?" To be more precise, "Is it true that all kinds of human suffering are the results of sin and is it possible that some forms of suffering are parts of the created order?"

The Reality and Complexity of Suffering in the Biblical Perspective

Similar to the Buddhist teaching, the Christian Scripture testifies that human suffering is a complex reality. Though suffering is not at the center of the biblical teaching, innumerable examples of suffering can be found throughout the Scripture, for example, physical pain, toil, guilt, premature death, oppression, loss in battle, disaster, illness, conflict, punishment, and spiritual torment. The list could go on.[41] These biblical examples are not abstract teachings about suffering, but they are actual experiences of men and women who tried to make sense of their predicament and sought to be freed from it. Therefore, suffering in the biblical perspective is not illusory, but it is an undeniable fact.[42] Even though the term suffering in the Bible does not contain as wide a range of meaning as the term *dukkha*, the complexity of suffering is clearly

---

They Saying about the Theology of Suffering?; Surin, *Theology and the Problem of Evil*; and Whitney, *What Are They Saying about God and Evil?* For specific positions concerning evil and suffering, see Cobb and Griffin, *Process Theology: An Introductory Exposition*; John Hick, *Evil and the God of Love*; Kushner, *When Bad Things Happen to Good People*; Lewis, *The Problem of Pain*; Moltmann, *The Crucified God*; Plantinga, *God, Freedom, and Evil*; and Sölle, *Suffering*.

41. See, for example, Gerstenberger and Schrage, *Suffering*.
42. See Hall, *God and Human Suffering*, ch. 1.

revealed through its various expressions. Scripture uses many different words to convey this idea, for instance, affliction, agony, anguish, distress, hardship, oppression, pain, trouble and tribulation. These terms are derived from four main Hebrew and Greek roots that portray many faces of suffering, namely כאב, עמל, קצו, and πασχω.

כאב means "be in pain, cause pain, or ruin," and its nominal form כְּאֵב means "pain and anguish" (Jer 15:18; Isa 65:14), and מַכְאוֹב means "pain and suffering" (Exod 3:7; Ps 38:17; Isa 53:3-4). The translations, however, are not always consistent. Nominal forms are normally rendered "pain," but the more abstract "suffering" is also used (NRSV in Exod 3:7; Job 2:13; Lam 1:18). When they are translated "wound" or "diseases," the pain-causing factors are usually specified (NRSV in Isa 53:4; Jer 15:8). Both bodily sensation and inner feelings are entailed, but there is no precise distinction between the two. They can refer to the feelings of either an individual or a community. In all instances, they always diminish the life of individuals or communities to a certain extent and occasionally lead them near to death. The cause of the pain is complex. It can be attributed to preventable human actions (Exod 3:7; Ps 69:26, 29) or inescapable human nature (Prov 14:13; Eccl 1:18; 2:23). It may be an effect of divine discipline or judgment (Jer 30:15; Lam 1:12, 18), or it may be involved with the vocation of the servants or prophets (Isa 53:3–4; Jer 15:18, 45:3).[43]

עמל denotes "labor, often with an eye to its difficulty, its burdensome nature, hence toil." Thirteen of its sixteen occurrences are in Ecclesiastes. In Ecclesiastes 1:3, human life is described as a laborious task. Elsewhere in Ecclesiastes, however, it is difficult to discern if it denotes life itself or the labor of maintaining a livelihood. Outside Ecclesiastes, this term also refers to labor without a negative connotation (Jonah 4:10; Ps 127:1). Its nominal form עָמֵל can simply mean a worker (Judg 5:26; Prov 16:26), or it can refer to a sufferer or one who labors in misery (Job 3:20; 20:22). The most common derivation is the noun עָמָל, "distress, trouble, toil, effort, misfortune, misery, or adversity," which mainly occur in Ecclesiastes, Job, and Psalms. It can also mean "trouble associated with or caused by wickedness or to name that wickedness itself."[44]

---

43. Fretheim, "כאב," 575–576.
44. Thompson, "עמל," 435–436.

It is important to note that the term עמל in Ecclesiastes is closely related to the term הבל, which is usually translated "vanity or meaninglessness." Qohelet clearly judges עמל to be הבל. He says, "Meaningless! Meaningless! Utterly meaningless! Everything is meaningless. What does man gain from all his labor at which he toils under the sun?" (Eccl 1:2–3). He gives several reasons why toil is meaningless. For example, the person may work hard, but then die and must leave all he owns to someone who has not worked for it (Eccl 2:17–23). It is well known that הבל literally means "breath, breeze, vapor," but scholars have different opinions concerning its meaning for Qohelet. It has been suggested that this term in Ecclesiastes means "absurd, absurdity, futility, temporary, emptiness, frustration, vanity, or meaninglessness."[45] More work must be done about Qohelet's understanding of הבל, but suffice it to say that the term can be generally rendered "meaninglessness," but its specific meaning must be decided on the basis of the immediate context because it can be used differently in different contexts.[46]

צוק means "constrain, bring into straits, close or press in/upon or vex." It has several derivatives, which mean "restriction, distress, affliction, grief, tribulation, trial, suffering, straitness, straits, stress, plight, pressure, or oppression." This group of words indicates the terrible physical and psychological suffering of individuals and the whole Israelite nation caused by personal foes (Pss 25:2; 107:2; 119:139) or hostile nations, for instance, the conditions imposed on people in Samaria and Jerusalem during the siege by Assyria and Babylonia respectively (Isa 8:22; 9:1; 29:2; Jer 19:9). In addition, the horrifying siege conditions described by צוק and its derivatives are understood as God's judgment of his disobedient people (Deut 28:53, 55, 57; Jer 19:9).[47]

πασχω means "to suffer, or undergo, experience." Though this term includes the wide range of human experiences, it is frequently used in a negative sense. It is found forty-two times in the New Testament. Most of its occurrences refer to the sufferings of Christ and Christians for Christ's sake.[48] From this root, there are several derivatives, for example, παθημα, "suffering, affliction or misfortune" (e.g. Rom 8:18 and 2 Cor 1:5ff); κακοπαθεω, "suffer

---

45. See a discussion in Fox, "The Meaning of Hebel for Qohelet," 409–427; Longman, *The Book of Ecclesiastes*, 58–65; and Lorgunpai, "World Lover, World Leaver," 70–84.

46. Longman, *The Book of Ecclesiastes*, 64.

47. Swart and Wakely, "צוּק," 786–787.

48. Michaelis, "Πασχω," 904–923.

evil or endure hardship" (2 Tim 2:9; 4:5); and συνκακοπαθεω, "endure hardship with someone" (Heb 4:15; 10:34).[49]

Therefore, it can be said that both Buddhism and Christianity agree that suffering is real and complex. The problem of suffering is not only an intellectual problem that requires a logical explanation, but also a tangible challenge that demands a proper response. Moreover, various expressions and manifestations of suffering in both religious traditions reveal that it is more appropriate to speak of *the many problems* of human suffering rather than *a problem* of human suffering.

This understanding is clearly supported by concrete situations of human misery. Suffering can be classified in various ways. It can be distinguished by its different targets – individuals, communities, nations, regions or the whole human race. It can also be differentiated by the way in which it affects humanity, namely physically or non-physically. Physical suffering primarily influences a person's or community's bodily sensations, for example, physical pain, physical disability, hunger, thirst, disease and death. Non-physical suffering mainly affects their inner beings intellectually, emotionally, psychologically and spiritually. It is revealed in conflict, anxiety, depression, disappointment, abandonment, shame, guilt and so on. Nevertheless, these types of suffering are closely connected since humanity consists of both physical and non-physical dimensions. Pain unquestionably affects a person holistically. Finally, suffering can be classified by its degree of intensity. It ranges from minor personal pain to severe regional or global hardship caused by poverty, illiteracy, starvation, environmental pollution, natural disasters, oppression, war, terrorism or AIDS. History shows that the Holocaust is not the only witness to the radical reality of human suffering. While we are uncertain about the exact number, we know that in this century alone millions suffered and died under brutal and inhumane political leaders around the globe. Furthermore, the United Nations Development Programme indicates that approximately 1 billion people are now living at the margins of survival on less than $1 US dollar a day, with 2.6 billion living on less than $2 US dollars a day, and around 10 million children dying each year before the age of five, the great majority from poverty and malnutrition.[50] For this reason,

---

49. Gartner, "Suffer," 719–722.
50. United Nations Development Programme, *Human Development Report 2007/2008*, 25.

suffering calls for a theological response that takes it seriously, a theology that is not just an academic exercise or merely addresses a particular kind of suffering without considering its diversity. This leads to the second question, "Does the traditional Christian understanding that attributes all suffering to sin provide an appropriate concept of this complex reality?"

Reexamination of the Traditional Theological Understanding of Suffering

Throughout the history of Christianity, it has been firmly maintained that all suffering is not and cannot be part of the divine intention for creation, but it is the consequence of Adam's transgression. Any attempt to alter this traditional understanding is often regarded as a deceptive and heretical effort. Nevertheless, a comparison with the Buddhist teaching that some types of suffering are inherent in human nature clearly brings this position into question. Christians are compelled to reconsider whether a suffering-free human life is a biblical truth or simply a denial of an unpleasant reality. It is also crucial to rethink if decay and physical death are natural consequences of birth rather than results of sin. Moreover, the traditional Christian understanding of suffering is greatly challenged by modern theologians who argue that the original creation was not free from suffering. Therefore, this section aims to show that it is too simplistic to attribute all suffering to sin, and it is possible that some forms of suffering are intrinsic parts of the human nature. In the final analysis, it will be seen that this understanding not only revitalizes a Christian theology of suffering, but also helps Christians be more receptive to the reality of human suffering.

The Traditional Theological Understanding of Suffering

The understanding that suffering came into existence as a result of the first sin is based on the story of creation and the fall as well as other passages in the Bible. The story of creation in Genesis 1 affirms that the entire universe was created by God and it was originally "very good" (Gen 1:31). The first appearance of suffering in this world can be traced back to the story of the fall in Genesis 3. When sin entered the world through the disobedience of humankind (Gen 3: 6–7), suffering was brought into being in the form of guilt, shame, conflict, pain, toil, and death. Adam and Eve's hiding from God, their excuses, enmity between the serpent and the woman, greater pain in childbearing, cursing of the ground, painful toil, and death are clearly outcomes of their disobedience (Gen 3: 15–19). In the New Testament, this concept is affirmed by Paul when he says that suffering, specifically death, entered the world through the sin of Adam (Rom 5:12–21; 1 Cor 15:21–22). He also declares that death is the wages of sin (Rom 6:23) and the last enemy to be destroyed by Christ (1 Cor 15:26). The Book of Revelation reveals that God will eventually bring suffering to an end: "He will wipe every tear from their eyes. There will be no more death or mourning or crying or pain, for the old order of things has passed away" (Rev 21:4).

Reflecting on the above passages, many theologians conclude that suffering, death in particular, cannot be part of the created order and human essence but is the result of sin. In the fifth century, Augustine said, "The first men were indeed so created, that if they had not sinned, they would not have experienced any kind of death; but that, having become sinners, they were so punished with death, that whatsoever sprang from their stock should also be punished with the same death."[51] In AD 418, the Council of Carthage affirmed the Augustinian view and rejected the Pelagian view that Adam was created mortal. The council declared, "If anyone should say that Adam the first man was created mortal so that, whether he sinned or not, he would have died physically, . . . let him be anathema".[52] This position is also confirmed by the Reformers. John Calvin, for example, stated, "Truly the first man would have passed to a better life, had he remained upright; but there would have been no separation of the soul from the body, no corruption, no kind of destruction, and, in short, no violent change."[53]

At the present, many biblical and theological scholars continue to uphold this tradition. Gordon J. Wenham indicates that, in Genesis 3, human mortality, pain in childbirth, and labor to produce food are viewed as the consequences of humanity's first sin. These consequences are both physical and spiritual. The spiritual outcome – alienation from God – immediately followed the act of disobedience, but the physical effects – toil, pain, and death – took longer to become apparent. These human characteristics are opposed to the background of Genesis 1, which ended by saying that the

---

51. Augustine, *The City of God*, 413.
52. Quoted in Nowell, *What a Modern Catholic Believes about Death*, 14.
53. Calvin, *Genesis*, 180.

whole creation was very good.⁵⁴ D. A. Carson understands God's verdict that all creation is very good to mean there is no sin and suffering in this world. The onset of suffering, toil, pain, and death follows the first human rebellion recorded in Genesis 3. He says, "All suffering, not least sickness and death, are tied to sin. If there had been no sin, there would have been no death, and no illness which is death's prelude."⁵⁵ James D. G. Dunn says that Paul's statements in Romans 5:12–21 reveal that death is not the proper end of human life, and it was not part of God's original plan for humankind.⁵⁶ While Stanley Grenz admits that all creatures are mortal in a biological perspective, he indicates that death is unnatural in a theological – particularly eschatological – perspective because it is contrary to God's ultimate intention for his creation.⁵⁷ Millard Erickson also maintains that physical death is a result of sin, but he speaks more cautiously of a pre-fallen human nature. He suggests that Adam was originally in the state of conditional immortality. Before the fall, he was not inherently immortal, but, given the right conditions, he could have lived forever. In other words, the potential of death and eternal life was within creation from the start. After he had sinned, Adam's death is no longer potential, but it became actual. In the past, he could die, but now he would die. In addition, Erickson says that a pre-fallen human body could become diseased, but sin brought about the diseases for humans to contract.⁵⁸

The Challenge of the Basic Buddhist Concept of Suffering

While a Christian theology of suffering in the Buddhist context is firmly rooted in theologies of creation and fall, it also reconsiders the traditional understanding in the light of the Buddha's teaching. Since the essence of the First Noble Truth is to accept the reality of suffering as it is, and to perceive life and the world as they are, ideas that suffering is exclusively the result of sin and a pre-fallen human is free from all sorts of suffering, especially decay and death, are highly questionable. Different from the traditional Christian understanding that regards all suffering as an intrusion into a perfect world,

---

54. Wenham, *Genesis 1–15*, 89–90.
55. Carson, *How Long, O Lord?*, 110.
56. Dunn, *Romans*, 288–289.
57. Grenz, *Theology for the Community of God*, 580.
58. Erickson, *Christian Theology*, 613.

the Buddha teaches that some kinds of suffering result from the impermanence of worldly existence, which is imperfect. While many Christians believe that human beings are originally immortal and exempt from pain and suffering, Buddhists understand that humankind is always mortal and subjected to pain and suffering.

In the First Noble Truth, the Buddha points out that suffering associated with birth, old age, and death is the natural state of suffering. This kind of suffering is unavoidable for all living creatures. Birth will naturally lead to decay, and, in turn, death. Moreover, the Buddha points out that all living beings must encounter physical suffering caused by the imperfection of the body, for example, suffering from weather, hunger, thirst, being impelled to urinate, and being impelled to defecate.[59] In the Three Characteristics of Existence, he indicates that all things are impermanent, non-static and instable. Nothing is the same at this moment as it was a moment ago and nothing will remain the same in the future. Human beings and all earthly existence are bound to this reality. For this reason, all things are within the state of suffering, not referring to the painful or frustrating experiences but the tense and contradictive state resulting from impermanence. Moreover, since nothing is perfect or constant, it cannot provide complete fulfillment to those who desire enjoyment but would cause suffering for those who attach to it.

These basic Buddhist principles can be beneficial for Christians. Even though ideas of five aggregates and soullessness found in these doctrines evidently contradict the Christian concepts of human soul and eternal life,[60] the Buddha's concepts of impermanence and suffering point to the true nature of all finite things. These teachings cannot deliver humankind from suffering, but they are able to free it from being bothered by the reality of human suffering. They also prevent humankind from unnecessary suffering caused by attaching to someone or something. While many Christians, especially those in the western world, are very much troubled by the existence of death

---

59. Vajirananavarorasa, *Dhammawijarn*, 13.

60. While Christianity holds that the soul is part of human nature, this understanding must be distinguished from Platonic idea of the natural immortality of the soul. For Christianity, the soul is not divine, but it is part of the created human nature. Therefore, the soul's immortality is dependent on the will of the Creator. For the soul to participate in the immortal life of God, it needs to be illuminated and elevated by the Spirit of God. See a discussion in Pannenberg, *Systematic Theology*, 2:181–231.

and various types of physical discomfort because they insist that life according to God's original plan should be suffering-free, Buddhists simply accept them as natural parts of human life. In this sense, Buddhists seem to have a healthier perspective of life because they view themselves as being under neutral bodily limitations while Christians view themselves as being inside an evil and sinful body. Consequently, the basic Buddhist concept of suffering compellingly urges theologians to rethink if the Bible really denies the possibility of suffering in the ontology of creation.

A New Theological Understanding of Suffering

In the light of Buddhist teaching, it is crucial to reconsider the biblical passages as well as explore the various positions of contemporary theologians concerning the possibility of suffering in the original creation. An assessment of biblical evidence for the traditional position reveals that there is no explicit statement on whether a pre-fallen human is immortal or free from all suffering. In fact, the traditional conclusion that humans were originally immortal and free from suffering is not a certainty, but speculation.[61] On the other hand, the Bible does not clearly identify the existence of suffering before the fall, yet some passages undoubtedly allude to this reality. Therefore, it is more likely that humans were mortal and not spared from all suffering from the start.

The creation narrative reveals that some types of suffering can belong to the divine intention for a good creation. The affirmation that the creation is "very good" (Gen 1:31) is often used to support that the world was perfect and contained no suffering. However, "good," טוב in Hebrew, does not mean "perfect" or "free from suffering." The term טוב has a wide range of meanings such as "pleasant, practical, suitable, nice, friendly, just, and morally good," yet the context suggests that it means "appropriate."[62] Claus Westermann says, "In any case 'good' is not to be understood as indicating some fixed quality; the meaning is rather functional: 'good for. . . .' The world which God created and devised as good is the world in which history can begin and reach its goal and so fulfill the purpose of creation."[63] While the human mind cannot reconcile a good creation, as well as a good God, with the existence

---

61. See a discussion in Pannenberg, 2:265–275.
62. Westermann, *Genesis 1–11*, 166.
63. Westermann.

of suffering – and, thus, inevitably demands theodicy – God has declared in the first chapter of history that every aspect of his majestic work is good and the whole created order is very good according to his design, notwithstanding the presence of some kinds of suffering. Hence, the notion that God's creation includes particular types of suffering from the very beginning does not destroy Christian faith. Indeed, it strengthens Christian faith to the level that is large and courageous enough to embrace this paradoxical reality.

In recent years, an argument for suffering in the ontology of creation has been clearly spelled out by Douglas John Hall and Wendy Farley. In *God and Human Suffering*, Douglas John Hall interestingly points out that at least four forms of suffering have existed in this world since the creation. They are loneliness, limitations, temptation, and anxiety. Loneliness can be found in Adam's life as the Lord God said, "It is not good for the man to be alone. I will make a helper suitable for him" (Gen 2:18). This dimension of suffering enables us to understand the joy of human fellowship. Limitations are represented by the tree of the knowledge of good and evil, which humankind cannot eat from (Gen 2:17). They prepare the way for us to experience wonder, surprise, and gratitude. Temptation also exists due to the fact that the serpent, or Satan, is God's creature. It helps us understand "good" and "right." Anxiety is the condition that causes Eve to follow the advice of the serpent. Without anxiety, we would not be able to experience comfort, relief, and joy.[64] Hall says:

> What I am contending is that there are, in fact, forms of suffering which belong, in God's intention, to the human condition. Not *all* of what we experience as suffering is totally absurd, a mistake, an oversight, or the consequence of sin. There is something about a significant portion of suffering through which we pass that belongs to the very foundations of beings – something without which our human being would not and could not be what is meant to be.[65]

Consequently, Hall makes a distinction between suffering as becoming and suffering as burden. Suffering as becoming, or integrative suffering, inheres

---

64. Hall, *God and Human Suffering*, 54–62.
65. Hall, 57.

in the created order, but suffering as burden, or disintegrative suffering, came into being as the result of sin. The distinction between these types of suffering lies in the criterion of life. The former integrates human beings into life and makes them more truly and fully alive. The latter does not serve life but is destructive and detracts humankind from the fullness of life.[66]

Hall's description of integrative suffering is very helpful. It enables Christians to see that some sorts of suffering can belong to human nature from the beginning. It also reveals that suffering is not always wrong because it can serve life and enrich our relationship with God. Besides limited freedom represented by the tree of the knowledge of good and evil, it is likely that Adam and Eve experienced physical limitations due to the fact that they occupied earthly bodies. They would not be able to survive without oxygen, water, and food.[67] These constraints, in turn, bring about physical suffering. Therefore, physical discomfort such as hunger, thirst, being impelled to urinate, being impelled to defecate, and even pain, should not be regarded as strangers to a pre-fallen human. Admittedly, this kind of suffering is undesirable, yet it can inhere in a good creation because its purpose is to serve life not to destroy it. Hunger and thirst informs human beings when the water and nutrient volume of the body falls below a certain threshold and urges them to seek food and drink in order to avoid starvation and dehydration. Being impelled to urinate and defecate indicates that liquid and solid waste needs to be eliminated from human bodies. Physical pain serves as a natural defense mechanism that protects humankind from greater harm. Above and beyond serving life, physical suffering obviously reminds human beings that they are not independent creatures, but they must always rely on the creator and sustainer of life (cf. Ps 104). Consequently, it can be said that some types of suffering are not only possible, but also necessary for human existence. However, we must be aware that, before the fall, these expressions of suffering may not be regarded as suffering as we now understand the term.

In *Tragic Vision and Divine Compassion*, Wendy Farley argues that suffering is not necessarily the consequence of sin or indication of the broken

---

66. See Hall, chs. 2–3.

67. Notice that God said, "I give you every seed-bearing plant on the face of the whole earth and every tree that has fruit with seed in it. They will be yours for food" (Gen 1:29). If humankinds were immortal and without any physical need, they would not need any food. Thus, this statement would be irrelevant to them.

world order. Tragic vision understands that creation is good, but it has a tragic structure that makes suffering possible and inevitable prior to any action of humankind. Finite existence gives rise to decay, frustration, hurt, and death. The variety and diversity of the world bring about conflicts between creatures. The fragility of human freedom is caused by inescapable anxiety and desire. Therefore, the structure that makes human existence possible also makes us subject to suffering. However, Farley indicates that evil causes the rupture of creation by sin and radical suffering. Sin is an evil in human existence that corrupts the human spirit by indifference to or desire for evil. Radical suffering is unjust suffering that destroys the human spirit. Consequently, human beings are not simply passive victims of original sin, but they must be responsible for what they do.[68]

Similar to the creation story, the fall account does not deny the possibility of suffering in the original creation. It is commonly held that God's pronouncement in Genesis 3:14–19 marks the beginning of suffering in this world, but this may not be the case. It is not correct to use the oracle for the woman to prove that pain in childbirth is the result of sin. God said, "I will *greatly increase* your pains in childbearing . . ." (Gen 3:16), but he did not say, "I will *give* you pain in childbearing." Here, it makes more sense to conclude that giving birth to a child will always include pain, but the pain will be greatly increased because of sin. Therefore, sin does not introduce pain to childbearing. It is also invalid to use the death of Adam mentioned in Genesis 3:19 to justify that humankind was originally immortal. God said to Adam, "By the sweat of your brow you will eat your food until you return to the ground, since from it you were taken; for dust you are and to dust you will return." The essence of this sentence is that, because of sin, Adam must endure toil until he dies, not that he will die. Here, death is assumed rather than introduced.[69] Gerhard von Rad says:

> The curses do not speak of death as a primary issue, but rather of life, and they affirm that hardship and wretchedness will continue *until* man in death returns again to the earth. One cannot say that man lost a "germ of immortality" any more than one can say that a material modification occurred in him,

---

68. See Farley, *Tragic Vision and Divine Compassion*.
69. Fretheim, "Genesis," 364.

as a consequence of which he must now fall prey to death; the narrator already said in ch. 2.7 that man was created of dust.[70]

Grounded on these observations, Terence E. Fretheim warns Christians against overstating the differences between conditions before and after the fall. He remarks, "Descriptions of paradise have, at times, been drawn in overly romantic terms. . . . For example, suffering is often considered to be only part of the broken world. But it would be truer to the text to speak of the effects of sin as an intensification of suffering, so that it becomes a burden, tragic, no longer serving of life. Eden, though, does include suffering."[71]

The understanding that sin does not lead to human mortality is also supported by Paul Tillich and Karl Barth. Paul Tillich says that sin does not bring about death, but it gives death, "the power which is conquered only in participation with the eternal. The idea that the 'Fall' has physically changed the cellular or psychological structure of man (and nature?) is absurd and unbiblical."[72] Karl Barth argues that human finitude is not the result of sin, but it is intrinsic to the original God-given nature. He says:

> This means that [death] also belongs to human nature, and is determined and ordered by God's good creation, and to that extent right and good, that man's being in time should be finite and man himself mortal. . . . Death is not in itself the judgment. It is not in itself and as such the sign of God's judgment. It is so only *de facto*. Hence, it is not to be feared in itself, or necessarily, but only *de facto*.[73]

A closer look at the New Testament passages also shows that the writers do not necessarily endorse the immortality of a pre-fallen human. In Romans 5:12, Paul says, "Sin entered the world through one man, and death through sin, and in this way death came to all men, because all sinned" (cf. 1 Cor 15:21–22). This declaration is the most significant basis for the traditional

---

70. Rad, *Genesis*, 95. He also points out that the threat of God's command in 2:17 is "you will surely die," not "you will become mortal." See also Hamilton, *The Book of Genesis*, 203; Skinner, *Critical Commentary on Genesis*, 84; Vawter, *On Genesis*, 85; and Westermann, *Creation*, 103.

71. Fretheim, "Genesis," 366.

72. Tillich, *Systematic Theology*, 2:66–67.

73. Barth, *Church Dogmatics*, 3:632.

conclusion that suffering and death do not originally belong to human nature. However, this argument is weakened by two main reasons. First, Paul's statement is not intended to be an explanation for human mortality. While it is impossible to provide a detailed exposition of this passage, it is sufficient to mention its basic theme.[74] The context clarifies that Paul aims to highlight the power of Christ's righteous act that overcomes the consequences of Adam's transgression.[75] The notion that sin and death entered the world and reigned over all people through one man, Adam, is to be viewed in contrast to the reign of grace, righteousness, and eternal life through Jesus Christ. Hence, Paul does not attempt to explain Adam's nature before the fall, but he aims to illustrate his theological understanding of Christ's power over the reigning of sin and death.[76]

Second, the term death, "θάνατος," cannot be restricted to the physical in this context but signifies both physical and spiritual death. It is linked to "condemnation" (vv. 16, 18), and it is contrasted with "eternal life" (v. 21). Indeed, Paul may have in mind the threat of Genesis 2:17 that Adam will die if he transgresses God's command.[77] Douglas J. Moo says, "Paul frequently uses 'death' and related words to designate a 'physico-spiritual entity,' – 'total death,' the penalty incurred for sin. Here, then, Paul may focus on physical death as the evidence, the outward manifestation of this total death; or, better, he may simply have in mind this death in both its physical and spiritual aspects."[78]

A very helpful theological description of death and its relation to sin can be found in Ray Anderson's *Theology, Death and Dying*. Differentiating between human nature and human person, Anderson indicates that the death of human nature is the natural death of a human as a biological creature. On the other hand, the death of the human person is the death of a relationship between person and God due to human sin. He says:

---

74. For a detailed study of Romans 5:12–21, see Dunn, *Romans*; Moo, *The Epistle to the Romans*; and Schreiner, *Romans*.

75. Moo, *The Epistle to the Romans*, 315.

76. A theological account of suffering, particularly God's response to human suffering and appropriate responses of believers to this complex reality, will be discussed more fully in subsequent chapters.

77. Schreiner, *Romans*, 272.

78. Moo, *The Epistle to the Romans*, 320.

> The original human *nature* of Adam before the fall was mortal and subject to the corruption and decay of all created forms of what we call the natural world. Sin did not cause human nature to become finite and mortal. The biological organism was given its own temporal and finite life-span in both the human and non-human natural form. Sin caused a separation between the human person and the life-sustaining promise and gift of immortality which issues from God alone. This is the death which entered into the human race as a consequence of sin, and it is to this death that natural death now points with its fatal finger.[79]

For Anderson, the human person is a biological creature, who is subjected to all of the conditions of a creaturely nature – decay, disease, and death – as other creatures. Death of the human nature is the limitation which God established upon the human person's earthly existence.[80] However, the biological death is not fatalistic because it is not the end of personhood. God will uphold the human person in this limitation through a personal and spiritual relationship with him. Different from non-human creatures, the human person is not entirely determined by the fate of biological death because the human person is created in the image and likeness of God and is given the gift of freedom to be for and with God and to be for and with other persons.[81]

Contrary to the death of human nature, the death of the human person was not ordained by God but is the consequence of sin. It is the death of the personal and spiritual relationship that the person has with God. The divine command in Genesis 2:17, "But you must not eat from the tree of the

---

79. Anderson, *Theology, Death and Dying*, 51.

80. This is similar to Hall's understanding that limitations may not be the results of sin, but they can be integral to human existence. It is also important to note that Anderson locates disease within the nature of biological creatures. However, if disease refers to sickness caused by infection or other unnatural means, not natural illness caused by decay, it is doubtful that it belongs to the original creation. While it is possible to accept that decay, natural illness, and death belong to God's good intention for finite creatures, it is difficult to hold that disease, especially life-threatening disease, is part of a pre-fallen human nature. Hall's criterion of life is helpful here. It is clear that disease does not serve life, but it deliberately threatens and shortens life. Thus, it should not inhere in the structure of creation. It is also interesting that the Buddha does not include disease in the first Noble Truth. For him, the built-in suffering consists of birth, decay, and death, but not disease. Consequently, it is inappropriate to regard disease as part of the original human nature.

81. Anderson, *Theology, Death and Dying*, 47–49.

knowledge of good and evil, for when you eat of it you will surely *die*," is to be understood as a warning against this kind of death. Therefore, Adam and Eve's transgression brings about the death of their communion with God and with each other. Nevertheless, sin does not simply affect a human's spiritual life, but it has an impact on the entire person – one's spiritual orientation to God and one's physical orientation to creation. With the death of their relationship with God, the biological death of human beings becomes fatalistic because there is no longer hope for the gift of immortality and fellowship with God beyond the earthly existence. Consequently, after the fall, the participation of the human person in the death of human nature becomes a threat to the human person.[82]

In light of this understanding, the death that entered the world through Adam's sin and came to all humankind (Rom 5:12) should be viewed primarily as the death of the human person, which also affects the human's biological death. It can be concluded that Paul neither affirms nor denies the physical death of humankind before the fall, but he confirms that the death of humans' relationship with God and biological death as fatalistic reality came into existence because of humans' transgression. Therefore, it is possible that some forms of suffering are natural aspects of human life from the very beginning.

Conclusion

In conclusion, the First Noble Truth enables Christians to better comprehend the reality and complexity of suffering, and to accept that some forms of suffering can be part of human nature. It prevents Christians from upholding the traditional theological understanding that all suffering is the result of sin without carefully examining biblical testimony. A reassessment of Scripture reveals that there is no explicit affirmation of pre-fallen human beings existing without suffering or in a state of immortality. In contrast, some biblical passages imply that humans experienced suffering before the fall. This suggests that some sorts of suffering are inherent in the structure of creation according to God's good intention. Various kinds of suffering related to physical limitations are not intrinsically evil, but they have naturally resulted from finitude and mortality. Moreover, these types of suffering exist to serve human life and

---

82. Anderson, 49, 56.

enrich our relationship with God. This is also true for decay, natural illness, and death. Even though they obviously shorten a human's biological life, and bring it to an end, they do not destroy a human's spiritual life. Quite the reverse, they free the human person from the limitations of human nature, to use Anderson's terms, so that the human person can fully enjoy relationship with God forever. Consequently, Christians should no longer attribute all suffering to sin, but we should accept that humans' earthly existence inevitably brings about certain forms of suffering.[83]

A new perspective on human suffering has several advantages. It releases Christians from being under the illusion that human life must be free from any kind of suffering – which often leads to the problem of theodicy – and helps them be more open to the reality of human suffering, specifically suffering that is tied to finite existence. Viewed from a Buddhist perspective, this position prevents Christians from attaching to an unrealistic view of life which, in turn, leads to unnecessary suffering. The idea that some kinds of suffering can belong to, and have a positive role in, God's good creation also makes Christian faith flourish. It encourages Christians to move beyond shallow belief that can only accept good from God, and not trouble (cf. Job 2:10), to genuine faith that continues to trust the divine goodness and wisdom that surpasses human knowledge, even when facing inescapable human misery.[84]

In addition, a new perspective on human suffering points to the fact that the whole created order is in a finite state and God alone is infinite, as Paul says: "[God] alone is immortal . . ." (1 Tim 6:15). The whole creation must always depend on God for its earthly existence and participation in the eternal life of the trinitarian God. Colin E. Gunton argues that creation is not naturally immortal. The doctrine of creation affirms that nothing is eternal and infinite but God.[85] Creation is not perfect in the beginning, but it is a project that is created to go somewhere. However, by virtue of the fall, creation can

---

83. While the basic Buddhist concept of suffering helps Christians be more open to the possibility of suffering in the original creation, it is important to stress that this is not the Buddha's concern. The Buddha would not care whether suffering was inherent in creation or was totally the result of sin. His teaching is designed to show people how to overcome suffering, not to understand its creation origin. In Christian theological terms, as Terry Muck puts it, the Buddha's teaching is soteriological in nature, not metaphysical.

84. This is a foundation of a proper Christian response to inexplicable suffering which will be elaborated in the next chapter.

85. Gunton, *The Triune Creator*, 224.

reach its original goal only by redemption and transformation through an ongoing work of the Triune creator. Therefore, creation, including human beings, must rely on the redemptive work of Christ and the transformative work of the Holy Spirit in order that it may be redeemed and transformed to completion.[86]

Nevertheless, this is not to say that the traditional theological understanding of suffering should be totally disregarded. This study refuses the notion that all suffering is the consequence of sin and cannot be an intended part of creation, yet it agrees that, in the fallen world, suffering that was not caused by sin as such is now greatly impacted by human transgression, with various examples of suffering clearly indicating evil forces behind them. Consequently, a Christian theology of suffering cannot simply accept the reality of suffering without addressing the truth of sin and attempting to respond to it in a right and proper manner. To this, the subsequent chapter will study the Second Noble Truth – the truth of the cause of suffering – in comparison with retribution theology. It will examine the Buddhist concept of *tanhā* (craving or desire), *avijjā* (ignorance), and the law of *kamma* (the law of cause and effect). Then, these concepts will be compared and contrasted with retribution theology in Christianity. Moreover, it will point out that, in many cases, suffering can remain a mystery that transcends the law of cause and effect and retribution theology. As a result, a proper response to one's affliction may not be dealing with his or her tanhā, avijjā, or sin, but to sustain his or her faith in God in the midst of inexplicable suffering.

---

86. Gunton, 11–12.

CHAPTER 3

The Causes of Suffering

In the previous chapter, I have suggested that the First Noble Truth has much to teach Christians about suffering. It reminds Christians that the problem of the human predicament is a complex reality that demands not only a rational explanation but also a proper response. A Christian theology of suffering in the context of Theravada Buddhism in Thailand can no longer follow the traditional approach that generalizes suffering and discusses it under the problem of evil and theodicy. On the contrary, it must specifically address different kinds of suffering and attempt to respond to them appropriately. Furthermore, the basic Buddhist concept of suffering prompts Christians to reexamine the traditional theological understanding that regards all suffering as an intrusion into a perfect world and to be more open to the possibility of suffering in the ontology of creation. I have concluded that it is biblically and theologically sound to affirm that some forms of suffering can belong to the divine intention for a good creation. This understanding, however, must be supplemented by the idea that suffering not caused by sin as such is severely impacted by sin in the fallen world, and many expressions of suffering are undoubtedly the results of human transgressions.

Consequently, this chapter will pay attention to suffering that does not belong to the original creation with the purpose of developing a Christian theological understanding of the causes of suffering that is relevant to the context of Theravada Buddhism in Thailand. It will begin with an exploration of the Second Noble Truth, the Truth of the Cause of Suffering (*Samudaya*), together with the Buddhist concept of *tanhā* (craving or desire), *avijjā* (ignorance), and the law of *kamma* (the law of cause and effect). Then, it will study some of the causes of suffering according to Christian theology in comparison with the Second Noble Truth. While there are various interpretations of the causes of suffering in Christianity, this chapter will focus on three major causes: sin, oppression, and mystery. To illustrate these themes, I will use retribution theology, liberation theology, and the Book of Job respectively.

I will argue that the Buddhist and Christian interpretations of the causes of suffering are similar in some aspects but different in essential aspects. The law of kamma is comparable with the principle of retribution, yet these concepts are not identical because the former is essentially the natural law of cause and effect whereas the latter advocates a Sovereign God who is the supreme judge and a Trinitarian God who is higher than the rigid law of cause and effect. While the Second Noble Truth teaches that the individual suffers because of his or her own tanhā, liberation theology witnesses to the reality of suffering caused by injustice and oppression. Moreover, the Book of Job challenges both the law of kamma and retribution theology by proclaiming that the cause of an individual's misery can remain a mystery.

Grounded in the method of a trinitarian comparative theology of religions, I maintain that differences between these religious traditions should not be diluted but must be taken seriously. The adherents of each religion should accept that their interpretations of the causes of suffering are really different, but they should approach these differences with respect and should humbly learn from one another. For Christians, this comparative study will open their eyes to an alternate interpretation of the causes of suffering. At the same time, it will enable them to have a clearer vision of some of the Christian explanations for the causes of the human predicament, specifically sin, oppression, and mystery. As a result, this understanding will lead to a more appropriate response to different types of suffering. In the final analysis, this chapter will argue that people may suffer because of their sins; they may be innocent sufferers who are oppressed by others; or they may endure hardship because of unknown reasons. Therefore, experiences of suffering may demand repenting from one's sin, liberating other people from oppressive situations, or sustaining one's faith in God.

The Truth of the Cause of Suffering (*Samudaya*)

After the Buddha acknowledges the reality of suffering, he moves to the second truth, namely the truth of the cause of suffering. While there are several possible causes of human suffering, the Buddha moves beyond those superficial causes and highlights tanhā (craving or desire) as the fundamental reason for suffering.[1] He says:

> This, O Monks, is the Noble Truth of the Cause of Suffering: Craving, which leads to rebirth, accompanied by pleasure and lust, finding its delight here and there. It is the craving for pleasure, the craving for existence, the craving for non-existence or self-annihilation.[2]

In order to accurately understand the truth of the cause of suffering, one must understand the correct meaning of the term tanhā, the types of tanhā, and how tanhā leads to suffering. Moreover, one must understand the doctrine of ignorance (*avijjā*) and the law of kamma which are closely related to the Second Noble Truth.

Tanhā

While tanhā is rendered "craving or desire," the Buddha clearly states that it refers to craving or desire in two specific manners: craving which leads to rebirth and craving which is accompanied by, and constantly finds its delight in, pleasure and lust. In the first place, tanhā is the craving which provides the binding force that captures humankind in the circle of birth and death (birth, decay, illness, and death or *samsara*).[3] In the second place, tanhā is the craving which exceeds the natural needs of human beings. For example, the desire for ordinary food to cease one's hunger is not considered tanhā, but the desire for delicious, colorful, and expensive food is certainly tanhā. It can be generally said that any desire that involves enjoyment and satisfaction is considered tanhā. From this understanding, the desire to be free from suffering is also regarded as tanhā, but it is a good tanhā that leads to the extinction of tanhā itself. In other words, tanhā is like a boat that one uses to go across the river. When one reaches the other side of river, the boat is no longer needed. In the same way, once the goal of nibbāna is reached, all kinds of tanhā will be quenched.[4]

---

1. See Muthukan, *Buddha-Sart*, 2:45–49.
2. SN LVI.11.
3. Humphreys, *Buddhism*, 91.
4. Chandngarm, *Arriyasatsee*, 68–70.

From this teaching of the Buddha, craving is divided into three kinds: craving for sensual pleasure (*kāma-tanhā*), craving for existence (*bhava-tanhā*), and craving for non-existence (*vibhava-tanhā*).

*Craving for Sensual Pleasure (*Kāma-tanhā*)*

Craving for pleasure is a desire for the sensual pleasures of the world that arises from the objects of the five senses: form (*rūpa*), sound (*sadda*), smell (*gandha*), taste (*rasa*), and touch (*photthabba*). Kāma-tanhā can be translated "desire for it to come." It is the desire for the coming of a particular sensual pleasure.[5] This kind of craving brings about suffering in many ways. It causes anxiety and struggle to obtain pleasure from the desired objects. It sometimes leads to hardship, danger, sickness, competition, and conflict. When one's particular desire is not fulfilled, one suffers. If it is fulfilled, one is temporarily satisfied but will strive for other sensual pleasures. Hence, a person will never be completely satisfied. Finally, this kind of craving causes rebirth, in which human beings continue to have the five groups of existence and, in turn, remain in a state of suffering.[6]

*Craving for Existence (*Bhava-tanhā*)*

Craving for existence is generally understood as the desire for having and being. It is one's desire to have what one wants to obtain and desire to be what one wants to become. It brings about suffering when a person cannot acquire what he or she wants and when he or she cannot accomplish his or her goal. Nevertheless, recent Buddhist scholars indicate that craving for existence should be viewed as the desire to hold the existence of oneself or one's possession.[7] It is the desire to sustain one's life, to be born in the next life, and to keep the persons or things that one loves forever. Bhava-tanhā can be translated "desire for it to remain." It is the desire for the ongoing presence of the desired objects.[8] Grounded in this understanding, this kind of craving causes suffering in terms of the fear of losing the persons or things that one

---

5. Chandngarm, 77.
6. Chandngarm, 71–72.
7. Chandngarm, 73; Dhammapitaka, *Dictionary of Buddhism*, 73.
8. Chandngarm, *Arriyasatsee*, 77.

loves, the struggle to keep them, and the sorrow resulting from losing them. More importantly, craving for existence eventually leads to rebirth.⁹

*Craving for Non-existence (*Vibhava-tanhā*)*

Craving for non-existence is often misunderstood as "not desire for being or having." In fact, this kind of craving refers to "desire for non-being or non-having." It explains one's longing to avoid or get out of unpleasant condition or situations. For instance, one may be getting old, but one desires not to become old. It is obvious that the result would be suffering since one's desire contradicts one's real being.¹⁰ Vibhava-tanhā can be rendered "desire for it to go." It is the desire for the extermination of the undesired objects.¹¹ This kind of craving causes suffering in terms of the anxiety to get rid of persons or things that a person hates, the struggle to destroy them, and the trouble caused by their presence.¹²

Avijjā

Even though the cause of suffering in the Second Noble Truth is tanhā, the Buddha explains further in the doctrine of Dependent Origination (*Paticcasamuppāda*) that the cause of tanhā can be traced back to ignorance (*avijjā*), which is the ultimate cause of suffering. The Buddha states:

> When there is this, that is. With the arising of this, that arises.
> When this is not, neither is that. With the cessation of this, that ceases.¹³

> With Ignorance as condition, there are Volitional Impulses.
> With Volitional Impulses as condition, Consciousness.
> With Consciousness as condition, Body and Mind.
> With Body and Mind as condition, the Six Sense Bases.
> With the Six Sense Bases as condition, (sense) Contact.
> With Contact as condition, Feeling.
> With Feeling as condition, Craving.

---

9. Chandngarm, 73.
10. Muthukan, *Buddha-Sart*, 2:56–57.
11. Chandngarm, *Arriyasatsee*, 77.
12. Chandngarm, 75.
13. SN II.28, 65.

> With Craving as condition, Clinging.
> With Clinging as condition, Becoming.
> With Becoming as condition, Birth.
> With Birth as condition, Aging and Death,
> Sorrow, Lamentation, Pain, Grief and Despair.
> Thus is the arising of this whole mass of suffering.
>
> With the complete abandoning of Ignorance, Volitional Impulses cease.
> With the cessation of Volitional Impulses, Consciousness ceases.
> With the cessation of Consciousness, Body and Mind cease.
> With the cessation of Body and Mind, the Six Sense Bases cease.
> With the cessation of the Six Sense Bases, Contact ceases.
> With the cessation of Contact, Feeling ceases.
> With the cessation of Feeling, Craving ceases.
> With the cessation of Craving, Clinging ceases.
> With the cessation of Clinging, Becoming ceases.
> With the cessation of Becoming, Birth ceases.
> With the cessation of Birth, Aging and Death,
> Sorrow, Lamentation, Pain, Grief and Despair cease.
> Thus is there a cessation to this whole mass of suffering.[14]

In its essence, the Law of Dependent Origination is an explanation of the process of the arising and cessation of suffering. In the *Abhidhamma* texts and Commentaries, this principle is known as *Paccayakara*, the interdependent nature of things. It consists of twelve factors, counting from ignorance to aging and death, since sorrow, lamentation, pain, grief, despair, and other forms of suffering are merely the results of the last factor. However, it is important to state that these factors are interdependently linked in the form of a cycle, not a linear sequence. There is no beginning or ending. Ignorance is located in the beginning of the process because it is considered the most practical starting point, not because it is the first cause of all things.[15] In other words, it is regarded as the root cause only in a figurative manner. It is a starting point in an exposition of all existence, the foundation of all life-affirming actions,

---

14. Vin. I.1–3; SN II.1, 65.
15. Dhammapitaka, *Buddhadhamma*, 83.

evil, and suffering.[16] As the Buddha says, "No beginning can be found, monks, to ignorance, thus: 'Before this point there was no ignorance, but then it arose.' In this case, it can only be said, 'Dependent on this, ignorance arises.'"[17]

For the Buddha, ignorance refers to "not knowing the four truths, namely, suffering, its origin, its cessation, and the way to its cessation."[18] It is the primary root of all suffering in the world, veiling humans' mental eyes and preventing them from seeing the true nature of things. It is an illusion that makes life appear to be permanent, happy, and beautiful. It prevents humankind from seeing that everything is actually impermanent, bound to suffering, and intrinsically impure.[19] Consequently, it is only through complete abandoning of ignorance that one will be able to experience the cessation of all suffering.

The Law of Kamma

The truth of the cause of suffering is closely related to the law of kamma. The term "kamma" literally means "action or doing," but, in Buddhism, it generally refers to "action based on intention" or "deed willfully done."[20] There are two main types of kamma. First, *Akusala-kamma*: actions which are unskillful, not good, or evil; specifically, actions which are caused by *akusala-mula*, the roots of unskillfulness, which are greed, hatred, and delusion. Second, *kusala-kamma*: actions which are skillful or good; specifically, actions which are caused by the three *kusala-mula*, the roots of skill, which are non-greed, non-hatred, and non-delusion.[21] According to the Buddha, good kamma produces good effects, and bad kamma produces bad effects. Therefore, the law of kamma is the natural law of cause and effect, of action and reaction. It indicates that human beings receive the fruits of their actions according to the natural process.[22] This principle is summarized in the well-known Thai

---

16. Nyanatiloka, *Buddhist Dictionary*, 60.
17. A.V. 113; Vis. M. 525.
18. SN XII.4.
19. Nyanatiloka, *Buddhist Dictionary*, 59–60.
20. Dhammapitaka, *Buddhadhamma*, 157. The term *kamma* does not mean the result of action as many people commonly and wrongly use it. Hence, we must distinguish between *kamma* and the fruit, or result, of *kamma*. For a more comprehensive understanding of this term, see 157–222.
21. Dhammapitaka, *Dictionary of Buddhism*, 60.
22. Dhammapitaka, *Buddhadhamma*, 156.

phrase, *tum dee dai dee tum chua dai chua*: "good actions bring good results, bad actions bring bad results."

It is significant to understand that the law of kamma does not merely describe a direct and immediate connection between actions and results because it also teaches that the results of one's kamma can take place later in this life or in lives to come. The Buddha says:

> He who kills and is cruel goes either to hell or, if reborn as man, will be short-lived. He who torments others will be afflicted with disease. The angry one will look ugly, the envious one will be without influence, the stingy one will be poor, the stubborn one will be of low descent, the indolent one will be without knowledge. In the contrary case, man will be reborn in heaven or reborn as man, he will be long-lived, possessed of beauty, influence, noble descent and knowledge.[23]

He also indicates that the process of kamma fruition is very complex, even to the point that is beyond most people's comprehension. However, the Buddha affirms that the law of kamma is certain, and one's kamma will eventually come to fruition. In *Maha-kammavibhanga Sutta*, the Buddha says that those who live a moral life may not immediately have a good life in the next life because of their evil kamma earlier or later, or their wrong view at the time of death. Similarly, those who live an immoral life may not reborn in a bad place because of their good kamma earlier or later, or their right view at the time of death. Nevertheless, the individuals will surely reap the fruits of their kamma in some subsequent existence.[24]

It is also crucial to mention that kamma is not the spiritual or divine being who will provide reward or punishment but "the power of a voluntary

---

23. MN 135. For the readers who are not familiar with Buddhism, this understanding can also be seen in the following illustrations. In the first story, a man was angry with his dog, so he kicked it until its leg was broken. Suddenly, his dog bit him at his leg. He clearly suffered because of his evil kamma that he had just committed with his dog. In the second story, another man was angry with his dog, so he kicked it until its leg was broken. One year later, that man was hit by a truck and his leg was broken. That incident can also be interpreted as the result of his evil kamma that he had committed with his dog in the past. In the third story, a man who had never harmed any person or animal was hit by a truck and his leg was broken. That event can also be viewed as the fruit of his evil kamma that he had committed in the previous life. Therefore, it can be seen that the law of kamma does not just describe a direct relation between deed and consequence.

24. MN 136.

thought, word, physical action, or dominant attitude to produce a fitting consequence in the life of its author or possessor."[25] Rahula makes a clear distinction between the law of kamma and the idea of moral justice, or reward and punishment, which arises out of the belief in a God who is a law-giver and who decides what is right and wrong. He says:

> The theory of karma is the theory of cause and effect, of action and reaction; it is a natural law, which has nothing to do with the idea of justice or reward and punishment. Every volitional action produces its effects or results. If a good action produces good effects and a bad action bad effects, it is not justice, or reward, or punishment meted out by anybody or any power sitting in judgment on your action, but this is in virtue of its own nature, its own law.[26]

This implies the rejection of the idea of a Sovereign God who is the supreme Judge. Moreover, the individual must be responsible for oneself. No one can help others escape from the law of kamma. Therefore, the idea of a Savior has no place in the Buddhist worldview. An individual must control and be responsible for his or her own destiny. This understanding is the foundation for the Third and Fourth Noble Truths, in which the Buddha insists that one must be dependent upon oneself in dealing with suffering. He says, "The truth of suffering is to be compared with a disease, the truth of the cause of suffering with the cause of the disease, the truth of extinction of suffering with the cure of the disease, the truth of the path with the medicine."[27]

In summary, Buddhism teaches that suffering is basically caused by human craving (*tanhā*) and ignorance (*avijjā*). Under the natural law of kamma and dependent origination, craving and ignorance bring about feelings of suffering in this life, and they enslave human beings in the circle of birth and death. Craving for pleasure is the desire for the sensual pleasures of the world, which leads to anxiety, struggle, disappointment, incomplete satisfaction, and continuing desire. Craving for existence is the desire to hold the existence of oneself or one's possession. This type of craving causes the fear of losing the persons or things that a person loves, the struggle to keep them,

---

25. King, *Buddhism and Christianity*, 113.
26. Rahula, *What the Buddha Taught*, 32.
27. Vis. M. XVI.

and the sadness resulting from losing them. Craving for non-existence is the longing to avoid or get out of unpleasant conditions or situations. This kind of craving brings about suffering resulting from the presence of the persons or things that one hates and the struggle to avoid or get out of those situations. Ignorance refers to unawareness of the true nature of all existence and not knowing the Four Noble Truths of the reality of suffering, its origin, its cessation, and the way to its cessation. Ignorance prevents humankind from seeing that all things are impermanent and will bring about suffering to those who attach to them. Moreover, it averts humans' mental eyes from the Four Noble Truths which can free them from suffering.

Consequently, in the Buddhist worldview, the individual's experiences of suffering are to be viewed in light of his or her own kamma – both in this life and from previous lives. No one can deliver others from the law of kamma, but each person must be responsible for himself or herself. In order to be free from the circle of birth and death and, in turn, suffering, one must not attach to anything or anyone, and a person must depend upon one's self in dealing with one's desire and ignorance. This teaching reveals that Buddhism is an atheistic and humanistic system that locates human beings at the center of their existence and believes that humankind can overcome the problem of human suffering by their own endeavors. It also implies the denial of a supreme God who gives rewards and punishments and a Savior who delivers humankind from suffering.

In the following section, the Buddhist understanding of the causes of suffering will be compared and contrasted with some of the Christian interpretations of the causes of suffering, namely sin, oppression, and mystery. The comparison will reveal that Buddhism and Christianity perceive the reasons for human suffering very differently, but there are some similarities between them. The similarities and differences between them can help Christians better comprehend the theological and biblical explanations for human misery and enable them to properly respond to different kinds of suffering.

Theological Understanding of the Causes of Suffering

Based on a comparative theology's commitment to specificity, this section will not explore all Christian interpretations of the causes of suffering, but it will focus on three Christian explanations for suffering in responding to the Second Noble Truth. Moreover, it will not examine these explanations in detail, but it will highlight the central message of each approach and compare it with the Buddhist understanding of the causes of suffering. First, this section will study the essence of retribution theology that attributes suffering to sin. Second, it will discuss the core of liberation theology that emphasizes suffering caused by exploitation and oppression. Finally, it will examine the message of the Book of Job which testifies that the cause of suffering can remain a mystery.

This comparative study will argue that both Buddhism and Christianity affirm that many forms of suffering are not part of human nature but rather the result of a person's illegitimate actions. Some aspects of Buddhist and Christian conceptions of the causes of suffering are similar. However, each religious tradition has unique insight into the relationship between wrongdoings and suffering. Moreover, Buddhism and Christianity advocate different responses to suffering. Grounded in a trinitarian approach to a Christian theology of religions, this section will uphold the Christian understanding of the causes of suffering, yet it will engage with and learn from the Buddhist interpretation with humility and respect. It will show that similarities and differences between Buddhist and Christian conceptions of the causes of suffering can help the Christian develop a deeper understanding of a Christian theology of the causes of suffering, which will lead to a more appropriate response to different types of suffering.

Suffering Is the Result of Sin: The Message of Retribution Theology

The first Christian interpretation of the causes of suffering which is comparable to the Buddhist understanding is a theology of retribution. While Buddhism views the individual's affliction within a framework of the law of kamma, retribution theology perceives it in relation to God's retributive justice. While Buddhism attributes suffering to tanhā, retribution theology ascribes it to sin. Therefore, both religions similarly affirm that immoral deeds, influenced by an unwholesome force that is at work in human life, will lead to suffering according to the system that governs human life. However, a careful comparison between these doctrines reveals that each religion has a unique understanding of the causes of suffering and how one should respond to them. For Buddhism, a person's tanhā leads to suffering under the natural law of cause and effect; therefore, he or she must be dependent upon himself or herself in dealing with his or her tanhā. For Christianity, the individual's sin brings about suffering under God's retributive justice; hence, the individual must turn from his or her sin to God. To be more precise, a person must repent from his or her sin, and enter a relationship with God the Father as his child through the cross of Christ and power of the Spirit.

Retribution theology is closely related to the traditional Christian understanding of suffering that attributes all suffering to sin. In the same way that affliction in a general sense first occurred in this world because of sin, a theology of retribution maintains that particular afflictions occur in people's lives because of their sins. More precisely, suffering is perceived as God's punishment for human sinfulness. It is a punishment that is not simply an expression of God's wrath and vengeance but is an affirmation of the retributive justice of God that acts against human sin and guilt.[28] Therefore, retribution theology emphasizes the role of God as judge, his commandments as a moral standard, and the covenantal obligations of his people. It involves divine judgment given in response to Israel's violations of God's law.[29]

Although the idea of God's retributive punishment of the sinner is often rejected by many people in the present day, it can be found throughout the Bible. In the Old Testament, there are numerous references to the retributive dimension of divine punishment of sinners – in both narratives and didactic material. Examples are to be found in the narratives of the flood, the destruction of Sodom and Gomorrah, the death of Aaron's sons Nadab and Abihu, the stoning of Achan and his family, and the destruction of Samaria and Jerusalem, to mention a few. Didactic passages are frequently found in Deuteronomy, Chronicles, the prophetic books, and the wisdom literature.

In Deuteronomy, the scheme of reward and punishment is apparent. Prosperity and long life were rewards for people's faithfulness to God. Disaster and turmoil were the result of their sins. In Deuteronomy 30:15–20, the Israelites were given two choices by Yahweh. If they chose to obey him, they

---

28. Inbody, *The Transforming God*, 59. In Old Testament theology, the concept of retribution depicts a correspondence between divine reward and human obedience as well as divine punishment and human disobedience; however, this term is often used to refer to the divine punishment for human sin.

29. Eichrodt, *Theology of the Old Testament*, 2:425.

would be blessed. If they chose to turn away from him, they would be cursed and destroyed.

In 1 and 2 Chronicles, the author clearly articulates the idea that sin always leads to judgment and disaster, while obedience and righteousness brings peace and prosperity (e.g. 1 Chr 28:8b–9; 2 Chr 7:14; 12:5; 15:2; 20:20). However, the Chronicler does not propose an unalterable law of retribution. Judgment and disaster do not immediately follow the transgression. They usually happen after the prophets have warned the people and offered them God's mercy. In addition, enemy invasions are not always viewed as the consequences of their sins (e.g. 2 Chr 16:1; 25:13; 32:1).[30]

In the prophetic books, the prophets consistently reminded the people, their leaders in particular, that the God of Israel is a God of justice who rewards obedience with worldly blessing and punishes disobedience with disaster for the whole nation; therefore, they must turn back from their sins (e.g. Isa 3:11; Jer 17:10; 50:15; Ezek 7:8). Nevertheless, the prophets also testify that the law of retribution is not absolute. A final restoration of Israel after the judgment of suffering and exile is not solely the result of the people's repentance and obedience but is primarily understood as "a unilateral manifestation of God's mercy over his judgment which transcends the scheme of reward and punishment" (see Isa 54:7–10; 55:3; Jer 23:5–6; 31:31–34; Ezek 36:22).[31]

Biblical wisdom literature offers a more complex theological understanding of retribution. While the Book of Proverbs advocates retribution theology, Ecclesiastes and Job put it into question.[32] While several sayings in Proverbs emphasize God's retributive punishment and reward, many passages concentrate on a direct correlation between human deed and its consequence rather than divine intervention. Thus, the Book of Proverbs witnesses to both judicial and act-consequence aspects of retribution.[33] God's role as judge is affirmed in the teaching that wrongdoers will not go unpunished (e.g. Prov 6:29; 11:21; 16:5; 17:5; 19:5) and that the wise and righteous will be granted

---

30. See Dillard, "Reward and Punishment in Chronicles."

31. Beker, *Suffering and Hope*, 43.

32. The message of the Book of Job will be discussed in the final section of this chapter. Since suffering is not prominent in Ecclesiastes, for purposes of this dissertation, this book will not be considered. For a detailed study, see Longman, *The Book of Ecclesiastes*. For a comparative study of Ecclesiastes and Buddhism, see Lorgunpai, "World Lover, World Leaver."

33. These types of proverbs are also described as forensic and dynamistic. See Hubbard, *Proverbs*, 149–150.

what they desire and will be delivered from harm (e.g. Prov 10:2, 24, 30; 11:4; 13:25). A close connection between deed and consequence is revealed in many proverbs. For instance: "Lazy hands make for poverty, but diligent hands bring wealth"(Prov 10:4–5); "Like a north wind that brings unexpected rain is a sly tongue – which provokes a horrified look" (Prov 25:23); "Whoever digs a pit will fall into it; if someone rolls a stone, it will roll back on them" (Prov 26:27).[34]

Although less frequently than in the Old Testament, the principle of retribution can still be found in the New Testament. Here, the focus is shifted from temporal retribution to a future and final judgment.[35] God is still regarded as a just God. It is believed that evil will be punished and good will be rewarded, but this may not happen until the end.[36] Several passages reveal that God's justice will be fully executed at Christ's second coming (e.g. Matt

---

34. Based on a clear relation between cause and effect, sowing and reaping, in these passages, some scholars, for example, Klaus Koch and Gerhard von Rad, suggest that retribution in the Old Testament should not be viewed as divine punishment, but it should be understood as the synthetic interpretation of life or a sphere of action which creates fate. In their view, action and consequence are aspects of one reality. There is an intrinsic correlation between the good deed and the good result, between the bad act and the bad result. Retribution, therefore, comes upon the person from the action itself, not from somewhere else. God does not directly intervene, but he has established this process, and he will bring it to its goal.

Here, it is not possible to provide a detailed examination of this view, but suffice it to say that it is too simplistic to disregard the judicial model of retribution. However, it is also incorrect to deny the act-consequence view of retribution because it is in harmony with many biblical passages about retribution. Consequently, as many scholars have pointed out, it is not necessary to choose between these two views of retribution because both of them have been operative in Israel's experience, and they complement each other. If the consequences of good or bad deeds are not somehow extrinsic to human agency, then there is no room for God to demonstrate justice. On the other hand, if the consequences of immoral deeds are not in some way intrinsic to human agency, then God is made responsible for all human disobedience and suffering. Stephen B. Chapman remarks, "The general theological perspective is clear: God's free and dynamic character enacts justice, yet God has also ordered creation in such a way that particular human actions normally have predictable moral consequences."

For further details, see Chapman, "Reading the Bible as Witness," 171–190; Koch, "Is There a Doctrine of Retribution in the Old Testament?," 57–87; Murphy, *The Tree of Life*, 115–118; and Rad, *Old Testament Theology*, 1:384–386.

35. Erickson, *Christian Theology*, 609.

36. This does not mean that the New Testament totally disregards immediate retribution. The death of Ananias, Sapphira, and Herod are the clearest examples (Acts 5:1–11; 12:23). This understanding is also supported by the teaching of God's discipline for his children in Hebrews 12:1–11. Here, the writer to the Hebrews focuses on a disciplinary dimension rather than retributive aspect of divine punishment. The portrait of God is changed from the judge to the father who loves and cares for his children. The purpose of punishment is not to demonstrate God's justice but to convince his people of their wrongdoing and turn them from it. Nevertheless, this passage affirms that the idea of God's temporal punishment is not absent from the New Testament.

24–25; Rom 2:1–16; 2 Pet 3:1–13; Rev 20:11–15; 21:1–8). Thus, believers will have to endure a certain amount of suffering with an assurance that one day they will receive their reward.[37] In addition, the New Testament message of the final judgment is closely related to an invitation to be reconciled to God through Christ.[38] People are called not only to repent from their sins but also to have a right relationship with God (e.g. Mark. 1:15; John 3:16–21; Acts 2:16–38; 2 Cor 5:10–11, 17–21; Heb 10:1–25).

In *Christ and the Judgment of God*, Stephen H. Travis argues that the concept of judgment in the New Testament should be perceived as a non-retributive theology of judgment because it centers on a relationship to God and to Christ. Though the language of judgment according to works is used (e.g. Matt 7:24–27; 25:31–46), the nature of the work is to be understood as evidence of a person's relationship to God (cf. Jas 2:14–26). The outcome of judgment is also expressed in terms of relationship to God – to be accepted into fellowship with God or rejected from that fellowship – rather than punishment from him (Matt 25:12, 21, 23, 30; Luke 13:25–27).[39] This understanding is obviously rooted in the doctrine of the Trinity. It reminds Christians that retribution theology must be viewed from a trinitarian perspective. The trinitarian God of Christianity is not the impersonal God of the philosophers, but he is the relational God who relates to the world through the Son and the Spirit. The trinitarian God's ultimate purpose is not to judge but to redeem and reconcile humankind and the whole creation to himself so that they may eternally participate in the life of the social Trinity.

A comparison between retribution theology and the law of kamma reveals both similarities and differences. On a surface level, these teachings are similar in two aspects. First, they affirm that much suffering is not intrinsic to human nature but is the result of human wrongdoing, which is influenced by sin or tanhā.[40] Second, the act-consequence aspect of retribution is very close

---

37. Simundson, "Suffering," 224.

38. God's response to suffering through the redemptive work of Christ will be discussed more fully in the subsequent chapter.

39. See Travis, *Christ and the Judgment of God*.

40. Nevertheless, the detailed study of sin or tanhā reveals that these concepts are very different, and each of them represents a unique worldview. For a good summary of the Christian understanding of sin see Erickson, *Christian Theology*, 561–600. For a thorough explanation of the Buddhist concept of tanhā and wrong kamma see Dhammapitaka, *Buddhadhamma*, 151–222.

to the law of kamma in the sense that it advocates an intrinsic correlation between deed and consequence, whether good or bad. Therefore, in my judgment, it is fair to say that retribution theology shares certain characteristics with the law of kamma, specifically the notions that every human act produces its effects and experiences of suffering come upon individuals from their wrongdoing itself, not from somewhere else.[41] It is also appropriate to hold that the Buddhist understanding of action and result is a kind of wisdom tradition which parallels that of the Old Testament. Bad kamma is comparable to the "foolish acts," mentioned in Proverbs, that produce bad results. This understanding is very helpful for Christians because it helps them realize that some of their experiences of suffering may be the direct result of their wrongdoing, not God's punishment. Therefore, they should not view God as a heartless judge who purposely afflicts pain on them, but they should be more responsible for their actions, knowing that their immoral actions will surely bring about suffering.

Notwithstanding, I will argue that retribution theology and the law of kamma are fundamentally different because of two main reasons. First, these doctrines perceive the relationship between wrongdoing and suffering in different manners. According to Buddhism, the law of kamma indicates that human beings receive the consequences of their actions according to the natural law of action and effect, not the judgment of God. The connection between action and consequence is also viewed as inexorable and mechanical. It is not under the control of any supreme being. Moreover, the process of kamma fruition is enigmatic. The individuals may not receive the result of their action immediately, but they will somehow reap its fruit later in their lives or in some subsequent existence.

On the contrary, the principle of retribution teaches that God is the supreme judge who gives reward and punishment, and he is also the creator and sustainer of the relation between act and result. Even though the act-consequence aspect of retribution is similar to the natural law of cause and effect, it does not deny the reality of God, and it does not divorce the correspondence

---

41. Commenting from the Buddhist perspective, Ven Phra Buddhadāsa Bhikkhu says that other religions also teach a law about kamma, but those teachings are not identical with the law of kamma in Buddhism. Bhikkhu, *Idappaccayatā*, 371.

between action and result from him.[42] In any case, Scripture leaves no room for a purely mechanical law of retribution. God is believed to be active in the association between human action and consequence.[43] The pattern that God has established is also viewed as a straightforward connection between deed and result (as reflected in several sayings in Proverbs), not a complex process that will somehow come to fruition at a later time. Moreover, retribution theology as a whole evidently points to the supremacy of God surpassing an unalterable connection between the two. In the final analysis, it is God – not any system – that determines the destiny of humankind. Through his mercy and grace, God does not respond to humankind according to their deeds. His forgiveness and restoration is available for those who truly repent from their sins (Pss 32:1–5; 103:1–13). More importantly, Christ's redemptive work on the cross obviously frees human beings from the results of their transgressions and reconciles them to God (Rom 5:6–10). The Holy Spirit frees them from being slaves to sinful nature and fear and testifies that they are God's children (Rom 8:12–16).

This difference clearly points to the unique understanding of Buddhism and Christianity concerning the fundamental problem of humankind. Buddhism emphasizes the natural law of cause and effect and teaches that human craving and ignorance are the root causes of humanity's predicament because they enslave human beings in the circle of birth and death. Christianity focuses on the relationship between God and humankind and upholds that sin is the primary cause of human suffering because it separates human beings from God. The different understandings of the basic problem of humankind leads to the second difference between retribution theology and the law of kamma.

The second difference between Buddhism and Christian retribution theology is that the law of kamma and retribution theology offer opposite solutions to suffering that is caused by human immoral deeds. According to the law of kamma, suffering is basically caused by human craving (tanhā) and ignorance (avijjā). No one can deliver others from this unchangeable law. Therefore, one must not attach to anything or anyone, but one must depend upon one's self

---

42. See Koch, "Is There a Doctrine of Retribution in the Old Testament?," 61; and Rad, *Old Testament Theology*, 1:384–386.

43. Murphy, *The Tree of Life*, 117; Preuss, *Old Testament Theology*, 184.

in dealing with one's desire and ignorance. In contrast, a theology of retribution teaches that suffering is God's punishment for human sin. Consequently, one must repent from his or her sins in order to receive God's forgiveness and, at the same time, enter into a genuine fellowship with him. Therefore, it is apparent that retribution theology and the law of kamma have different destinations. Retribution theology advocates a journey of faith that leads to genuine fellowship with the Triune God. The law of kamma proposes a path of detachment that leads toward a complete detachment, namely nibbāna.[44]

From this comparative study, a Christian theology of suffering in the context of Theravada Buddhism in Thailand must affirm that one of the causes of suffering is sin. Some of an individual's experiences of suffering can be viewed as direct results of wrongdoing and manifestations of divine retributive punishment. However, this understanding should not be confused with the law of kamma in Buddhism. Even though these doctrines concur that there is a connection between acts and consequences – whether good or bad – they understand this connection very differently, and they offer opposite solutions to suffering that is caused by human misconduct.

Consequently, I would argue that it is possible and appropriate for Thai Christians to use the term "the result of kamma" (Thai: *pon kum*) in place of the term "the result of sin" (Thai: *pon kong bab*) in communicating the gospel to the Thai people, yet they should not use these terms interchangeably as if they are identical when they describe the Christian faith. For instance, "the due penalty" mentioned in Romans 1:27 in the Thai Holy Bible is translated pon kum (the result of kamma). This translation is relevant to the Thai, but it is misleading because it signifies that the people mentioned suffer under the law of kamma rather than the judgment of God. Another example is an attempt to contextualize the Apostles' Creed in the Thai context by John Davis and fifty Thai seminary students in 1990. It is stated, "[A human] is incapable of attaining sufficient merit to liberate [himself or herself] and therefore, sowing what [he or she] reaps according to karma, [he or she] must perish."[45]

---

44. In the article, "The Divine Comedy," I have argued that *The Divine Comedy* of Dante Alighieri (1265–1321) clearly illustrates that, for Christianity, human life is a journey of attachment that moves from the lesser attachments of this world to the greater attachment to God. On the contrary, the Buddha's story reveals that human life is a journey of detachment that moves toward absolute detachment. See Boonyakiat, "The Divine Comedy," 237–239.

45. Davis, *Poles Apart?*, 146.

This statement is correct as far as it goes, yet it does not go far enough. There is no doubt that this statement relevantly speaks to the Thai, but it falls short in representing an authentic Christian belief. After all, human beings are accountable to God, not to the law of kamma.

On the contrary, Thai Christians should boldly, yet humbly, affirm the essence of retribution theology that much human suffering is the result of sin and many painful experiences of individuals can be the result of their sins. Therefore, when an individual faces hardship, that person should humbly and carefully examine himself or herself to see if the suffering is the result of sin. Then the individual must repent. This response to suffering also applies to those who have not been reconciled with God through Christ. People may be far from physical suffering, yet they constantly undergo spiritual suffering. This kind of suffering will ultimately lead them to God, the only person who can free them from the suffering that greatly afflicts their souls.

However, retribution theology is not the only Christian interpretation of the causes of suffering. The experiences of suffering of numerous people around the globe clearly reveal that they do not face hardship because of their misconduct, but because of injustice and oppression. A theology of liberation clearly witnesses to this reality and proposes another response to the problem of human suffering that Thai Christians cannot overlook.

Suffering Is the Result of Oppression: The Message of Liberation Theology

While the Second Noble Truth and retribution theology focus on suffering caused by individuals' wrongdoing, Scripture testifies that some kinds of suffering are the results of oppression. Many passages indicate that the innocent face hardship because of the actions of other persons. The death of Abel is the result of Cain's sin (Gen 4). Joseph's torture in many circumstances came from others' evilness (Gen 37–41). Israel was often attacked by other wicked nations. The most important account is the exploitation and oppression that the Jewish people experienced in Egypt (Exod 1–3). Among the Israelites, the weak and the poor were often oppressed by the strong and the rich and even by their own leaders. These testimonies, especially the Exodus account, become the paradigm for liberation theology that draws our attention to the reality of suffering resulting from injustice and oppression in society. It proclaims that this kind of suffering does not demand the sufferers' repentance but calls for the Church's solidarity with the sufferers in resisting oppressive social structures. This section will highlight key concepts of liberation theology and compare them with the law of kamma and retribution theology. It will argue that suffering can be the consequence of oppression, exploitation, and abuse. In other words, one's misfortune can be the result of others' sin – selfishness, indifference, hatred and cruelty. Moreover, it will suggest that Christians should respond to this type of suffering by showing solidarity with and becoming advocates for the oppressed.

Liberation theology is a movement that brings together theology and socio-political concerns rather than a school of theological theory. It has various expressions among different groups of people (for example, blacks, feminists, Asians, and Latin Americans), therefore, it is more accurate to speak of many theologies of liberation. Among these theological positions, Latin American liberation theology is the most significant because it is a forerunner that provides a model for other liberation theologies.[46] Even though liberation theologies have different socio-religious backgrounds and emphases, they are constructed on a foundation with three essential factors: theology as a critical reflection on praxis, orientation towards the poor and oppressed, and salvation as liberation.

In the first place, a theology of liberation views theology as a critical reflection on society and the Church. In *A Theology of Liberation*, the Magna Carta of Latin American liberation theology, Gustavo Gutiérrez indicates that theological reflection is "a criticism of society and the Church," and it is "a critical theory, worked out in the light of the Word accepted in faith and inspired by a practical purpose – and therefore indissolubly linked to historical praxis."[47] The starting points of theology are facts and questions obtained from the world and history, not only from revelation and tradition. The church must

---

46. Webster, "Liberation Theology," 635. For important works in liberation theologies, see Commission on Theological Concerns, *Minjung Theology*; Cone, *God of the Oppressed*; Cone, *A Black Theology of Liberation*; Gutiérrez, *A Theology of Liberation*; Bonino, *Doing Theology in a Revolutionary Situation*; Pieris, *An Asian Theology of Liberation*; and Segundo, *The Liberation of Theology*.

47. Gutiérrez, *A Theology of Liberation*, 9. Though Gutiérrez's use of Marxism has been criticized by many theologians and the Vatican in the 1980s, his approach still generally represents the main thrust of liberation theology, and his book remains one of the main resources of a liberation paradigm at the present. Therefore, this section will primarily focus on this important book.

be open to the world and be mindful of its historical changes, and theology must be continually renewed.[48] Theology as critical reflection on society and the church fulfills a prophetic role of the church because it explains to the people the true meaning of historical events according to God's will and plan. Consequently, theologians "will be personally and vitally engaged in historical realities with specific times and places. They will be engaged where nations, social classes, and peoples struggle to free themselves from domination and oppression by other nations, classes, and peoples."[49]

In the second place, a theology of liberation is oriented towards the poor and oppressed. Take Latin American liberation theology for example. Liberation theologians agree that the single most important feature of this region is poverty. This poverty is the result of sinful social structures that support the wealth and power of the few at the expense of the humanity of the majority.[50] In the Second General Conference of Latin American Bishops at Medellín, Columbia (CELAM II), in 1968, the bishops acknowledged that the church had allied with the oppressive ruling powers in the region and declared that, in the future, it would side with the poor.[51]

Gutiérrez clarifies that poverty can be understood in three ways: scandalous condition, spiritual childhood, or commitment to solidarity and protest. First, several terms used for poverty in the Bible connotes that poverty is a scandalous condition. The cause of poverty is not fate but the injustice of oppressors. Several passages condemn oppression in all forms (for example, Amos 2:6–7; 4:1; 5:7; 8:5; Mic 3:9–11; Job 24:2–12, 14). Moreover, the Bible gives instruction to prevent poverty (for example, Exod 22:25; Deut 24:19–21; Lev 23:22).[52] Second, poverty is used in a spiritual sense in referring to spiritual childhood. It is contrary to pride and self-sufficiency, but it is synonymous with openness to God, humility before him and total trust in him. The

---

48. Gutiérrez, 9–10.

49. Gutiérrez, 10.

50. Stanley J. Grenz and Roger E. Olson, *20th-Century Theology: God and the World in a Transitional Age* (Downers Grove, IL: InterVarsity Press, 1997), 216.

51. CELEM stands for "Consejo General del Episcopado Latinomericano" (General Council of the Latin American Episcopate). This council was founded in 1955 to study the specific problems of Latin America. The purpose of the second meeting in 1968 was to apply the principles of Vatican II (1965) to Latin America. This council is generally viewed as the birth of liberation theology. Cf. *The Church in the Present-Day*.

52. Gutiérrez, *A Theology of Liberation*, 165–168.

notion of spiritual poverty can be found in various passages (for example, Isa 66:2, and Zeph 2:3 and 3:12–13) but the clearest expression is found in the Beatitudes as Jesus says, "Blessed are the poor in spirit, for theirs is the kingdom of heaven" (Matt 5:3).[53] Finally, the deepest meaning of Christian poverty is commitment to solidarity with the poor and protestation against poverty.[54] Based on the fact that Christ emptied himself and took the nature of a slave (Phil 2:6–7) and that he became poor for our sakes (2 Cor 8:9), Vatican II declares in *Lumen Gentium 8* that "just as Christ carried out the work of redemption in poverty and under oppression, so the Church is called to follow the same path in communicating to others the fruits of salvation."[55] For this reason, the Church must reject poverty, which also encompasses all kinds of oppression, and voluntarily make itself poor in order to protest against it.[56] It must make a public denunciation of oppressive structures and every dehumanizing situation. This denunciation, moreover, must move from a verbal and external level towards concrete actions and commitments.[57]

Finally, a theology of liberation understands salvation primarily as liberation from exploitation. In a liberation paradigm, sin is not a private reality which requires only spiritual redemption without challenging the structure in which we live. In contrast, it is "a social, historical fact, the absence of fellowship and love in relationships among persons, the breach of friendship with God and with other persons, and, therefore, an interior, personal fracture."[58] Sin is the root of injustice and exploitation, and it requires a radical liberation. By his death and resurrection, Christ liberates humankind from sin and all its consequences. His liberating action touches the social order in its roots and basic structure. It is a radical liberation from all misery, breach, and oppression. Moreover, Christ brings human beings into communion with God and others.[59]

For Gutiérrez, salvation is qualitative and history is one. He suggests that Christians should move from the quantitative view of salvation – which holds

---

53. Gutiérrez, 169–171.
54. Gutiérrez, 172.
55. Flannery, *Vatican Council II*, 357–358.
56. Gutiérrez, *A Theology of Liberation*, 173.
57. Gutiérrez, 154.
58. Gutiérrez, 102–103.
59. Gutiérrez, 103.

that salvation is a cure for sin in this life that will be attained beyond this life – to the qualitative point of view – which asserts that salvation is not otherworldly but is an intrahistorical reality, the communion of human beings with God and among themselves that embraces all human reality, transforms it, and leads it to its fullness in Christ.[60] Since salvation is intrahistorical, Gutiérrez argues that there are not two histories, one profane and the other sacred, but there is only one history, a Christo-finalized history. Christ is Lord of it and salvation is at its center. He rejects a spiritualizing interpretation of Old Testament texts that turns the eschatological promises from historical to spiritual. He proposes that liberating historical events should be comprehended as "partial fulfillments" of the eschatological promises which lead to complete fulfillment. Creation and salvation are brought together on the basis of the historical and liberating experience of the Exodus. They are one salvific act. It is the termination of disorder and the creation of a new order. The God who turned chaos to cosmos is the same God who brought Israel from oppression to liberation. The work of Christ is also a part of this movement and brings it to completeness. It is a liberation from sin and from all its consequences, and it is a new creation of new humanity.[61]

This brief exposition admittedly does not do justice to liberation theology, but the accusation of oppression as the cause of suffering is relevant to the great majority of humanity, including the Thai people. Various faces of human suffering mentioned in the second chapter of this work undoubtedly testify to a social dimension of sin and the need for liberation from oppressive structures. Because of the existing system that causes economic, social, and political dependence of some social classes or countries on others, the gap between the rich and the poor and the distance between developed and developing societies always grows larger. Similarly, starvation is the scandal of this world. While there is enough food on this planet for its inhabitants, people are so obsessed with themselves and have no time to think about feeding the hungry. As a result, millions are left to endure malnutrition and starvation. In Thai society, oppression has various expressions. Besides poverty, people in the Kingdom of Thailand are oppressed by several factors. Ethnic minority people groups are often despised by the local Thai. People from the

---

60. Gutiérrez, 84–86.
61. Gutiérrez, 86–89.

countryside are usually looked down on by urban residents. Thai women are still under the dominion of Thai men and seldom receive equal opportunities, particularly in the workplace. People of lower statuses are obliged to follow the agenda of their superiors. The powerless and uneducated have become victims of child abuse, domestic violence, drug and sex trafficking, and corruption. The list could go on.

Within this context, liberation theologians are certainly right in accusing a traditional theology of generating artificial and irrelevant questions and producing answers that have little, if any, bearing upon real life. A theology of suffering that is limited to the problem of theodicy or other theoretical concerns falls short in addressing the concrete problem of human suffering. Liberation theology moves beyond the general problem of suffering to the actual human suffering caused by exploitation and oppression. It also dismisses a philosophical and theological debate on the subject of suffering and focuses on resisting dehumanizing situations and oppressive structures in a concrete manner. Instead of blaming God and focusing on the question, "Why does God allow such suffering?," believers are called to take a responsibility and ask, "How should Christians respond to this kind of suffering?"

A theology of liberation clearly challenges both retribution theology and the law of kamma that attribute people's affliction to their own misconduct, whether in this life or in previous lives. While these traditional interpretations are not mistaken, they can lead to indifference to social injustice, and, at the same time, they can ironically support oppressive structures. Therefore, a Christian theology of suffering in the context of Theravada Buddhism in Thailand can no longer stress the logical problems of suffering without taking into account the concrete problems of suffering in Thai society and responding to them in action.

At this point, we must be mindful that liberation theology is relevant to suffering caused by oppression but it is not *the* answer to other types of suffering. After all, liberation from oppressive situations does not guarantee freedom from spiritual suffering, and liberation from all kinds of slavery in this life will surely come to an end when people enter eternity. Moreover, liberation theology successfully gives the answer to Christians who are the observers, but it does not offer much help for the sufferers. Oppressive situations unavoidably compel the sufferers to make sense of their experiences. Several questions remain unanswered. "How should the oppressed respond to oppression?" "What if liberation does not come in this lifetime?" "Why does God allow such suffering?" "Where is God in the midst of unjust and inexplicable suffering?" These questions lead to another interpretation of the cause of suffering, together with another response that is indispensable to all sufferers.

Suffering Is a Mystery: The Message of the Book of Job

While Scripture affirms that human suffering can be the consequence of an individual's sin or oppressive social structures, it also reveals that suffering can be a mystery that is beyond human comprehension. The Book of Job is the clearest demonstration of this puzzling reality. This section will study the message of the Book of Job in relation to the Second Noble Truth, retribution theology, and a liberation approach.[62] It will begin by identifying the problem of suffering in the Book of Job. Then, it will examine the author's answers to the problem of suffering as found in the prologue, the three-circle dialogue, Yahweh's speeches, and the epilogue. This section will argue that the Book of Job challenges both traditional Christian and Buddhist interpretations of the cause of suffering by proclaiming that the reason for suffering ultimately found in divine wisdom, not in human knowledge. As a result, a proper response to suffering may not be repenting from one's sin or liberating others from oppressive situations but rather sustaining one's faith in God.

The Problem of Suffering in the Book of Job

The Book of Job is placed in the category of wisdom literature within the Hebrew Bible, yet it presents a peculiar kind of wisdom which is often called "a crisis of wisdom" that challenges the traditional ideas of divine justice and the doctrine of retribution which are firmly upheld in Proverbs.[63] It is obvious that the book addresses the problem of suffering, but it is not easy to determine the specific problem of suffering raised by the author because various

---

62. For a detailed study of the Book of Job, see Clines, *Job 1–20*; Clines, *Job 21–37*; Glatzer, *The Dimensions of Job*; Hartley, *The Book of Job*; Newsom, "The Book of Job"; and Wood, *Job and the Human Situation*.

63. Murphy, *The Tree of Life*, 34. While wisdom literature is identified as Job, Proverbs, and Ecclesiastes, it is scattered throughout Scripture in various forms, for example, sayings, riddles, poems, meditations on cosmological, and ethical questions. Andersen, *Job: An Introduction and Commentary*, 23–24. For more information on wisdom literature, see Murphy, *The Tree of Life*.

aspects of suffering are discussed and many insights can be found.[64] I will argue that the fundamental problem of suffering in the Book of Job is "*How should one respond to the reality of inexplicable suffering in this world?*" The author, however, guides the readers to this core question by beginning with a more famous question: "*Why does suffering happen?*" In other words, the Book of Job moves from the problem of the cause of suffering to the problem of the way to respond to suffering. In the final analysis, the readers will realize that the second question is far more important than the first.

The first question is an intellectual quest for the cause of affliction in one's life. Closely related to this question is whether there is such a thing as innocent suffering. While Job insisted on his piety, the friends firmly proclaimed that his anguish came about because of his sin. Their disputes, however, revolve around the cause of suffering. It seems that the Book of Job gives no answer to the *why* question; thus, it should not be regarded as the focus of the author.[65] After all, the answers of Job's friends are rejected by Job and, more importantly, by Yahweh (42:7). The speeches of Yahweh contain nothing about Job's predicament or its reason. At the end, Job remains ignorant of the reason for his calamities. However, a closer look at the Book of Job reveals that the author *does* answer the intellectual question about suffering in two manners. First, the rejection of the advice of Job's friends demonstrates the author's refusal of the rigid understanding of retribution. The Book of Job is a canonical corrective against an exaggerated and mechanical application of a proper retribution theology. It verifies once and for all that personal sin is not the only reason for suffering.[66] Second, the absence of an explanation for Job's suffering in Yahweh's speeches shows that the cause of suffering can remain a mystery.

---

64. For example, John Hartley proposes six prominent themes about human suffering. Larry Waters indicates sixteen truths in the book, in which fourteen of them are about suffering. See Hartley, *The Book of Job*, 450–451; and Waters, "Reflections on Suffering from the Book of Job," 450–451.

65. Clines says that there are three questions: Why suffering? Is there an innocent suffering? What am I to do when I am suffering? He indicates that the first question is not crucial for the book since no reason for human suffering is given. For the second question, he says that the book answers it, but it is still not the primary concern of the book. Finally, he believes that the last question is the primary problem of suffering in the Book of Job because it takes the whole book to answer. See Clines, *Job 1–20*, xxxviii–xxxix.

66. Dillard and Longman, *An Introduction to the Old Testament*, 208.

The second question is a more existential question concerning the proper attitude toward and response to one's misery. This is the primary question that the Book of Job tries to answer. The believers can continue to believe not because their faith gives them the explanation to the problem of suffering, but because it helps them cope with affliction on the practical level and not be crushed by it.[67] H. H. Rowley states it well:

> What the book of Job says is that there is something more fundamental than the intellectual solution of life's mysteries. The author has a message for the spirit rather than for the intellect.... When one is suffering it may be good to understand the cause; but it is better to be sustained to endure.[68]

This question, however, cannot be disconnected from the previous one. It is precisely within the milieu of inexplicable affliction that the Book of Job offers hope to the readers and teaches us *how* we should respond to that situation. Therefore, both questions are vital, and readers must pay attention to what the author has to say about the answers, particularly in the prologue, the three-circle dialogue, Yahweh's speeches, and the epilogue.

Answers to the Problem of Suffering in the Book of Job

The Prologue

The prose prologue (chs. 1–2) introduces the main characters and the setting and initiates the plot by raising the problem that needs a solution: Job's innocent suffering. It also takes the readers behind the scenes into the council of Yahweh (1:6–12; 2:1–6). The readers know what the reason behind Job's misery is while the characters do not. Thus, the issue which appears to Job and the readers is different. For Job, the major question is *why* he intensely suffered despite his innocence. For the readers it is *how* a righteous person is to respond when he or she is undeservedly afflicted. While Job did not know the answer, the readers can see both answers in the prologue.

What is the reason for Job's suffering? At the very beginning, the author makes clear that Job was "blameless and upright; he feared God and shunned evil" (1:1) and the reason for his severe affliction was Satan's questions about

---

67. McKeating, "The Central Issue of the Book of Job," 246–247.
68. Rowley, "The Intellectual Versus the Spiritual Solution," 124.

his integrity (1:6–12; 2:1–6). The point that the author wants to stress here is not the trial caused by Satan, but it is the fact that Job's suffering was not caused by his sin. He was truly an innocent sufferer. The author is proclaiming that there is such a thing as innocent suffering. Therefore, right at the beginning of his work, he courageously challenges the common and long established belief of his time, the notion that one suffered because of one's sins. More specifically, he argues that "the connection is not often obvious, and life is much more complex than this simple formula. Human suffering is more than a system of rewards and punishments."[69] In the context of Theravada Buddhism in Thailand, the Book of Job indicates that not all sufferers are guilty of bad kamma. It is possible that individuals suffer in spite of their innocence. The law of cause and effect may work in a general sense, but it is too simplistic in the light of the complex reality of suffering.

How should one respond to one's undeserved afflictions? Job's reactions are prime examples for all innocent sufferers. When the first trial struck, Job's response was remarkable:

> At this, Job got up and tore his robe and shaved his head. Then he fell to the ground in worship and said: "Naked I came from my mother's womb, and naked I will depart. The Lord gave and the Lord has taken away; may the name of the Lord be praised." In all this, Job did not sin by charging God with wrongdoing. (1:20–22)

After the second trial came and Job's wife told him to curse God and die, his feedback indicated that he still held on to his integrity. He replied, "You are talking like a foolish woman. Shall we accept good from God, and not trouble?" (2:10). Moreover, the author reaffirms, "In all this, Job did not sin in what he said" (2:10). He not only emphasizes Job's piety, but also shows the readers that when they are facing unjust suffering, they can and should hold on to their integrity. They must learn to trust God and give him glory in all things – what he gave and what he has taken away – and all circumstances – good and bad. As Clines says, "Sufferers who can identify with Job's acceptance of his suffering, neither ignoring the reality of suffering by

---

69. Andersen, *Job*, 67.

escaping into the past, nor so preoccupied with present grief as to ignore past blessing, are fortunate indeed."[70]

In addition, Job's response surpasses the liberation paradigm that is preoccupied with resisting unjust actions, yet provides little help to the sufferers. Parts of Job's suffering are the results of the attacks of the Sabeans and Chaldeans (1:14–15, 17). The author, however, neither condemns that cruel acts nor suggests a liberative response that will bring back Job's possessions. In contrast, through Job's response, the author wonderfully helps the readers grasp the fact that the victims of unjust suffering, while not necessarily being passive, can learn to accept their afflictions by holding on to their integrity and trusting God and giving him glory in all circumstances. In doing so, the sufferers are already liberated by God in the midst of their calamities!

The Three-Circle Dialogue

The lengthy dialogue between Job and his friends indicates the significance that the author attaches to it. Its purpose is to allow the author to develop fully the discussion of proper responses to misery as well as the cause of suffering, particularly the limitation of retribution and the reality of innocent suffering. David F. Ford interestingly points out that this dialogue and debate may represent the attempt of a tradition to face its limitations and move through a crisis. In other words, the author tries to hold together traditional belief with a new experience. The readers are immersed in a complex argumentative exchange, and they are given considerable responsibility to wrestle with the complexity and make sense of it.[71]

Through Job's lament in the monologue and his arguments in the dialogue that follow, the author suggests another response to suffering: we must let suffering direct us towards God. Before the friends speak, Job begins with a monologue in the form of a radical lament. With bitterness and anger, he curses the day of his birth and prefers death to life (ch. 3). This lament springs from very profound and unbearable suffering, but it directs Job to God, not away from him. This is another example that innocent sufferers can follow. Clines says:

---

70. Clines, *Job 1–20*, xxxviii–xxxix.
71. Ford, *Christian Wisdom*, 122–123.

> There are not two Jobs, but there is more than one right way of coping with innocent suffering: when Job cannot bow in pious submission to the divine theft of his children, his property and his reputation he can still, with a piety equal but different, assert that it is with God and no other that he must treat and demand that from God and no other his innocence be vindicated, since not even his own complete assurance of his innocence can satisfy him.[72]

Moreover, Job's cry echoes the prayers of lament found in other passages of the Old Testament, for example, Psalms 13, 22, 88, 137, Jeremiah 20:14–18, and Lamentations. The prayers of the afflicted may be filled with resentment, reproach, questions, and protest, but they actually draw the afflicted closer to God whom they address. It shows the personal relationship of Israel with their God and indicates that "in prayer, Israel is completely, even stunningly, honest with God."[73] Gustavo Gutiérrez similarly argues that "this manifestation of irrepressible feeling expresses, even if in an unconventional form, a profound act of self-surrender and hope in God."[74] In his lament, it is clear that Job curses the day of his birth but does not curse God. His lament does not destroy his faith in the Lord but helps him sustain his faith in the Lord.

In the dialogues that follow, it can be seen that Job does not give up his faith and hope in God in spite of all his calamities and protests. It is interesting that, throughout the dialogues, the three friends speak to Job but never speak to God. Job responds to them, but he often turns from them to address God directly.[75] For instance, in his reply to Eliphaz's first speech (chs. 6–7), Job addresses his comforter only in the first half of his talk, and then he redirects his attention to God. Though he begins to speak to God directly in 7:7, verses 1–6 should be understood as an introduction to his speech to God. They are spoken in the direction of God, not the friend.[76] Job briefly responds to Bildad's first argument and turns to God for the rest of chapters

---

72. Clines, *Job 1–20*, 66.
73. Billman and Migliore, *Rachel's Cry*, 26.
74. Gutiérrez, *On Job*, 10.
75. Murphy, *The Tree of Life*, 38.
76. Clines, *Job 1–20*, 183.

9 and 10. Perhaps the most well-known speech that Job directs to God is in 19:25–27. Job says:

> I know that my Redeemer lives, and that in the end he will stand upon the earth. And after my skin has been destroyed, yet in my flesh I will see God; I myself will see him with my own eyes – I, and not another. How my heart yearns within me! (19:25–27)

Furthermore, Job admits that it is hopeless to compel God to vindicate him (ch. 9), but he constantly appeals to God for vindication. In chapter 9, he imagines himself with God in court. Job recognizes that he could not prove his innocence before God; therefore, he wishes that there were a mediator or arbiter to mediate between him and God. In chapter 13, Job calls upon God to enter into a lawsuit with him and asks God to show him his offense and sin. Finally, in chapter 23:3–7, he says:

> If only I knew where to find him; if only I could go to his dwelling! I would state my case before him and fill my mouth with arguments. I would find out what he would answer me, and consider what he would say. Would he oppose me with great power? No, he would not press charges against me. There an upright man could present his case before him, and I would be delivered forever from my judge. (23:3–7)

Consequently, in spite of his grumbles and protest, Job did not forsake his faith and hope in God. In contrast, suffering directed him towards God whom he presented with his case. Gordis rightly comments:

> In spite of all his calamities Job does not yield to atheism. He cannot deny the clear evidence of his senses – his bitter suffering is a challenge to the justice of God. But neither can he surrender the prompting of his heart. In his darkest hour he retains the faith that behind the cruel God who is afflicting him stands the righteous God who will ultimately vindicate him.[77]

Apart from giving the answer for the question of how one should respond to severe and incomprehensible suffering, the author discusses more fully the question, "Why does suffering happen?" He argues that not all suffering

---

77. Gordis, *The Book of God and Man*, 152.

can be attributed to the result of sin and one may be afflicted despite one's integrity. Since dialogue is at the heart of the Book of Job, the author does not simply mention the reality of innocent suffering and totally disregard traditional retribution theology. In contrast, he describes the conventional view with unsurpassed eloquence and fairness, notably in the speeches of Eliphaz, Bildad, and Zophar. The basic premise is "if the person sins, then he or she will suffer." It must be admitted that there is truth in this principle and that Scripture affirms that both obedience and sin have consequences. The three friends, however, reverse cause and effect and say, "If the person suffers, he or she must have sin." In doing this, they go beyond the general idea of retribution and assert that *all* suffering is caused by sin.[78]

Even before the author proves that the friends were wrong through Job's responses, he signifies the inadequacies of their arguments through their structure and contents. First, while the order of the friends' speeches is always Eliphaz, Bildad, and Zophar, it is interesting that their speeches get shorter in the third cycle and Zophar does not speak at all. It may be true that this is a result of an error in textual transmission, but it is likely that the author purposely conveys that the three friends have run out of arguments against Job.[79] Second, they keep on repeating the same arguments through the several series of speeches. It is possible that the author is trying to tell the readers by this tiresome repetition that their orthodoxy is "an exhausted mine and that it keeps turning in place like a serpent biting its own tail. The only thing that changes in their speech is the tone, which becomes steadily more hostile and intolerant."[80]

Job's arguments against his friends clearly reject an overstated retribution doctrine that they firmly maintain. While the friends continually accuse him of his sin, Job asks them to point it out for him specifically. Of course, his friends are unable to fulfill Job's request. They constantly return to a general principle of retribution or merely tell Job that he has a secret sin (e.g. 11:6). In addition, Job argues that, in numerous cases, the wicked are not punished but prosper (Job 21 and 24). In the final analysis, Job's situation and real life

---

78. Dillard and Longman, *An Introduction to the Old Testament*, 209.
79. Dillard and Longman, 203.
80. Gutiérrez, *On Job*, 28.

experiences forcefully prove that human suffering is much more complex than a simplistic system of rewards and punishments.

Yahweh's Speeches

The divine reply from the whirlwind is the climax of the Book of Job (chs. 38–41). Through its content and its occurrence in the book, the author clearly provides answers to the why and how questions concerning the problem of suffering. In terms of the content, even though God does not explicitly mention anything concerning Job's suffering, he implicitly answers Job's quest for a reason behind his suffering. At the same time, he indirectly leads Job to a proper response to incomprehensible suffering. Here, God shows that the cause of suffering can remain a mystery and one can go through incomprehensible suffering by faith in God. For its inclusion, God's conversation with Job clearly indicates that the appeal of Job, though characterized by complaints and protests, is indeed heard and answered by God. In addition, it reveals that innocent sufferers need not feel that they are expelled from God's presence. When they need the sustaining presence of God, they will still have it.[81]

Strictly speaking, the author refuses to offer any justification for suffering from a human point of view, but he does far more. He helps the readers move beyond a rigid system of retribution to embrace the mystery of life. More importantly, he presents us with a new point of view of human life and the reality of suffering that God, not any human or power, is the true center of all things. He is the Creator whose "wise and loving purpose guides all things to their final consummation, so that those who endure in faith while within the human situation, share in the ultimate triumph of the Living God Who is working out His gracious purpose in the world of [humans]."[82]

In his speeches, Yahweh neither blames Satan nor gives the reason for Job's suffering. In contrast, he proclaims the mystery and complexity of creation which is beyond human comprehension in order to remind Job that humankind has no right to accuse God as unjust. God proclaims that he structured the world according to his blueprints (Job 38:4–8) in order to show that justice is also in the structure of the universe. He declares that the whole

---

81. Rowley, "The Intellectual Versus the Spiritual Solution," 125.
82. Wood, *Job and the Human Situation*, 21.

of creation is under his control (Job 38:16–39:30); as a result, he wisely and caringly watches over people just as he wisely manages the entire universe and caringly provides for creatures.[83] These speeches, therefore, affirm God's graciousness and kindness to all the works of his hands.

Through his encounter with God, Job finds a new power which is able to sustain him in the midst of his predicament. He does not discover any explanation for his suffering, but he gains a new attitude to life. Turning from his concern to a larger world and wider providence, Job eventually realizes that God is the true center of all things and nothing is beyond his concern. All things are created by him and are dependent on him. In all circumstances, God is still fully present at the center, directing and sustaining all things, seen and unseen. Consequently, human destiny is in the hand of God.[84] Human life is within the divine cosmic purpose. God's purpose, however, is far beyond what humans could ever comprehend. Responding to God's speeches, Job admits:

> I am unworthy – how can I reply to you? I put my hand over my mouth. I spoke once, but I have no answer – twice, but I will say no more. (40:4–5)

> I know that you can do all things; no plan of yours can be thwarted. You asked, 'Who is this that obscures my counsel without knowledge?' Surely I spoke of things I did not understand, things too wonderful for me to know. (42:2–3)

Throughout the dialogues, Job is confident that he knows the answers to the questions in life. Here, God's reply from the whirlwind makes Job aware that he overstepped the boundary between God and humankind. Job's confidence in his own knowledge is an insult to the true owner of knowledge, Yahweh.[85] It is this that is brought out in Job's closing remarks. He says, "My ears had heard of you but now my eyes have seen you. Therefore I despise myself and repent in dust and ashes" (42:5–6). Though there are differences in rendering the word מאס (despise, reject, abase, or retract) and the phrase על ונחמתי (I repent upon . . . , I am comforted concerning . . . , or I have changed

---

83. Hartley, *The Book of Job*, 49.
84. Wood, *Job and the Human Situation*, 20.
85. Glatzer, *The Dimensions of Job: A Study and Selected Readings*, 7.

my mind about . . .),[86] the context suggests that Job's final statement should be rendered, "Therefore, I abase myself and I am comforted concerning dust and ashes."[87] Here, Job humbled himself before the Lord and declared that he was comforted even in his present suffering. Rowley concludes:

> More significant is his recognition that, with all the loss and the pain he had suffered, he had gained something even from his agony. In his prosperity he thought he had known God. Now he realizes that compared with his former knowledge his present knowledge is as the joy of seeing compared with a mere rumor. All his past experience of God was nothing compared with the experience he had now found. He, therefore, no longer cries out to God to be delivered from his suffering. He rests in God even in his pain.[88]

The Epilogue

The epilogue (42:7–17) returns to the style of the prologue. It can be divided into two parts: the condemnation and restoration of the three friends (42:7–9), and Job's restoration and God's blessings for him (42:10–17). The author brings the story to a conclusion as well as reinforces the answers to the problem of suffering that he has proposed throughout the book. In the first part, the disapproval of uncritical retribution theology is clearly reaffirmed in Yahweh's approval of Job and his wrath for the friends. In 42:7–8, he calls Job "my servant" four times. This is the same title that the Lord uses to refer to Job in 1:8 and 2:3. Hence, Job's integrity is also confirmed at the end of the story. In contrast to Job, in the same verses, the Lord tells the three friends twice that "you have not spoken of me what is right, as my servant Job has." Because of their rigid understanding of retribution, they could only explain Job's affliction as the result of sin with the only solution being repentance.

---

86. See Newsom, "The Book of Job," 628–629; Hartley, *The Book of Job*, 535–537; and Clines, "Job," 484.

87. This translation fits well with the contents of Yahweh' speeches, but other translations are also possible since they convey Job's total submission to God. However, if the word "repent" is used, it is important to note that Job did not repent of any sin that had brought on his suffering, but he repented of his charges against God and of the doubts he had. See Rowley, "The Intellectual Versus the Spiritual Solution," 125.

88. Rowley, 125–126.

Since they urged Job to repent in order to get away from suffering and receive God's blessing, they were ironically tempting Job to use God for his own benefits. If Job followed their advice, he would confirm Satan's accusation that Job was self-serving in his fear of God.[89]

In the final part of the epilogue, the author points out that God, in his freedom and through his grace, will also rescue those who trust and hope in him. Thus far, the Book of Job asserts that when innocent sufferers endure inexplicable suffering with faith and hope in God, and when they bring their agony to his throne, even with anger and protest, they will surely find that God has never forsaken them but always loves and cares for them. Here, the author adds that the afflicted who do not give up their faith and hope in God will receive his blessings. Job's restoration and God's abundant blessings for him clearly indicate the author's point. Nevertheless, the author does not suggest these are God's rewards for Job' endurance of his suffering or God will *always* bless those who trust in him. What the writer is saying is God delights in bestowing blessings upon those who believe in him. It is God's act of grace, not what he is compelled to do.[90]

In summary, the Book of Job testifies that suffering can be a mystery that is beyond human comprehension. It also reveals that the most important question about human suffering is not "Why does suffering happen?" but "How should one respond to the reality of inexplicable suffering in this world?" According to the Book of Job, it is Job's encounter with God – not the understanding of his affliction – that brings comfort and transformation to his life. Therefore, appropriate responses to suffering may not be repentance or showing solidarity with the sufferers but holding on to one's integrity, drawing near to God, and sustaining one's faith in him.

---

89. Hartley, *The Book of Job*, 48–49.

90. Clines, "Job," 484. Many scholars disregard this final part because it is anticlimactic and unrealistic. It seems to support the traditional understanding of retribution which contradicts the message of the book. However, this is not the case. It is important to note that the author discards *naive* retribution theology, not retribution theology itself. He argues that this doctrine cannot be inserted into a narrow system of rewards and punishments, but it still contains a valid principle for believers. The three friends insisted that the righteous *always* prosper and the wicked are *always* promptly punished. Job's experience does not support this argument because he was a righteous person who suffered greatly but he was finally restored and blessed by God. Therefore, this final part should be perceived as an integral part of the Book of Job as a whole. In any case, Job's restoration is the public vindication from God that he has longed for. It is a divine approval of his faith and integrity in the midst of brutal and unfathomable suffering.

Conclusion

In conclusion, both Buddhism and Christianity agree that some forms of suffering do not belong to human nature. This kind of suffering is the result of humanity's immoral deeds. Buddhism views individuals' affliction within a framework of the law of kamma and attributes suffering to craving (*tanhā*) and ignorance (*avijjā*). No one can liberate others from the law of kamma, but each person must be responsible for himself or herself. In order to be free from suffering, one must not attach to anything or anyone, and one must depend upon one's self in dealing with one's desire and ignorance. This teaching reveals that Buddhism locates humans as the center of their existence and believes that human beings can overcome the problem of human suffering by their own efforts. It also implies the denial of the supreme God who gives rewards and punishments and the Savior who delivers humankind from suffering.

While there are many Christian interpretations of the cause of suffering, this chapter focuses on three interpretations that are relevant to the context of Theravada Buddhism in Thailand. Retribution theology perceives individuals' suffering in relation to God's retributive justice and ascribes it to the individuals' sin. In this view, one must repent and surrender to God in order to be freed from suffering. Liberation theology emphasizes the reality of suffering caused by injustice and oppression in society and proclaims that believers must be in solidarity with the sufferers and denounce oppressive social structures through their words and actions. The Book of Job witnesses to the realities of inexplicable suffering and innocent sufferers. It shows that believers should respond to the problem of the cause of suffering, but they should pay more attention to the ways to respond to suffering, which is more important. According to the Book of Job, proper responses to suffering include holding on to one's integrity, drawing near to God, and trusting him.

In this chapter, I have argued that the Buddhist and Christian interpretations of the causes of suffering are similar in some aspects, but they are fundamentally different. The law of kamma is similar to the principle of retribution, but they are not identical: the former is essentially the natural law of cause and effect whereas the latter advocates for a sovereign God who is the judge and a Triune God who is higher than the unbending law of cause and effect. While the Second Noble Truth teaches that individuals suffer because of their cravings and ignorance, liberation theology points to suffering caused by injustice and oppression. It rightly affirms a cause of suffering that Buddhism apparently ignores – the oppression of others. The Book of Job challenges both the law of kamma and retribution theology by proclaiming that the cause of the individual's misery can remain a mystery. Moreover, it insists that the creator God – not the system of reward and punishment or the law of cause and effect – is the true center of all things. A merciful God watches over humankind and has a good and eternal purpose for all human beings. Therefore, it is not individuals who can control their destiny and deliver themselves from suffering. God is the only person who can ultimately help human beings amidst the unavoidable and complex problem of suffering.

Grounded in the method of a trinitarian comparative theology of religions, I have proposed that the followers of both religions should accept that their interpretations of the causes of suffering are truly different, but they should respectfully learn from one another. At the same time, they should humbly contribute their unique insights to each other. For this reason, a Christian theology of suffering in the context of Theravada Buddhism in Thailand affirms that much suffering does not belong to original human nature. It resists any attempt to generalize suffering and declares that suffering is a complex reality that can be attributed to several causes, for example, sin, injustice and oppression, and mystery. It also refuses any narrow-minded approach to suffering that limits suffering to a particular cause and overlooks other reasons behind it. In contrast, it proposes that Christians should address the problem of suffering in its complexity and respond to it in a more holistic manner.

Moreover, the comparative study in this chapter reveals that differences between Christian and Buddhist understandings of the cause of suffering lead to very different and even opposite solutions to the problem of human suffering. While Buddhism teaches that human effort is the answer, Christianity believes that only God can ultimately deliver humankind from suffering. Here, it is important to ask, "According to the Buddhist tradition, how does human endeavor liberate human beings from suffering?" and "In Christianity, how does God save humankind from suffering?" To these questions, the final chapter will study the Third and Fourth Noble Truth – the truth of the extinction of suffering and the way to the extinction of suffering – in comparison with the Christian understanding of God's response to the problem of human suffering as found in Martin Luther's theology of the cross, together with contributions from Kazoh Kitamori, Jürgen Moltmann, and Kosuke Koyama.

It will point out that humans properly responding to suffering can deliver themselves from suffering to a certain degree. Nevertheless, God is the only person who can ultimately and eternally save humankind from suffering.

CHAPTER 4

The Ways to the Extinction of Suffering

A comparison between the Buddhist and Christian concept of the causes of suffering in the previous chapter reveals that both religions agree that much suffering does not belong to human nature and is resolvable. It is mentioned that Buddhism and Christianity give unique interpretations of the causes of suffering and propose different solutions to the problem of human suffering. Moreover, a brief description of the Buddhist answer and some Christian proposals have been discussed. Buddhism teaches that humans' cravings and ignorance are the basic causes of the human predicament because they enslave human beings in the circle of birth and death. Hence, human beings must deal with their cravings and ignorance in order to be freed from suffering. Christianity offers various reasons for suffering, for example, sin, injustice and oppression, and mystery. These Christian interpretations, however, revolve around the notion that God is the center of all things; thus, human beings must walk in right relationship with him and continue to trust him even in the midst of inexplicable suffering.

In this chapter, the Buddhist teachings of the extinction of suffering (the Third Noble Truth) and the way to the extinction of suffering (the Fourth Noble Truth) will be examined more fully. Then, these teachings will be compared and contrasted with a theological understanding of the way to the extinction of suffering. The focus will be given to a Christian understanding of God's response to the problem of human suffering as found in a theology of the cross. Besides examining Luther's theology, this chapter will take into consideration the theologies of Kazoh Kitamori, Jürgen Moltmann, and Kosuke Koyama that enable Christians to better comprehend the relationship between the cross of Christ and human suffering. The purpose of this final chapter is to bring this comparative study to the central points of both religions' answers to the problem of human suffering, the core of Buddhalogy and a Christian theology of suffering.

Over and against a theocentric or pluralistic position that all religions are merely different paths to the one Ultimate Reality and salvation, I will argue that Buddhism and Christianity are different paths that lead to different Ultimate Realities and salvations. Admittedly, these roads intersect at many points, yet they move in opposite directions and eventually take the voyagers to different destinies, namely an absolute detachment at nibbāna for Buddhism or eternal fellowship with God for Christianity. Contrary to the pluralistic axiom that forces the participants in an interfaith dialogue to give up their absolute truth claims, this study – rooted in a trinitarian comparative theology of religions – maintains that Christians should engage and learn from Buddhist insights, yet they should not privatize the Christian faith and keep it within the church.

Consequently, this chapter will argue that a Christian theology of suffering in the context of Theravada Buddhism in Thailand affirms that human effort can certainly deliver humankind from suffering to a certain degree, yet only God can save humankind from sin and enable humanity to experience true freedom from suffering. Therefore, human beings should respond to God's saving work by repenting from their sin and trusting in him. Moreover, they should learn to participate in the suffering of Christ and the suffering of other people by seeking to work for social transformation in obedience to Christ and in the power of the Spirit.

The Buddhist Way to the Extinction of Suffering

After the Buddha pointed out the truth of suffering and its cause, he proclaimed the truth of the extinction of suffering (*nirodha*) and the path leading to the extinction of suffering (*magga*). He said:

> This, O Monks, is the Noble Truth of the extinction of Suffering:
> It is the complete fading away and extinction of this craving,
> its forsaking and giving up, liberation and detachment from it.
>
> This, O Monks, is the Noble Truth of the Path which leads to the extinction of suffering: It is the Noble Eightfold Middle Path,

that is to say, Right Belief, Right Aspiration, Right Speech, Right Conduct, Right Means of Livelihood, Right Endeavor, Right Mindfulness, Right Meditation.[1]

Even though the Buddha referred to the Third Noble Truth as the extinction of suffering, he specifically defined it as the extinction of craving. This indicates that craving is intrinsically suffering, and it causes other forms of suffering. Therefore, the extinction of craving is the extinction of suffering as well as the cause of suffering.[2] While the term nirodha is used in the Third Noble Truth, the ultimate goal of Buddhism is generally referred to as nibbāna, which literally means to become extinct, to cease, to blow out, or to become extinguished. The term nibbāna portrays the extinction of fire or heat, showing the heart's condition as calm, fresh, cheerful, and not anxious.[3] Therefore, it is an "absolute extinction of that life-affirming will manifested as greed, hate and delusion, and convulsively clinging to existence; and therewith also the ultimate and absolute deliverance from all future rebirth, old age, disease and death, from all suffering and misery."[4]

In order to better understand nibbāna, it is important to understand the two types of nibbana, as well as the four categories of the noble persons (*ariya-puggala*). The first type of nibbāna is nibbāna with the substratum of life remaining (*saupādisesa-nibbāna*). This type of nibbāna is understood in two ways. First, it is the extinction of desire, but the five groups of existence still remain. It describes the nibbāna of the Worthy One (*arahanta*) who is still alive. Second, it is a nibbāna that still consists of some desire. It represents nibbāna of the Stream-Enterer (*sotāpanna*), the Once-Returner (*sakadāgāmī*), and the Non-Returner (*anāgāmī*). Chandngarm indicates that these interpretations are both valid because the term *upādi* in Tipitaka is used in referring to both desire and the five groups of existence. Hence, it can be concluded that *saupādisesa-nibbāna* is the experience of the mind in the high state of

---

1. SN LVI.11. In this chapter, the Third Noble Truth will not be examined in detail, but it will be considered together with the fourth Noble Truth since the Buddha mentioned it only briefly and focused more on the final truth. For a detailed study of the Third Noble Truth, see Chandngarm, *Arriyasatsee*, ch. 7; and Rahula, *What the Buddha Taught*, ch. 4. For a detailed discussion on nibbāna, see Dhammapitaka, *Buddhadhamma*, chs. 6–10.
2. Chandngarm, *Arriyasatsee*, 79–80.
3. Dhammapitaka, *Buddhadhamma*, 261.
4. Nyanatiloka, *Buddhist Dictionary*, 201.

the noble persons who are still alive, interacting with external factors, and consuming physical satisfaction.[5] The soul in the high state is characterized by insight into the Three Characteristics of Existence as well as purity, peace, and compassion. Therefore, this type of nibbāna can be attained within this lifetime.[6] As the Buddha said:

> Enraptured with lust (*raga*), enraged with anger (*dosa*), blinded by delusion (*moha*), overwhelmed, with mind ensnared, man aims at his own ruin, at the ruin of others, at the ruin of both, and he experiences mental pain and grief. But if lust, anger and delusion are given up, man aims neither at his own ruin, nor at the ruin of others, nor at the ruin of both, and he experiences no mental pain and grief. Thus is Nibbana visible in this life, immediate, inviting, attractive, and comprehensible to the wise.[7]

The second type of nibbāna is nibbāna without any substratum of life remaining (*anupādisesa-nibbāna*). If the term upādi is rendered "the five groups of existence," this type of nibbāna means nibbāna without the five groups of existence still remaining, i.e. that of the Worthy One (*arahanta*) who has passed away. If the term upādi is translated "desire," this type of nibbāna refers to nibbāna of the Worthy One (*arahanta*) who does not have any desire.[8]

The understanding of the two types of nibbāna is closely related with four categories of the noble persons. These categories are differentiated by one's achievement in practicing the Threefold Training (*sikkhāttaya*) and in overcoming desire or bondage (*samyojana*). There are ten kinds of bondage that enslave humankind in the circle of birth and rebirth: false view of individuality (*sakkāyadiṭṭhi*), doubt (*vicikicchā*), adherence to mere rules and rituals (*sīlabbataparāmāsa*), sensual lust (*kāmarāga*), repulsion or irritation (*paṭigha*), attachment to realms of form (*rūparāga*), attachment to the formless realm (*arūparāga*), pride (*māna*), distraction (*uddhacca*), and ignorance (*avijjā*).[9] The four categories of the noble persons consist of the

---

5. Buddhist scholars usually prefer the word "mind" to the word "soul" which carries the connotation of "immortal entity" which contradicts the principle of *anattā*.

6. Chandngarm, *Arriyasatsee*, 80–82.

7. AN III.55.

8. Chandngarm, *Arriyasatsee*, 82.

9. Dhammapitaka, *Dictionary of Buddhism*, 329–330.

Stream-Enterer (*sotāpanna*), the Once-Returner (*sakadāgāmī*), the Non-Returner (*anāgāmī*), and the Worthy One (*arahanta*).

The Stream-Enterers (*sotāpanna*) are those who have perfectly practiced the Middle Way and can overcome the first three bondages: the false view of individuality (*sakkāyadṭṭhi*), doubt (*vicikicchā*), and adherence to mere rules and rituals (*sīlabbataparāmāsa*). These noble persons remain in laity, but they are approaching *arahanta*. They will be reborn not more than seven lives.[10]

The Once-Returners (sakadāgāmī) are those who have perfectly practiced the Middle Way and can overcome the first three bondages like the Stream-Enterer. Moreover, they can reduce lust (*raga*), anger (*dosa*), and delusion (*moha*). They will be reborn as human for one more time. Hence, they are called the Once-Returners.[11]

The Non-Returners (*anāgāmī*) are those who have perfectly practiced the Middle Way and can overcome two more bondages: sensual lust (*kāmarāga*) and repulsion or irritation (*paṭigha*). Hence, they can conquer the first five bondages. After death, the Non-Returners will be reborn in the realm of *suddhāvāsa*, where they will reach nibbāna.[12]

The Worthy Ones (*arahanta*) are those who have perfectly practiced the Middle Way, completed the Threefold Training, and can overcome the first five bondages of life in the same way as anāgāmī. Moreover, they can defeat the attachment to realms of form (*rūparāga*), attachment to the formless realm (*arūparāga*), pride (*māna*), distraction (*uddhacca*), and ignorance (*avijjā*). Therefore, they are free from all bondages of life and reach nibbāna, being free from samsara.[13]

While the exact condition of arahanta who have entered *parinibbāna*, the final or complete nibbāna, is commonly questioned, the Buddha did not give a clear answer for he regarded this reality as a metaphysical truth that cannot be proved or disproved. However, it can be said that nirodha, or nibbāna, as the experience of the mind in the high state in this life or as the state after

---

10. Chandngarm, *Arriyasatsee*, 82–84.
11. Chandngarm, 83–84.
12. Chandngarm.
13. Dhammapitaka, *Buddhadhamma*, 286.

parinibbāna, is the most significant experience which is beyond anything and is worthy to be diligently sought after.[14]

In order to reach this ultimate goal, the Buddha teaches that one must go through the path that leads to the extinction of suffering. This doctrine is commonly called the Middle Way (*majjhimā-paṭipadā*) because it avoids the two extremes of sensual indulgence (*kāmasukhallikānuyoga*) and exaggerated asceticism (*attakilamathānuyoga*). The Buddha personally tested these extremes and found they could not liberate humankind from the problem of suffering. Consequently, he proclaimed the Middle Way of Life which will lead to enlightenment and deliverance from suffering. Venerable Phra Dhammapitaka indicates that the Middle Way is the life principle for those who practice and those who understand the reality of life, not those who blindly believe. The outcome is happiness, purity, brightness, calmness, and freedom. Therefore, Buddhism is a religion of action and perseverance, not that of praying or expecting. The Buddha's teaching aims for realistic outcomes so its followers can truly manage their life in this world, right here and right now. If one is concerned about one's next life, one must actualize the good life that one expects with today's concrete actions. Hence, one will have an assurance for the life to come.[15]

The Noble Eightfold Path consists of (1) Right Understanding, (2) Right Thought, (3) Right Speech, (4) Right Action, (5) Right Livelihood, (6) Right Effort, (7) Right Mindfulness, and (8) Right Meditation. These aspects, however, are not to be practiced sequentially, but simultaneously. They are closely connected with and support one another in promoting the three essentials of the Buddhist training and discipline, which is called "the Threefold Training" (*Sikkhāttaya*): Ethical Conduct (*sīla*), Mental Discipline (*samādhi*), and Wisdom (*paññā*).[16]

---

14. Chandngarm, *Arriyasatsee*, 84–87.

15. Dhammapitaka, *Buddhadhamma*, 5–6.

16. Rahula, *What the Buddha Taught*, 46. Ethical Conduct (*sīla*) includes Right Speech, Right Action, and Right Livelihood (numbers three, four, and five in the list). Mental Discipline (*samādhi*) consists of Right Effort, Right Mindfulness, and Right Meditation (numbers six, seven, and eight in the list). Wisdom (*paññā*) includes Right Understanding and Right Thought (numbers one and two in the list). For the purpose of this dissertation, the essence of each aspect will presented without discussing its details. For a thorough explanation of the Noble Eightfold Path see Bodhi, *The Noble Eightfold Path*; and Dhammapitaka, *Buddhadhamma*, chs. 19–21.

Right Understanding (*Sammādiṭṭhi*)

Right Understanding, or Right view, refers to the adoption of the Buddha's teachings about the world and the human condition. More specifically, it indicates the understanding of the truth of suffering, the cause of suffering, the extinction of suffering, and the way to the extinction of suffering, i.e. the understanding of the Four Noble Truth. The Buddha said:

> And what, monks, is right view? Knowledge with regard to suffering, knowledge with regard to the origination of suffering, knowledge with regard to the stopping of suffering, knowledge with regard to the way of practice leading to the stopping of suffering: This, monks, is called right view.[17]

This knowledge, however, is the lower level of understanding, conception, not higher levels of understanding, namely insight and enlightenment.[18] In *Mahavedalla Sutta*, the Buddha indicates that Right View is arisen from two conditions: the voice of another (*paratoghosa*) and appropriate attention (*yonisomanasikāra*).[19] The former is to listen, have conversation, study, and learn from others. The latter is to critically reflect, logically think, and carefully analyze the situations or problems according to their real conditions and causes.[20] Moreover, right view can be cultivated in three ways, corresponding to the three types of *paññā*, wisdom, knowledge, or understanding. It can be cultivated through studying or learning from others (*sutamaya-paññā*). It can be developed by reflecting, reasoning, and thinking (*cintā-paññā*). It can be gained through meditation (*bhāvanāmaya-paññā*).[21]

Right Thought (*Sammāsankappa*)

Right Thought refers to the wholesome thoughts (*kusala-vitakka*), which are threefold. First, the thought of renunciation (*nekkhamma-vitakka*). It means the thought that is free from selfish desire and the intention to be free from desire. Second, the thought free from hatred (*abyāpāda-vitakka*). It is the

---

17. SN XLV.8.
18. Chandngarm, *Arriyasatsee*, 92.
19. MN XLIII.
20. Dhammapitaka, *Dictionary of Buddhism*, 35.
21. D. III.219. See Chandngarm, *Arriyasatsee*, 93; Dhammapitaka, *Dictionary of Buddhism*, 96.

thought free from hatred, anger, or revenge and characterized by compassion. Third, the thought free from violence (*avihimsā-vitakka*). It refers to the decision not to harm or take advantage of others but to help them. As the Buddha said, "And what is right thought? The thought of renunciation, of freedom from hatred, and of harmlessness: This is called right resolve."[22]

Right Speech (*Sammāvācā*)

Right Speech means abstaining from unwholesome words. The Buddha said:

> And what is right speech? Abstaining from lying, abstaining from divisive speech, abstaining from abusive speech, abstaining from idle chatter: This, monks, is called right speech.[23]

While the first two aspects of the Middle Way describe inner qualities, this third aspect marks the beginning of behaviors that can be clearly seen and involve other persons.[24] Right Speech has four characteristics, which are fully described in the wholesome course of action (*kusala-kammapatha*) in the *Majjhima Nikaya*, or Middle-length Discourses of the Buddha.[25] First, it is to avoid lying and not to speak a lie for the sake of oneself or other persons. Second, it is to abstain from malicious speech, but to unite the discordant, to encourage the united, and to create harmony. Third, it is to refrain from harsh speech, but to speak with gentleness and love. Fourth, it is to desist from frivolous talk, but to say at the appropriate moment, in accordance with facts, reason, and usefulness.[26]

Right Action (*Sammākammanta*)

Right Action is abstaining from the killing of living beings, dishonesty, and sexual misconduct. The Buddha said, "And what, monks, is right action? Abstaining from taking life, abstaining from stealing, abstaining from unchastity: This, monks, is called right action."[27] Similar to Right Speech, this aspect of the Middle Way is explained in the wholesome course of action

---

22. SN XLV.8.
23. SN XLV.8.
24. Chandngarm, *Arriyasatsee*, 97.
25. MN I.287.
26. Dhammapitaka, *Dictionary of Buddhism*, 234–235.
27. SN XLV.8.

(*kusala-kammapatha*) in the *Majjhima Nikaya*.[28] First, it is to abstain from the destruction of life and to be compassionate to other living beings. Second, it is to renounce stealing, but to respect others' rights to their belongings. Third, it is to refrain from sexual misbehavior.[29]

Right Livelihood (*Sammā-ājīva*)

For Right Livelihood, the Buddha briefly explained, "And what, monks, is right livelihood? There is the case where a disciple of the noble ones, having abandoned dishonest livelihood, keeps his life going with right livelihood: This, monks, is called right livelihood."[30] Saeng Chandngarm proposes that Right Livelihood should be divided into two kinds according to the statuses of laity and clergy. For lay people, Right Livelihood means any occupation that is legal, moral, and does not harm others, both directly or indirectly.[31] In the business circle, there are five trades (*vaṇijjā*) that one should avoid: trade in weapons, human beings, animals for meat, alcoholic drinks, and poison.[32] For the clergy, Right Livelihood refers to using the four requisites for comfort just as needed and not seeking them by improper means, for example, by flattering, implying, imposing, or gambling.[33]

Here, it is important to note that the Ethical Conduct (*sīla*) of Right Speech, Right Action, and Right Livelihood reveals that Buddhism should not be perceived as a passive and subjective religion that is involved with individuals' moral conduct and neglects helping other sufferers through concrete actions.[34] It is obvious that Buddhist Ethical Conduct promotes a noble way of life that will be beneficial to those who practice it as well as other people in society. It prevents Buddhists from oppressing others in their words, deeds, or careers. At the same time, it encourages them to contribute to society and

---

28. MN I.287.
29. Dhammapitaka, *Dictionary of Buddhism*, 234–235.
30. SN XLV.8.
31. Chandngarm, *Arriyasatsee*, 99.
32. AN III.207.
33. Chandngarm, *Arriyasatsee*, 100.
34. Dhammapitaka, *Buddhadhamma*, 761–762.

help the poor. The support that Buddhists always give to Buddhist monks and the poor is the clearest example of the active role of Buddhism in society.[35]

Right Effort (*Sammāvāyāma*)

The Buddha explained that Right Effort is seen in four manners. In the first place, it is an effort to prevent evils that have not yet arisen. In the second place, it is an endeavor to abandon evils that have arisen. Then, it is an attempt to create noble qualities that have not yet arisen. Finally, it is an effort to maintain and develop good qualities that have arisen. He said:

> And what, monks, is right effort? (i) There is the case where a monk generates desire, endeavors, activates persistence, upholds and exerts his intent for the sake of the non-arising of evil, unskillful qualities that have not yet arisen. (ii) He generates desire, endeavors, activates persistence, upholds and exerts his intent for the sake of the abandonment of evil, unskillful qualities that have arisen. (iii) He generates desire, endeavors, activates persistence, upholds and exerts his intent for the sake of the arising of skillful qualities that have not yet arisen. (iv) He generates desire, endeavors, activates persistence, upholds and exerts his intent for the maintenance, non-confusion, increase, plenitude, development, and culmination of skillful qualities that have arisen: This, monks, is called right effort.[36]

Right Mindfulness (*Sammāsati*)

Sati is often translated as "recollection." However, this term is broader than an aspect of memory – an ability to recall in contrast to forgetfulness. It also refers to the ideas of "non-carelessness, non-distraction, and non- confusion," which signify the positive qualities of "care, circumspection, alertness to one's duties and the condition of being constantly present in the awareness of the various things which come into contact with one and responding to them

---

35. In this sense, as Aloysius Pieris has pointed out, Buddhism shares values with the liberation movement because it teaches voluntary poverty for monks as well as the responsibility of lay people to support those monks. Therefore, Pieris calls this an "Asian liberation theology." See Pieris, *An Asian Theology of Liberation*, 74–80.

36. SN XLV.8.

appropriately."[37] Therefore, Right Mindfulness is the awareness of one's bodily actions, feelings, mind, and mental qualities. It is constant care and caution, not allowing oneself to fall into harmful ways or to miss any opportunity for improvement. It is recognizing things that need to be done and performing one's daily responsibilities with sincerity and effort towards improvement.[38]

In *Maha-satipatthana Sutta*, the Buddha teaches four foundations of mindfulness (*satipaṭṭhāna*). First, contemplation of the body (*kāyānupassanā-satipaṭṭhāna*) or mindfulness in regard to the body. This can be done through mindfulness of breathing (*ānāpānassati*), of posture (*iriyāpatha*), of consciousness (*sampajañña*), of the body's impurity (*paṭikūla-manasikāra*), of the body's element (*dhātu-manasikāra*), and of the nine different states of a corpse. Second, contemplation of feelings (*vedanānupassanā-satipaṭṭhāna*) or mindfulness in regard to feelings. It is the discernment of one's true feelings that requires one remain focused on feelings in and of themselves. Third, contemplation of mind (*cittānupassanā-satipaṭṭhāna*) or mindfulness in regard to mental conditions. It is the awareness of one's true mental condition that requires one remain focused on one's mental qualities in and of themselves. Finally, contemplation of Dhamma (*dhammānupassanā-satipaṭṭhāna*) or mindfulness in regard to Dhamma. It is the mindfulness of the reality of five principles: the Five Hindrances *(nīvaraṇa)*, the Five Groups of Existence (*pañcakkhandha*), the Twelve Spheres (*āyatana*), the Seven Factors of Enlightenment (*bojjhanga*), and the Four Noble Truths (*arriyasacca*).[39]

Right Meditation (*Sammāsamādhi*)

Right Meditation, or Right Concentration, means bringing one's consciousness to a single point in meditation.[40] The Buddha said:

> And what, monks, is right concentration? (i) There is the case where a monk – quite withdrawn from sensuality, withdrawn from unskillful (mental) qualities – enters and remains in the first jhāna: rapture and pleasure born from withdrawal, accompanied by directed thought and evaluation. (ii) With the stilling

---

37. Dhammapitaka, *Buddhadhamma*, 804–805.
38. Dhammapitaka, 805.
39. D. 22.
40. Dhammapitaka, *Buddhadhamma*, 824.

of directed thought and evaluation, he enters and remains in the second jhāna: rapture and pleasure born of concentration, unification of awareness free from directed thought and evaluation – internal assurance. (iii) With the fading of rapture, he remains in equanimity, mindful and alert, and physically sensitive of pleasure. He enters and remains in the third jhāna, of which the Noble Ones declare, "Equanimous and mindful, he has a pleasurable abiding." (iv) With the abandoning of pleasure and pain – as with the earlier disappearance of elation and distress – he enters and remains in the fourth jhāna: purity of equanimity and mindfulness, neither pleasure nor pain. This, monks, is called right concentration.[41]

There are two methods in Buddhist meditation: the development of serenity (*samatha-bhavana*) and the development of insight (*vipassana-bhavana*). Both methods share preliminary requirements: moral discipline must be purified, obstacles must be removed, and the meditator must seek a suitable place and correct instruction (preferably from a personal teacher). Then, the meditator has to select an object of meditation, something to be used as a focus for developing concentration. In Buddhism, the subjects of meditation are grouped into a set of forty, called "places of work" (*kammatthana*), consisting of ten *kasinas*, ten unattractive objects (*dasa asubha*), ten recollections (*dasa anussatiyo*), four sublime states (*cattaro brahmavihara*), four immaterial states (*cattaro aruppa*), one perception (*eka sañña*), and one analysis (*eka vavatthana*).[42]

Right Meditation is the last and most important aspect of the Middle Way. It can be said that other aspects are simply instruments of Right Meditation.[43]

---

41. SN XLV.8.

42. The ten *kasinas* mentioned in the Suttas are the earth, water, fire, wind, blue, yellow, red, white, space, and consciousness. The ten unattractive objects are corpses in various stages of decomposition. Concentrating on these objects is similar to the contemplation of bodily decay in the mindfulness of the body. The ten recollections are recollections of the Buddha, Dhamma, Sangha, morality, generosity, heavenly beings, death, body, breathing, and peace. The four sublime states are social attitudes: loving-kindness, compassion, unselfish joy, and equanimity. The four immaterial states are the bases of infinite space, infinite consciousness, nothingness, and neither-perception-nor-non-perception. The one perception is the perception of the repulsiveness of food. The one analysis is the contemplation of the body's element. For more information see Bodhi, *The Noble Eightfold Path*, ch. 7.

43. Chandngarm, *Arriyasatsee*, 106.

Through the concentration of one's mind, one can enter the state of serene contemplation or absorption (*jhāna*). This state is divided into two types and each type consists of four levels. The first type is jhānas of the Fine-Material Sphere (*rūpa-jhāna*). It consists of the First Absorption – rapture and pleasure born from withdrawal, accompanied by directed thought and evaluation – the Second Absorption – rapture and pleasure born of concentration, unification of awareness free from directed thought and evaluation – the Third Absorption – the fading of rapture, the remaining in equanimity, mindful and alert, and physically sensitive of pleasure – the Fourth Absorption – the abandoning of pleasure and pain, the purity of equanimity and mindfulness, neither pleasure nor pain. The second type is jhānas of the Immaterial Sphere (*arūpa-jhāna*), which consists of the Sphere of Infinity of Space (*ākāsānañcāyatana*), Sphere of Infinity of Consciousness (*viññāṇañcāyatana*), Sphere of Nothingness (*ākiñcaññāyatana*), Sphere of Neither Perception Nor Non-Perception (*nevasaññānāsaññāyatana*).[44]

It is only through Right Meditation that one can enter the state of serene contemplation that enables one to fully realize the truth of the Three Characteristics of Existence. This realization, in turn, frees one's mind from attachment to the five groups of existence. Consequently, one can attain the goal of nibbāna, freedom from the wheel of birth and death and, in turn, suffering.

To summarize, the ultimate goal of Buddhism is to attain nibbāna, an absolute extinction of desire and the bondages of life as well as the extinction of the five groups of existence. To reach this aim, the Buddha teaches that one must overcome one's craving and ignorance by practicing the Noble Eightfold Path (*magga*), or the Middle Way (*majjhimā-paṭipadā*), which consists of Right Understanding, Right Thought, Right Speech, Right Action, Right Livelihood, Right Effort, Right Mindfulness, and Right Meditation. To know this Path is not enough, one must truly embrace it into one's life. Rahula says:

> [The Noble Eightfold Path] is a way of life to be followed, practised, and developed by each individual. It is self-discipline in body, word and mind, self-development and self-purification. It has nothing to do with belief, prayer, worship or ceremony. In that sense, it has nothing which may popularly be called

---

44. D. III.224.

"religious." It is a Path leading to the realization of Ultimate Reality, to complete freedom, happiness and peace through moral, spiritual and intellectual perfection.[45]

Hence, the Buddhist solution to the problem of suffering brings us back to the heart of Buddhism. It is truly an atheistic and humanistic system that locates human beings at the center of their existence and believes that humankind can overcome the reality of suffering by their own endeavors. Grounded in its firm belief in the law of kamma, it proclaims that no one can deliver others from the consequences of their wrong actions. In contrast, each person must be responsible for himself or herself. One must not attach to anything or anyone, and one must depend upon one's self in dealing with one's desire and ignorance in order to be free from the circle of birth and death and, in turn, suffering.

The Noble Eightfold Path certainly brings about realistic outcomes for those who practice it. Proper attitudes and actions can prevent individuals from unnecessary suffering, for example, Right Understanding of the impermanence of all earthly things helps individuals realize that decay and death is unavoidable. Instead of resisting this reality, they should accept it and learn not to attach themselves with impermanent persons or things. Similarly, correct attitudes and actions enable the sufferers to overcome their painful feelings, for instance, Right Thought – thought free from hatred, anger, and revenge – can quench the resentment and bitterness caused by an unforgiving heart. Moreover, the Noble Eightfold Path indirectly averts the suffering of other people in society. As mentioned, the Buddhist Ethical Conduct of Right Speech, Right Action, and Right Livelihood prevents Buddhists from oppressing other people through their words, actions, or careers, and it encourages them to contribute to society and help the poor. Therefore, each aspect of the Middle Way has an important role in helping individuals overcome different forms of suffering in this life, and, if individuals truly practice all aspects of the Middle Way, they will eventually be free from all forms of suffering.

The Buddhist understanding of the way to the extinction of suffering is a context for developing a Christian theology of the way to the end of suffering that is relevant to the context of Theravada Buddhism in Thailand. In the

---

45. Rahula, *What the Buddha Taught*, 50.

following section, the Middle Way will be compared and contrasted with a Christian way to the extinction of suffering. It will be seen that Buddhism and Christianity share some responses to the problem of human suffering, yet each religion offers a unique solution to this problem.

The Theological Understanding of the Way to the Extinction of Suffering

In this section, we shall examine a Christian theological understanding of the way to the end of suffering. While Buddhism teaches that the path leading to the extinction of suffering lies in human effort, Christianity believes that Jesus Christ is the only way in which humankind can find genuine freedom from suffering. This section, therefore, will attempt to answer the most important question for a Christian theology of suffering: "How does God respond to human suffering?" In addition, it will take into consideration the Buddhist concept of the Middle Way in order to formulate a Christian answer to the problem of human suffering that is truly relevant to the context of Theravada Buddhism in Thailand. In the final analysis, Christians' only hope and focus is the fact that the God in whose image we have been created is the person who shares our suffering in the trinitarian sense and frees us from suffering.

I will argue that Buddhism and Christianity share some responses to the problem of human suffering because several aspects of the Middle Way are very similar to biblical teachings. Therefore, Buddhists and Christians can learn from one another and help one another in overcoming suffering. From a Christian standpoint, it can be said that the Noble Eightfold Path can also help Christians overcome suffering to a certain extent. Nevertheless, I will propose that Buddhism and Christianity ultimately offer opposite solutions to the problem of suffering. Buddhism teaches that it is human effort that leads humankind to nibbāna. In contrast, Christianity believes that only God, through Christ, can deliver humankind from suffering. While proper attitudes and actions can empower sufferers and prevent unnecessary suffering to a certain degree, only God's redemptive work can bring suffering to a complete extinction. For this reason, a responsibility of humankind is to turn from sin to God and actively participate in the suffering of Christ and others.

A comparison between the eight aspects of the Middle Way and biblical teachings clearly reveals that Buddhism and Christianity share a great deal of ethical concerns. This understanding clearly supports a trinitarian comparative theology of religions that affirms God's truth and the presence of the Holy Spirit in world religions. Both religions give similar preventatives and solutions to suffering. For instance, the second and third meaning of Right Thought – the thought free from hatred, but filled with compassion, and the thought free from violence, but full of mercy – is comparable to the Beatitudes, in which the meek, the merciful, the pure in heart, and the peacemakers are blessed (Matt 5:5, 7–9).[46] Right Speech – abstaining from unwholesome speeches – is equivalent to Paul's teaching in Ephesians 5:4, "Nor should there be obscenity, foolish talk or coarse joking, which are out of place, but rather thanksgiving." Right Action – abstaining from the killing of living beings, dishonesty, and sexual misconduct – is similar to the sixth and seventh commandments, "You shall not murder" and "You shall not commit adultery" (Exod 20:13–14), as well as other warnings against sexual immorality (e.g. Prov 5:7–23; 1 Cor 6:9; Rev 21:8).[47] Right Livelihood corresponds to various biblical passages concerning work ethic (e.g. Prov 12:24; 21:25; Eph 4:28; 2 Thess 3:6–13).[48] Consequently, Buddhists and Christians should learn from one another about these particular doctrines. Furthermore, they should work together in promoting and executing these beneficial concepts to Thai society. For Christians, they should not reject aspects of the Middle Way that do not contradict Christian faith. After all, some of them are identical with biblical teachings.

However, acknowledging the fact that the work of the Spirit in other religions must be consistent with the persons and works of the Father and Jesus Christ, one must carefully examine if the Middle Way as a whole really corresponds with the Christian faith. I will argue that it is incorrect to take these Buddhist and Christian teachings out of their original context and claim that

---

46. The first meaning of Right Thought, "the thought free from selfish desire," corresponds to biblical teachings, but "the intention to be free from all desire" is different from Christian teachings.

47. However, the sixth commandment of Yahweh forbids the killing of humans, not other living beings.

48. In *Christ Mind, Buddha Heart*, Dale A. Johnson interestingly compares the Noble Eightfold Path to the Beatitudes and other biblical teachings. His comparison reveals many points of contact between the two. Nevertheless, his argument is weakened by his pluralistic approach that does not do justice to the teachings of both religious traditions. I do not think Buddhists and Christians can agree with much of his interpretation of the Noble Eightfold Path and the Beatitudes. See Johnson, *Christ Mind, Buddha Heart*.

both religions offer the same solution to the problem of suffering. Considering the Middle Way and corresponding biblical teachings in light of their guiding vision indicates that they are similar on a practical level, but they are very different in their essence. Therefore, they suggest different, and even opposite, solutions to the problem of suffering. While Buddhalogy suggests that human beings can eliminate suffering by relying on their own efforts, particularly by practicing the Noble Eightfold Path, a Christian theology of suffering teaches that only God can ultimately save human beings from suffering.

Since the cross of Christ is the clearest expression of God's response to human suffering, we shall discuss the theology of the cross more fully in order to see how God responds to human suffering through the cross. It is important to note that theologians of the cross do not present a theodicy, but they attempt to show how God has responded to evil and suffering in the world and, in turn, how Christians should respond to this issue. In other words, they do not focus on the cause of suffering, but they emphasize the end of suffering and the path leading to its termination. This section, therefore, will examine the theology of the cross presented by Luther, Kitamori, and Moltmann. It will also take into consideration the contributions of Kosuke Koyama, who has greatly enriched a theology of the cross and contextualized it into an Asian context.

Martin Luther's Theology of the Cross

It is generally accepted that *theologia crucis*, theology of the cross, is the key to Luther's whole theology.[49] The formulation of the theology of the cross took place over a period of several years, and it was catalyzed by Luther's initial difficulty concerning how the idea of a righteous God could be good news for sinful humankind.[50] Luther's theology of the cross consists of three major aspects: it is a theology of revelation; it holds that God makes himself known through suffering; and it is a theology of faith.

In the first place, the theology of the cross is a theology of revelation. It stands in sharp contrast to speculation.[51] For Luther, the true knowledge of God can be found only in God's self-revelation. This revelation, however,

---

49. McGrath, *Luther's Theology of the Cross*, 1.
50. McGrath, 99.
51. Loewenich, *Luther's Theology of the Cross*, 22.

is indirect and hidden in the suffering and the cross of Christ. The concept of the hidden God is at the center of the theology of the cross. In Thesis 20 of the Heidelberg Disputation, Luther's reference to the *posteriora Dei*, the rearward parts of God, serves as an emphasis that in the same way that Moses was allowed to see God only from the rear (Exod 33:23), we can only see the indirect revelation of God in suffering and the cross. Even though God is revealed in the passion and the cross of Christ, he is not immediately recognizable as God. As a result, anyone who attempts to speculate on the created order through human reason is incapable of discerning God's revelation and does not deserve to be called a theologian. In contrast, the person who is able to discern God's revelation through the suffering and the cross of Christ deserves to be called a theologian.[52]

In the second place, the theology of the cross maintains that God makes himself known through suffering. For Luther, God is active in this matter, and suffering is seen as the means by which human beings are brought to God. Luther differentiates between two kinds of love: *amor Dei*, God's love, and *amor hominis*, human love. God's love and human love are paradoxical. Human love is oriented towards something that people believe they can enjoy, but God's love is directed towards something that does not exist in order to create something new. Luther sometimes refers to the love of God as *amor crucis*, the love of the cross, which "turns in the direction where it does not find good which it may enjoy, but where it may confer good upon the bad and needy person."[53]

Luther explains further that the works arising from human love appear to be beautiful, but they lead to death. In contrast, God's works that flow out of God's love often appear to be ugly and unattractive. Here, Luther introduces the dialectic between *opus alienum Dei*, God's alien work, and *opus proprium Dei*, God's proper work. The alien works mean "putting down, killing, taking away hope, leading to desperation, etc." and the proper works mean "forgiving, giving mercy, taking up, saving, encouraging, etc." Luther sometimes calls the alien works, "the works of the left hand," and the proper works, "the works of the right hand."[54] However, Luther maintains that these

---

52. McGrath, *Luther's Theology of the Cross*, 149.
53. *HDT*, 28; *LW* 31:57.
54. Kärkkäinen, "Evil, Love and the Left Hand of God," 222.

works result from the same love of God, and the proper works are veiled in the alien works and take place concurrently with them.[55] Referring to Isaiah 53:2 and 2 Samuel 2:6, Luther indicates that God makes us nothing and foolish to reveal his real love to us.[56] Actions which are alien to God's nature result in actions which belong to his very nature. Consequently, the passion of Christ (*passiones Christi*) and human suffering (*Anfechtung*) represent the alien works of God through which he works out his proper work. Luther also regards God himself as the source of Anfechtung.[57]

This paradox can be seen in the justification of individuals. In order that humankind may be justified, they must humble themselves before God. It is God who both humiliates and justifies. He makes humankind sinners in order that he may make them righteous.[58] Through the experience of the alien works of God, the sinners find themselves driven to despair under the wrath of God, yet they learn to trust only in God through the cross of Christ which enables them to be justified. As Luther says, Anfechtung (assault, temptation, or a state of hopelessness and helplessness),[59] "in so far as it takes everything away from us, leaves us nothing but God: it cannot take God away from us, and actually brings him closer to us."[60] Therefore, the theologian of the cross regards such suffering not as an invasion into this world but as the most precious treasure that reveals the hidden God. However, it is important to note that although Luther considers all Anfechtung to originate from God, he differentiates between satanic Anfechtung and divine Anfechtung.

Finally, the theology of the cross is the theology of faith and of faith alone. For Luther, the theologian of the cross is the person who, through faith, discerns the presence of the hidden God in the suffering and the cross of Christ. At the cross, Christ suffered the same Anfechtung on our behalf, and he took upon himself our sin, in order that we might possess his righteousness. However, it is through faith alone that the true significance of the cross is understood and through faith alone that its power can be appropriated. While the unbeliever only sees the helplessness and hopelessness of a dying

---

55. *HDT*, 16; *LW*, 31:50.
56. Kärkkäinen, "Evil, Love and the Left Hand of God," 222.
57. McGrath, *Luther's Theology of the Cross*, 151.
58. McGrath, 151.
59. McGrath, 170.
60. *WA* 5.165.39–166.1. Cited in McGrath, 152.

man upon the cross, the believer recognizes the presence and work of the crucified and hidden God who is present in human suffering and actively works through it.[61]

Kazoh Kitamori's *Theology of the Pain of God*

Another person who significantly shapes a theology of the cross is Kazoh Kitamori. Even though Luther had clearly indicated that the theologian of the cross must discern the presence of the hidden God in the suffering and the cross of Christ, the concept of *the suffering God* was brought to new prominence in the mid-twentieth century by Kitamori's *Theology of the Pain of God*. The first English edition of his formative work was released in 1946 in the aftermath of World War II. Many people might have thought that this book came primarily from the suffering and defeat of the Japanese, yet Kitamori insists that the idea is predominantly rooted in Scripture and is impacted by Japanese and Buddhist traditions.[62]

Kitamori explains a theology of the pain of God by differentiating the three orders of divine love: love of God, pain of God, and love rooted in the pain of God. The first order of God's love is his immediate love of those who are worthy of receiving it. Christ and humankind were originally objects of this order of love, but now Christ is the only object because humankind has fallen away from it due to rebellion and sin. The second order of God's love is his pain which resulted from his response to human sin. His response brings about pain for two reasons. First, he forgives and loves sinful human beings who should not be forgiven. Second, he sends his only Son to suffer and die. The third order of God's love is love rooted in the pain of God. It describes God's mediated love – in contrast to his immediate love as in the first order – that redeems humankind from sin and makes them his sons and daughters with Christ.[63] According to Kitamori, only those who are embraced by the love rooted in the pain of God can pursue the theology of the pain of God.[64] Consequently, he concludes his masterpiece with this prayer:

---

61. McGrath, 174–175.

62. Kitamori cites various biblical passages to support his argument. However, his basic texts are Jeremiah 31:20 and Isaiah 63:15. An exegetical work of these passages is given in an appendix of his book. See Kitamori, *Theology of the Pain of God*, 151–167.

63. Kitamori, 117–121.

64. Kitamori, 149.

> My prayer night and day is that the gospel of love rooted in the pain of God may become real to all [humans]. All human emptiness will be filled if this gospel is known to every creature, since the answer to every human problem lies in the gospel. Therefore I pray, "May thou, O Lord, make known to all [humanity] thy love rooted in the pain of God." The greatest joy and thanksgiving comes from the knowledge that this prayer is being granted and that step by step this gospel is becoming real to [humankind].[65]

Perhaps the most significant contribution that Kitamori has made is his argument against a traditional Christian theology that maintains divine immutability and impassibility. He clearly accomplishes the task of a theology of the pain of God, which is "to win over the theology which advocates a God who has no pain."[66] Kitamori points out that Western Christianity is overly dependent upon Greek philosophy that perceived God as immutable and impassible.[67] He argues that, at the cross, both the Father and the Son experienced pain because of their essential unity. He says:

> The death of God the son can be called the pain of God because the person of the Father lived. Pain can only be experienced by the living, not by the dead who are already freed from suffering. Because God is essentially one in his essence, although Father and Son differ in the persons of the Trinity, it is possible that the Father still lives even in the death of his Son. Thus the pain of God arises.[68]

Though many theologians disagree with Kitamori's idea that the pain of God is caused by an internal conflict within God's own nature, his attack on the doctrine of divine immutability has created a profound impact in Christian theology.[69] It has been echoed and elaborated by many contemporary theologians. In fact, Jürgen Moltmann admits that Kitamori's suggestion is a

---

65. Kitamori, 150.
66. Kitamori, 22.
67. Kitamori, "The Problem of Pain in Christology," 85.
68. Kitamori, *Theology of the Pain of God*, 115.
69. One example of a theologian who disagrees with the notion that the pain of God lies in his essence is Choan-Seng Song. He argues that if God's pain is only about an internal struggle

basis for his understanding of the crucified God.⁷⁰ To this, we shall examine Moltmann's theology, which is one of the most, if not *the* most, powerful voices of a theology of the cross at the present.

Jürgen Moltmann's *The Crucified God*

Grounded in Luther's foundation and Kitamori's contribution, Jürgen Moltmann brings a theology of the cross to its fruition through *The Crucified God: The Cross of Christ as the Foundation and Criticism of Christian Theology*. As the subtitle of this book indicates, Moltmann argues that the crucified Christ is the foundation and criterion of true Christian theology. All Christian statements about God, creation, sin, and death have their center in the crucified Christ. All Christian statements about history, the church, faith and sanctification, the future, and hope spring from the crucified Christ.⁷¹ He says, "Whatever can stand before the face of the crucified Christ is true Christian theology. What cannot stand there must disappear."⁷² This is especially true of what we understand about God. Christ died on the cross crying, "My God, my God, why have you forsaken me?" (Matt 27:46). For Moltmann, this cry of abandonment is not the end of theology, but it is the beginning of a truly Christian theology – a liberating theology which makes Jesus' experience of God on the cross the foundation for all our ideas about God.⁷³

Since the crucified Christ is the center of the Christian theology of God, Moltmann points out that "what is manifested in the cross is God's suffering of a passionate love for his lost creatures, a suffering prepared for sacrifice."⁷⁴ Grounded in Luther's *theologia crucis*, Moltmann maintains that God reveals himself to humankind through suffering and the cross, not through power and glory. The passion and cross of Christ is the visible revelation of God which is set over against the invisible things of God in created things that the theologian of glory is searching for. However, instead of asking just what God means for humankind in the cross of Christ, he also asks, "What

---

of God between love and wrath, then it has little implication for humankind. See Choan-Seng Song, *Third-Eye Theology*, 84–85.

70. Moltmann, *The Crucified God*, 47.
71. Moltmann, 204.
72. Moltmann, x.
73. Moltmann, x.
74. Moltmann, x.

does the cross of Jesus mean for God himself?" For Moltmann, this Christ event is a God event. On the cross, God has not just acted externally, but he has acted in himself and has suffered in himself.[75] Thus, the crucified Christ reveals the crucified God, and the suffering of Christ manifests the suffering of God himself.

For Moltmann, the theology of the cross must replace philosophical theism and atheism. For philosophical theism, the nature of divine being is characterized by its unity, lack of beginning and ending, and immutability. Thus, suffering and death must be excluded from the divine being. This philosophical concept of God has been adopted by Christian theology until the present. However, if this notion is applied to Christ' death on the cross, his death cannot be explained in theological terms because God cannot suffer and die. Christian theology, therefore, can no longer uphold this metaphysical concept of God. It is the time to differentiate between the Father of Jesus Christ and the God of the pagans and the philosophers. While philosophical theism holds that God cannot suffer and die, a theology of the cross affirms that "God suffered in the passion of Christ and he died on the cross of Christ."[76]

In atheism, an unjust, evil, and suffering world does not speak of a good and righteous God, but an unpredictable demon, blind fate, damning rule, or annihilating emptiness. Moltmann sees atheism as "the brother of theism" for it also sees the world as the reflection of a higher being. Whereas theism sees the righteous God through the created order, atheism perceives the nothingness in the reality of suffering and evil.[77] While theism neglects the history of suffering in this world as something to be tolerated or something that will be compensated for in heaven, atheism chooses the non-existence of God as an excuse for God in view of the suffering world. This is atheism as a theodicy! Here, a protest for atheism sets God and suffering in opposition and it becomes an atheistic protest "for God's sake." This protest, however, is eliminated by a theology of the cross which views God as the suffering God in the passion of Christ. At the same time, this theology cries out with the Godforsaken Jesus, "My God, my God, why have you forsaken me?" For the theology of the cross, God and suffering are not contradictions because

---

75. Moltmann, 205.
76. Moltmann, 214–216.
77. Moltmann, 220–221.

"God's being is in suffering and the suffering is in God's being itself, because God is love."[78]

Moltmann's understanding of the suffering God also challenges the Hellenistic apathetic theology that has greatly influenced the Christian concept of God. The term *apatheia* means incapable of being affected by external influences, incapable of feeling, or the freedom of the spirit from needs and drives. In the physical sense it means unchangeability; in the psychological sense, insensitivity; and in the ethical sense, freedom.[79] Since Plato and Aristotle, God's perfection has been described as apatheia. God is good; therefore, he cannot be the cause of evil. God is perfect; thus, he has no needs. God is sufficient; hence, he needs neither love nor hate. God knows neither wrath nor grace. Nothing can make him suffer. God is absolutely free.[80] Moltmann points out that this notion contradicts the idea of God in Scripture because the Old Testament often speaks of the wrath of God and the New Testament emphasizes the passion story of Jesus Christ.[81]

Rooted in the Jewish theologian Abraham Heschel's idea of the prophets' proclamation of God as *pathetic theology*, Moltmann indicates that the pathos of God is grounded in his freedom and interest in his creation and people. God takes human beings seriously to the point that he suffers from their actions and can be injured through them. At the core of the prophetic proclamations is the assurance that God is interested in the world to the point of suffering. The prophets, however, never identified God's pathos with his essence, but with the form of his relationship to the created orders.[82] Therefore, the history of God cannot be separated from the history of his people.[83] In view of the pathos of God, human beings become the compassionate people who enter into a sympathetic union with God.[84]

Moltmann explains further that the cross of Christ must be viewed from a trinitarian perspective. This is a solution for the paradox that God is dead on

---

78. Moltmann, 225–227.
79. Moltmann, 267.
80. Moltmann, "Crucified God," 10.
81. Moltmann, 11.
82. Here, Moltmann departs from Kitamori's understanding that God's pain lies in his essence.
83. Moltmann, *The Crucified God*, 270–271.
84. Moltmann, 272.

the cross and yet is not dead. He says, "The material principle of the doctrine of the Trinity is the cross of Christ. The formal principle of knowledge of the cross is the doctrine of the Trinity," and "The theology of the cross must be the doctrine of the Trinity and the doctrine of the Trinity must be the theology of the cross, because otherwise the human, crucified God cannot be fully perceived."[85] According to Mark, Jesus died with a cry of Godforsakenness (Mark 15:34). For Paul, the Father has abandoned and delivered up the Son for godforsaken people (Rom 8:32). From this understanding, Moltmann interestingly points out:

> It may therefore be said that the Father delivers up his Son on the cross in order to be the Father of those who are delivered up. The Son is delivered up to this death in order to become the Lord of both dead and living. And if Paul speaks emphatically of God's "own Son," the not-sparing and abandoning also involves the Father himself. In the forsakenness of the Son the Father also forsakes himself. In the surrender of the Son the Father also surrenders himself, though not in the same way. For Jesus suffers dying in forsakenness, but not death itself; for men can no longer 'suffer' death, because suffering presupposes life. But the Father who abandons him and delivers him up suffers the death of the Son in the infinite grief of love. We cannot therefore say here in patripassian terms that the Father also suffered and died. The suffering and dying of the Son, forsaken by the Father, is a different kind of suffering from the suffering of the Father in the death of the Son. Nor can the death of Jesus be understood in theopaschite terms as the "death of God." . . . The Son suffers dying, the Father suffers the death of the Son. The grief of the Father here is just as important as the death of the Son. The Fatherlessness of the Son is matched by the Sonlessness of the Father, and if God has constituted himself as the Father of Jesus Christ, then he also suffers the death of his Fatherhood in the

---

85. Moltmann, 241.

death of the Son. Unless this were so, the doctrine of the Trinity would still have a mono-theistic background.[86]

From this understanding, Moltmann concludes that the spirit of life, love, and election to salvation arise from the cross of Christ. The concrete history of God in the death of Jesus on the cross can be understood as the history of history because it contains within itself all the depths of human history. Consequently, there is no suffering that is not God's suffering; no death that has not been God's death on the cross; and no life and joy which have not been integrated into the eternal life and eternal joy of God.[87] Whoever suffers without reason always feels that he or she is abandoned by God. However, whoever cries out to God in this suffering joins in the death-cry of Jesus. For this person, then, God is the human God who cries with him or her and intercedes for him or her.

For Moltmann, the individuals who suffer do not only protest against their fate. They suffer because they live. They are alive because they love. When we suffer because we love, God suffers in us. Those who enter into love, and through love experience suffering and death, enter into the history of God because their forsakenness is lifted away from them in the forsakenness of Christ. As a result, they can continue to love and can sustain suffering and death.[88] To recognize God in the crucified Christ means to comprehend the trinitarian history of God and to understand oneself and this suffering world as existing in it.[89] For eschatological faith, the trinitarian history of God is open to the future. It moves towards eschatological consummation so that the Trinity may be all in all. God is in us. God suffers in us. We are participating in the trinitarian process of the history of God. In the same way that we participate in the suffering of God, we will participate in the joy of God when he brings his history to completion.[90]

---

86. Moltmann, 243. However, several theologians have expressed strong concerns about Moltmann's trinitarian theology, especially the danger of tritheism and patripassianism. See a discussion in Kärkkäinen, *The Trinity*, ch. 8.

87. Moltmann, *The Crucified God*, 246.

88. Moltmann, 253–254.

89. Moltmann, "Crucified God," 18.

90. Moltmann, *The Crucified God*, 255.

Kosuke Koyama

Another theologian who greatly enriched a theology of the cross is Kosuke Koyama from Japan.[91] Even though Koyama's theological discussions include many different subject matters since he aims to provide a *theologia in loco*, specifically theology relevant to an Asian context, it is apparent that his entire theological program centers on the cross of Christ. This fact is clearly demonstrated in the title of one of his books, *No Handle on the Cross: An Asian Meditation on the Crucified Mind*. In a preface to the twenty-fifth anniversary edition of *Water Buffalo Theology*, he also states that "*Water Buffalo Theology* tries to combine the biblical moral endeavor with the unconditional grace manifested in the form of *theologia crucis*. I hold that there cannot be true religion apart from self-discipline *and* an open acceptance of grace."[92] In this section, I will propose that Koyama's major contribution to a theology of the cross is his vision of the crucified mind.[93] This concept enables Christians to move beyond passively acknowledging God's presence in the passion of Christ and the suffering of humankind to actively participating in the suffering of Christ and that of others.

Koyama argues that all Christians must have a crucified mind. He points out that the unique spiritual insight that the Judeo-Christian tradition contributes to humankind is that God does not "handle" history, but he comes to history through his involvement with human beings throughout history and through the incarnation of Christ.[94] Based on the image of Jesus carrying a heavy cross with no handle, not a lunch-box or business briefcase with nice

---

91. During his career, Dr. Koyama was a lecturer at Thailand Theological Seminary (now McGilvary College of Divinity at Payap University), director of the Association of Theological Schools in South East Asia (now the Association for Theological Education in South East Asia: ATESEA), dean of the South East Asia Graduate School of Theology (SEAGST), editor of the South East Asia Journal of Theology, senior lecturer in religion at the University of Otago (New Zealand), and professor at Union Theological Seminary in New York City. It is my privilege to serve the Lord in the same institution where Dr. Koyama once served. I am grateful for his profound theological heritage, which speaks directly to the Thai context. His insights are involved with several theological topics. A thorough examination of his theology is certainly beyond the scope of this study. Hence, I will focus on his contribution to a theology of the cross, specifically his concept of a crucified mind. See Koyama, *No Handle on the Cross*; Koyama, *Three Mile an Hour God*; and Koyama, *Water Buffalo Theology*. For an appraisal of Koyama's theology, see Irvin and Akinade, *The Agitated Mind of God: The Theology of Kosuke Koyama*.

92. Koyama, *Water Buffalo Theology*, xii. Emphasis in the original.

93. Kärkkäinen indicates that the concept of the crucified mind is the heart of Koyama's theology. Kärkkäinen, *The Doctrine of God*, 288.

94. Koyama, *No Handle on the Cross*, 13.

handle, Koyama suggests that the cross without a handle signifies extreme inconvenience, ugliness, inefficiency, insecurity, pain, and self-denial. Hence, those who would follow Christ must deny themselves and receive the mind of the crucified Lord, a crucified mind. As Jesus says, "If anyone would come after me, he must deny himself and take up his cross and follow me" (Matt 16:24).[95]

Reflecting on various New Testament passages, especially Paul's statements in 1 Corinthians 1:18–25 and 2:2, and Philippians 2:5–11, Koyama indicates that a crucified mind is the mind which "has decided to live by the power of the crucified Lord," "desires to seek understanding through the wisdom of the crucified Lord," and "speaks of Jesus Christ through the influence of the spirituality and mentality of the crucified Lord."[96] He explains further:

> The crucified mind, then, is not a sickly mind. It is not suffering from a persecution complex. It is not a mutilated mind. . . . It is a theologically inspired mind. It is an honest and careful mind. It is a believing mind. It is weak, yet a strong mind. It is foolish, yet a wise mind. It is the mind confessing, "I believe, help my unbelief!" Basically it is a mind of Jesus Christ who carried the cross "without a handle," and prepared deepening while he was "bent down."[97]

In sum, a crucified mind is a mind characterized by self-denial, following the mind of Christ (Phil 2:5) that compels him to enter human history, deny himself, participate in human suffering, and be crucified on behalf of sinful humankind. Hence, Christians who have this state of mind will be willing to deny themselves and participate in the suffering of Christ and of others.

Koyama indicates that the crucified mind is essential for Christians who seek to communicate the gospel of Christ to people of other faiths. He wonderfully depicts this mentality in the final chapter of *Water Buffalo Theology*. Recalling his conversation with a Thai Buddhist monk, Koyama retells the monk's reaction to John 1:1, "In the beginning was the Word, and the Word was with God, and the Word was God." The monk said:

---

95. Koyama, 1–2.
96. Koyama, 8.
97. Koyama, 12.

> My friend, this is quite a *noisy* religion. I am afraid that we are getting further and further away from the bliss of tranquility and detachment. At least in the beginning there must have been Nirvanic silence, deep tranquility and *non-attachment*.[98]

Koyama agrees that Christianity is a *noisy* religion. Indeed, the Bible witnesses a progression of God's "noisy attachment." The progress of attachment is intensified when "the Word became flesh and made his dwelling among us" (John 1:14). All things are reconciled, or *attached*, to God through Jesus Christ, and this is accomplished by "his blood, shed on the cross" (Col 1:20). Here, a theology of the cross summarizes the paradox of God's glory in the suffering and death of Christ. Therefore, Christians must demonstrate the quality of Christ's glory in suffering through the three models of Christian presence: stumbling presence, "discomforted" presence, and "unfree" presence.[99]

Christian stumbling presence refers to the fact that Christians bear a stumbling message of salvation through the crucified Christ, which is contradictory to human reason. Koyama says:

> It is difficult to stake one's life on a man who was crucified between two thieves outside the gate of Jerusalem, trusting him to be the Lord in whom alone God's final restoration of all things was effected (Eph 1:10). . . . With sheer good sense the very people from whom Christ came stumbled at him (Rom 9:32, 33; Matt 13:57). With sheer good sense, the people who lived at a distance from Abraham stumbled at him (Acts 17:32). With sheer good sense the people who live in proximity to the Buddha stumble at Christ as well. The lordship of Christ in the theology of the cross – the crucified lordship! – is universally "sheer nonsense" to humans (Gal 5:11).[100]

In this sense, Christians are those who have overcome the stumbling block of the crucified Christ. Christian presence is established upon the glory of the crucified Christ, yet, at the same time, it is a stumbling presence because it witnesses to the paradoxical reality of the cross. For Koyama, Christ's cry on the

---

98. Quoted in Koyama, *Water Buffalo Theology*, 160. Emphasis in the original.
99. Koyama, 161–163.
100. Koyama, 163.

cross, "My God, my God, why have you forsaken me?" (Mark 15:34), reveals a Christ who is stumbling at the forsaking of the Father, yet who firmly trusts in him. Christian stumbling presence, therefore, is given to them by God. It guards Christians against a superficial triumphalism of faith that prevents them from seeing a crucified Lord. However, it is precisely in the stumbling presence that Christians can better communicate with other people.[101]

Since the term "stumble" conveys the idea of unbelief, it may not be appropriate to use it to describe the first Christian presence. It seems to me that Koyama's concept of a stumbling presence is closer to the terms "paradoxical presence, protesting presence, or believing presence." It is the presence of both *opus alienum Dei* and *opus proprium Dei*, to use Luther's terms. It describes an ability to discern the hidden God in the suffering of Christ. It illustrates Job's cry and believers' prayers of lament which are full of pain and anger yet refuse to turn away from God. This attitude clearly represents a crucified mind that endures suffering through the power of the crucified Lord and responds to it through the wisdom of the crucified Lord.

Christian "discomforted" presence refers to the fact that Christians must participate in the suffering of Christ. Christians are comforted people because they belong to Jesus Christ. However, this particular belonging entails both Christological comfort and Christological discomfort because, "We are to live sharing the pain *pathos* of God's saving will expressed in the striking images at the crucial moments of salvation-history."[102] In the same way that Paul understands that he is called to participate in Christ's suffering (e.g. Rom 8:17; 2 Cor 6:4–10; Phil 3:10), people with a crucified mind should participate in Christ's discomfort and suffering. Moreover, in the suffering world, they should follow an example of the crucified Lord who suffers for others by participating in the suffering of other people.[103] For this reason, I would propose that Christian discomforted presence can also be called "Christian suffering presence." Christians are to be in solidarity with suffering creation – the whole environment, and suffering people in particular.

Christian "unfree" presence indicates that Christians must give up their freedom in order to serve God and others. Christians are freed because Jesus

---

101. Koyama, 165.
102. Koyama, 166.
103. Koyama, 167.

Christ has redeemed them from the power of darkness. However, a theology of the cross asks a crucial question, "Should not this freedom be crucified, following the Son of God who crucified his freedom for others in the form of a servant?" (Phil 2:7; Luke 22:27; Isa 53). Consequently, Christians with a crucified mind live in freedom from "the basic principles of the world" (Gal 4:3), yet they live in "unfreedom" to be the servants of all. In addition, this "unfree" presence reveals that God frees Christians from other tables of saving messages in order that they may be *attached* to the Lord's table, which reminds them of Christ's suffering until he comes (1 Cor 11:26). This is to participate in the ministry of "reconciling all things" of the hidden God.[104]

"How does God respond to human suffering?" The study of a theology of the cross in this section reveals that God is not passive, but active concerning the matter of human suffering. The cross of Christ clearly points to the fact that the trinitarian God has assumed responsibility over the existence of evil and suffering in this world by becoming a suffering God. In contrast to philosophical theism, Scripture testifies that the Triune God of Christianity is not a detached observer who is characterized by immutability and impassibility, but he is a compassionate God who is present in the suffering of humankind.

Considering the cross from a trinitarian vantage point helps us grasp a clearer vision of God's participation in human suffering. It enables us to comprehend the truth that all persons of the Trinity actively participate in human suffering at the cross. The crucified Christ reveals the crucified God and the suffering Son manifests the suffering Father. Jesus suffers dying in forsakenness, and the Father suffers the death of the Son as well as suffering the death of his Fatherhood. The sacrifice of the Father and the Son is done through the Holy Spirit. At the same time, the Spirit is the link between the Father and the Son in their separation.[105] Therefore, it can be said that "the Father lets his Son sacrifice himself through the Spirit," to use Moltmann's terms.[106] Moreover, it can be concluded:

> The cross is at the centre of the Trinity. This is brought out by tradition, when it takes up the Book of Revelation's image of 'the Lamb who was slain from the foundation of the world' (Rev

---

104. Koyama, 168–170.
105. Moltmann, *The Trinity and the Kingdom*, 82–83.
106. Moltmann, 83.

5.12). Before the world was, the sacrifice was already in God. No Trinity is conceivable without the Lamb, without the sacrifice of love, without the crucified Son. For he is the slaughtered Lamb glorified in eternity.[107]

Consequently, it can be seen that God is interested in human suffering to the point of participating in our suffering. The history of God in the death of Jesus on the cross is truly the "history of history" because it includes not only the sin of the world but also all of humankind's suffering, pain, and death.

However, God does not simply suffer *with* human beings, but he suffers *for* us. At the cross, *opus alienum Dei* and *opus proprium Dei* are clearly in operation. Through Christ's death, God shares in human suffering in order to redeem humankind from sin and its consequences. It is at the cross that God walks alongside humankind in our suffering, and it is here that he works out his justification and salvation. This is indeed the new meaning of suffering. Christ's resurrection and glorification after he has suffered and died also affirms that God will eventually bring suffering to an end: "He will wipe every tear from their eyes. There will be no more death or mourning or crying or pain, for the old order of things has passed away" (Rev 21:4).

The trinitarian history of God on the cross is truly open to the future. It moves towards eschatological consummation so that God may be all in all. Therefore, when human reason causes people to see only a suffering and dying man on the cross, faith in God enables Christians to see the Savior who saves us from sin and suffering as well as a confidence in the ultimate freedom from suffering in the future. As we are in Christ, the Holy Spirit allows us to share Christ's victory through faith and baptism. The Spirit gives substantial healing to our lives, and bears witness that we are God's children, heirs of God and co-heirs with Christ. The Spirit grants us strength to endure and hope for the future. We share in Christ's suffering in this world, but we will also share in his glory in the future. Meanwhile, as we, and the whole of creation, wait eagerly for liberation from the bondage to decay and entrance into the glorious freedom of God's children, the Spirit helps us in our weakness and intercedes for us when we do not know what we ought to pray for (Rom 8:12–27).

---

107. Moltmann, 83.

Finally, the theology of the cross reveals that believers must move beyond knowing the new meaning of suffering – God heals human pain through his pain – to embracing the mind of Christ. Christians are to deny themselves, participate in the suffering of Christ, and walk alongside others in their suffering. In their misery, they will endure it through the power of the Holy Spirit and respond to it through God's wisdom. In so doing, they are forcefully proclaiming the message of the cross through their lives. Other sufferers will surely be challenged by their lives and be more open to the gospel. In their comfort, Christians will voluntarily suffer for Christ and for other people. Paul says, "For it has been granted to you on behalf of Christ not only to believe on him, but also to suffer for him" (Phil 1:29) and "Now I rejoice in what was suffered for you, and I fill up in my flesh what is still lacking in regard to Christ's afflictions, for the sake of his body, which is the church" (Col 1:24). They will no longer live for themselves, but they will live for Christ and other people. As Paul says, "And [Christ] died for all, that those who live should no longer live for themselves but for him who died for them and was raised again" (2 Cor 5:15; cf. Rom 14:7–8). In their freedom, they will be attached to God and become the servants of all: "You, my brothers, were called to be free. But do not use your freedom to indulge the sinful nature; rather, serve one another in love" (Gal 5:13). In short, they will no longer seek to escape from suffering, knowing that they are already freed from it, but they will embrace it for Christ and in the power of the Spirit in order to participate in the ministry of "reconciling all things" to God.

Conclusion

In this chapter, I have indicated that both Buddhism and Christianity agree that the problem of human suffering is resolvable, yet each tradition has a different view of the basic cause of suffering and offers a unique solution to this problem. Buddhism understands that the extinction of suffering is achieved in the absolute detachment at nibbāna; therefore, human beings must attempt to reach this goal by practicing the Middle Way, or the Noble Eightfold Path of Right Understanding, Right Thought, Right Speech, Right Action, Right Livelihood, Right Effort, Right Mindfulness, and Right Meditation.

A comparison between this teaching and biblical teachings reveals both similarities and differences. It is interesting that several aspects of the Middle

Way are very close to Christian teachings. It can be said that the Buddhist and Christian answers to the problem of human suffering are essentially different, but they do *not totally* oppose one another. Buddhists and Christians can learn from one another so that they may be able to respond to suffering more effectively. For Christians, aspects of the Noble Eightfold Path that do not contradict the Christian faith can help them develop their relationship with God as well as prevent them from unnecessary suffering. For instance, Right Thought will enable the pure in heart to see God (Matt 5:8) and avert the resentment and bitterness caused by an unforgiving heart. Therefore, a Christian theology of suffering in the context of Theravada Buddhism in Thailand agrees that dealing with the inward experience of the sufferers and enabling them to develop good attitudes and actions can empower sufferers and prevent unnecessary suffering to a certain degree.

Notwithstanding various commonalities, I have proposed that Buddhism and Christianity ultimately offer opposite solutions to the problem of human suffering. Buddhism teaches that it is a human's own effort that leads to nibbāna, but Christianity believes that Jesus Christ is the only Way to salvation. The Middle Way and the Way obviously lead to different goals. The former advocates an absolute detachment at nibbāna, but the latter promotes an absolute attachment – that of eternal fellowship with God. Therefore, in contrast to Buddhism, Christianity teaches that human beings must respond to God's saving work by repenting from their sin and trusting in him.

The answer to the question, "How does God save humankind from suffering?," lies in a theology of the cross. The theological heritage of Martin Luther, Kazoh Kitamori, Jürgen Moltmann, and Kosuke Koyama helps Christians better understand the relationship between the cross of Christ and human suffering. I have mentioned that the cross is the clearest manifestation that the trinitarian God of Christianity is a suffering God who actively participates in human suffering. The crucified Christ reveals the hidden God who was also crucified on the cross. It is here that all the suffering of humankind throughout history is embraced by God himself. Moreover, it is at the cross that Christ redeems humankind from sin and its consequences, especially suffering. In the suffering world, believers are encouraged by the fact that the trinitarian history of God on the cross is moving towards eschatological consummation. Christ's suffering, death, resurrection, and glorification reveals that God will surely and finally put an end to suffering. In the same way that the incarnation, crucifixion, and resurrection are factual events in history, Christ's second coming and final judgment will be factual events that bring history to an end. At the eschaton, God will be all in all. We will receive the beatific vision of God as we witness and experience a complete extinction of suffering. As John says:

> Then I saw a new heaven and a new earth, for the first heaven and the first earth had passed away, and there was no longer any sea. I saw the Holy City, the new Jerusalem, coming down out of heaven from God, prepared as a bride beautifully dressed for her husband. And I heard a loud voice from the throne saying, "Now the dwelling of God is with men, and he will live with them. They will be his people, and God himself will be with them and be their God. He will wipe every tear from their eyes. There will be no more death or mourning or crying or pain, for the old order of things has passed away." (Rev 21:1–4)

Another question that emerges from God's response to suffering is "How should humankind respond to the reality of suffering?" I have suggested that human beings should respond to God's saving act by repenting from their sin and trusting in him. Furthermore, they should learn to participate in the suffering of Christ and the suffering of other people, as well as of the whole created order. Following Koyoma's three models of Christian presence, believers should demonstrate the quality of Christ's glory by suffering while holding to their firm belief in the midst of affliction, practicing solidarity with the suffering of Christ and the whole of creation, and serving God and other people.

For this reason, a Christian theology of suffering in the context of Theravada Buddhism in Thailand affirms that proper attitudes and actions can certainly empower sufferers and avert preventable suffering to a certain degree, yet it sincerely and humbly declares that only the redemptive work of the Triune God can bring suffering to a complete extinction. This message is truly good news for the Thai people. It is a great comfort to know that humankind does not face suffering alone, but there is a compassionate God who is present in the suffering of humankind. It is a great hope to hear that beyond humans' limited ability to complete the Noble Eightfold Path leading to the end of suffering there is a Savior who is the Way to the end of suffering.

It is also a great encouragement to hear that human effort is not useless because, though it cannot free the individual from suffering, it becomes an act of participating in the suffering of the One who has already freed them from suffering. More importantly, it is a great joy to know that those who believe do not have to be afraid of suffering, but they can embrace it, knowing that in so doing they are participating in God's redemptive work for all humankind.

Conclusion

The problem of suffering is real and complex. Christianity and Buddhism each approach this inevitable reality in a different manner. In Thailand, the understanding and responses of the Thai people, including Christians, to suffering is greatly influenced by the Buddhist concept of suffering as reflected in the Four Noble Truths. A traditional Christian theology of suffering, which often emphasizes the problem of evil and theodicy, may be relevant to the context in which it was developed, the western world. Unfortunately, the traditional Christian theology of suffering falls short in addressing the needs of the Thai people who belong to the Buddhist world and perceive suffering differently. Furthermore, dealing with suffering in the broader framework of theodicy is important and necessary. However, it tends to create a hypothetical question, "*Why* does an omnipotent and loving God allow suffering?," that leads to theoretical answers that are not really beneficial for the sufferers, who do not merely seek to understand, but to be freed from, suffering.

Consequently, this dissertation has aimed to develop a Christian theology of suffering that is relevant to the context of Theravada Buddhism in Thailand. Grounded in a methodology of a trinitarian comparative theology of religions, I have proposed that a Christian theology of suffering that is truly relevant to this context must be firmly rooted in the biblical and theological concept of suffering, yet it should critically engage and learn from the Buddhist concept of suffering. The Christian concept of suffering is maintained, but it is reflected and enhanced by the insights gained from the Buddhist tradition. This study reveals four critical aspects of a Christian theology of suffering in the context of Theravada Buddhism in Thailand.

First, in the light of the First Noble Truth, a Christian theology of suffering in the context of Theravada Buddhism in Thailand acknowledges the reality and complexity of suffering and affirms that some forms of suffering can be part of human nature. A comparative study between the First Noble Truth and the basic Christian concept of suffering indicates that both religions agree that suffering is real and complex. The problem of suffering, therefore, should be viewed as a concrete challenge that demands a proper response rather than an intellectual question that requires a logical explanation. Additionally, it is more appropriate to speak of *many problems* of human suffering rather than *a problem* of human suffering.

The Buddhist teaching that some types of suffering are naturally connected to finitude and mortality leads to a reassessment of the traditional Christian understanding that the original creation was absolutely without suffering. Over the traditional view, I have argued that some sorts of suffering are located in the structure of creation according to God's good intention. Some types of suffering related to physical limitations – decay, natural illness, and even death – are not intrinsically evil but are natural results of finitude and mortality. These types of suffering exist to serve human life and enrich our relationship with God. Even though they shorten and finally end the human's biological life, they do not destroy the human's spiritual life. In contrast, they free the human person from the limitations of human nature, so that the human person can fully enjoy a relationship with God forever. Consequently, Christians should accept that humans' earthly existence inevitably brings about certain forms of suffering.

Second, reflecting on the Second Noble Truth, a Christian theology of suffering in the context of Theravada Buddhism in Thailand affirms that many forms of suffering do not belong to the original creation. However, a Christian theology of suffering in the context of Theravada Buddhism in Thailand resists any attempt to generalize suffering and declares that this complex reality can be attributed to several causes, for example, sin, oppression, and mystery. In addition, it refuses any narrow-minded approach that limits suffering to a particular cause and overlooks other possible causes, and proposes that Christians should address human suffering in a more holistic manner. Among many Christian interpretations of the causes of suffering, three positions have been presented in this study because they are more relevant to the context of Theravada Buddhism in Thailand: suffering as the result of sin, as caused by oppression, and as a mystery.

Retribution theology views the suffering of individuals in relation to God's retributive justice and ascribes it to the individuals' sin; therefore, a proper response to suffering is to repent and surrender to God. I have argued that the Buddhist and Christian interpretations of the causes of suffering are similar in some aspects, but they are fundamentally different. Retribution theology and the law of kamma share some similarities on a surface level, yet they are different in their essence. These doctrines are similar in two manners. First, they affirm that much suffering does not belong to human nature, but it is the result of human wrongdoing, which has been influenced by sin or tanhā. Second, the act-consequence aspect of retribution and the law of kamma advocate an intrinsic correlation between deed and consequence, whether good or bad. This understanding helps individuals realize that some of their suffering experiences should not be regarded as God's punishment, but the suffering should be perceived as consequences of their wrongdoing. Hence, individuals should not blame God for their affliction, but they should be more responsible for their actions, knowing that their immoral actions will oftentimes bring about suffering.

Notwithstanding their similarities, I have stated that retribution theology and the law of kamma are fundamentally different because of two reasons. First, they perceive the relationship between wrongdoing and suffering in different manners. According to the law of kamma, actions bring about results according to the natural law of action and effect; the connection between actions and results is inexorable and mechanical; and the process of kamma fruition is sophisticated – the individuals may somehow reap its fruit immediately, later in their lives, or in some subsequent existence. In contrast, the principle of retribution teaches that the connection between actions and results is established by God who is the supreme judge; it is a straightforward connection, not a complex process that will somehow come to fruition at a later time; and it is not an unalterable connection because God's grace and mercy surpasses it. Second, the law of kamma and retribution theology offer opposite solutions to suffering caused by immorality. The law of kamma holds that suffering is basically caused by human craving (*tanhā*) and ignorance (*avijjā*). Thus, one must depend upon one's self in dealing with one's desire and ignorance. A theology of retribution teaches that suffering is God's punishment for human sin. Hence, one must repent from sin and enter into a genuine fellowship with God.

Liberation theology highlights suffering caused by injustice and oppression in society. It challenges both retribution theology and the law of kamma which attribute people's affliction to their own misconduct. The traditional interpretation is not mistaken, but it is not the only reason behind suffering, and it can lead to indifference to injustice and oppression in society. Instead of asking the question, "Why does God allow such suffering?," Thai Christians should ask, "How should Thai Christians respond to injustice and oppression in Thai society?" Therefore, Thai Christians cannot overlook suffering caused by exploitation and oppression in Thai society, and they should respond to it by being in solidarity with the sufferers and denouncing oppressive social structures through their words and deeds.

The Book of Job testifies to the realities of innocent sufferers and inexplicable suffering. It challenges both the law of kamma and retribution theology by proclaiming that the cause of the individual's suffering can remain a mystery. It also proclaims that the creator God is the true center of all things. He watches over all human beings and has a good and eternal purpose for them. Therefore, God is the only person who can help human beings in their suffering. Moreover, the Book of Job reveals that the most important question about human suffering is not "*Why* does God allow suffering?" but rather "*How* should one respond to the reality of inexplicable suffering in this world?" According to the Book of Job, it was Job's encounter with God – not the understanding of his affliction – that brought comfort and transformation to Job's life. Therefore, proper responses to suffering may not be repenting or showing solidarity with the sufferers, but holding on to one's integrity, drawing near to God, and sustaining one's faith in him.

Third, responding to the third and Fourth Noble Truth, a Christian theology of suffering in the context of Theravada Buddhism in Thailand agrees that right attitudes and actions can help the individuals endure suffering and prevent unnecessary suffering to a certain degree, yet it affirms that only Jesus Christ can save humankind from sin and suffering and bring suffering to a complete extinction.[1] I have proposed that the Buddhist and Christian ways

---

1. However, it must be noted that suffering will be taken up into our worship in some sense. In Revelation 5, the Lion of the tribe of Judah who has triumphed is described as "*a Lamb, looking as if it had been slain*" (v. 6). Furthermore, the heavenly host praises him by singing, "You are worthy to take the scroll and to open its seals, because *you were slain*, and with *your blood* you purchased men for God from every tribe and language and people and nation. You have made them to be a kingdom and priests to serve our God, and they will reign on the earth. . . . *Worthy is the Lamb, who was slain*, to receive power and wealth and wisdom and strength and honor and glory and praise!" (vv. 9–10, 12). Emphasis added. In *The End of*

to the extinction of suffering are similar on a practical level. Several aspects of the Middle Way are very close to Christian teachings; therefore, they can be beneficial to Christians. Nevertheless, I have argued that the Buddhist and Christian answers to the problem of suffering are fundamentally different. Buddhism teaches that it is human effort that leads to nibbāna, but Christianity believes that human beings cannot break the bondage of suffering by themselves, but they can be delivered from it by God's redemptive work.

For this reason, the most important question in a Christian theology of suffering is not "*Why* does God allow suffering?" but "*How* does God respond to human suffering?" The answer to this question lies in the cross of Christ because it is the clearest manifestation of God's redemptive work. The cross of Christ reveals that God has assumed the responsibility over evil and suffering in this world by becoming a suffering God. It testifies that the God of Christianity is not a detached observer, but he is a merciful and gracious God who actively participates in human suffering.

Trinitarian theology enables us to comprehend the truth that all persons of the Trinity actively participate in human suffering at the cross. The crucified Christ reveals the crucified God and the suffering Son manifests the suffering Father. Jesus suffers dying in forsakenness. The Father suffers the death of the Son and the death of his Fatherhood. The sacrifice of the Father and the Son is done through the Holy Spirit who is the link between the Father and the Son in their separation. The Spirit of life proceeds from the cross of Christ, enabling it to contain within itself all the depths of human history. All suffering and death has been included on the cross, and life and joy has been integrated into the eternal life and eternal joy of God.

However, it is significant to stress that God does not simply suffer *with* human beings, but he suffers *for* us. Through Christ's suffering and death, God shares human suffering in order to redeem humankind from sin and suffering. As Kitamori says, "God in pain is the God who resolves our human pain by his own. Jesus Christ is the Lord who heals our human wounds by

---

Memory, Miroslav Volf argues that the memory of Christ's death and resurrection provides a framework for the sufferers to remember rightly a wrongdoing that they have suffered. First, it enables the victims to remember the wrongdoing not as righteous persons, but as sinners who are embraced by the righteous God. Second, it helps them remember the wrongdoing as already forgiven. Finally, it enables them to remember every wrongdoing in light of the future reconciliation with wrongdoers. Hence, remembering the Passion brings healing to the wronged in community with wrongdoers, not at their expense. See Volf, *The End of Memory*.

his own (1 Peter 2:24)."[2] More importantly, Christ's resurrection and glorification evidently confirms that he is the Savior of the world, and those who believe in him will share his triumph over sin and suffering. Christ' victory becomes the victory of believers through the Holy Spirit. The Spirit of life is the comforter who applies Christ's healing to humankind. The cross does not bring only justification but also regeneration to human beings. In the midst of suffering believers receive strength to endure and hope for the future from the Holy Spirit who dwells in their lives. They can be certain that they will finally be raised from the dead and share in Christ's glory. Moreover, believers can be assured that the whole creation will be restored and transformed by the Holy Spirit so that it may reach its completion according to the divine intention. Hence, the restored and transformed created order can truly bring glory to God.

The assurance given through the Holy Spirit is not speculation because it is based on a historical event on the cross that guarantees God's promise for the future. It is also not a result of completing God's commandments or adhering to any particular religious standard, but it is the free gift of a compassionate God for all humankind. This is the good news for the Thai people that Christians must humbly proclaim if they want to represent faithful and genuine Christian participation in an interfaith dialogue.

Finally, a Christian theology of suffering that is truly relevant to the context of Theravada Buddhism in Thailand cannot be limited to academia. Besides attempting to understand God's response to human suffering, it must ask another important question, "How should Christians respond to suffering?" The preceding discussion suggests that Thai Christians should respond to the reality of human suffering in three manners: faith, solidarity, and repentance.

Above all, Thai Christians should respond to suffering, especially incomprehensible suffering, by faith.[3] Different causes of suffering demand different kinds of responses, but faith must be the primary response of believers in all situations. This is the essence of the theology of the cross and of the Book of

---

2. Kitamori, *Theology of the Pain of God*, 20.

3. Here, faith does not refer to "what people believe," but it is "a heartfelt trust in God." As Calvin says, "[Faith] is a steady and certain knowledge of the Divine benevolence towards us, which, being founded on the truth of the gratuitous promise in Christ, is both revealed to our minds, and confirmed to our hearts, by the Holy Spirit." Calvin, *Institutes of the Christian Religion* (3.2.7).

Job. Faith is asserted throughout the Bible, and it is summarized in Hebrews 11. Believers can continue to believe, not because their faith gives them the explanation to the problem of suffering, but because it helps them cope with affliction on a practical level. However, faith does not require that we deny our feelings when we come to God. On the contrary, those who suffer can honestly protest and complain to their Lord. The example of Job or the prayers of lament mentioned above clearly affirm this idea. Our honest cry to God may be filled with anger and protest, but it does not destroy our faith and hope because it actually draws us closer to God. Responding to inexplicable suffering by faith is an expression of the crucified mind, particularly in the paradoxical presence. When Thai Christians endure hardship by faith and by relying on the power of the crucified Christ, they are witnessing to the message of the cross through their lives. Christian sermons about the cross may not make sense to other Thais, but Christian lives that genuinely reveal the message of the cross will surely challenge other sufferers and help them be more open to the gospel.

In order to sustain their faith in God in difficult times, Thai Christians must learn to cultivate an intimate relationship with God at all times. Here, they can benefit greatly by learning from the concept of Right Meditation. As many scholars have pointed out, Buddhist meditation is truly comparable to Christian spirituality.[4] Even though these concepts lead to different destinations, each of them has the same function in its tradition, namely to assist the individuals to overcome anything that hinders them from the highest goal. Right Meditation enables Buddhists to achieve the absolute detachment of nibbāna because it helps them detach their minds from all persons and things and fully realize Dhamma, particularly the Three Characteristics of Existence and the Four Noble Truths. Christian spirituality enables Christians to have genuine fellowship with God because it helps them detach their lives from the lesser attachments of this world and attach their whole being to God.[5] In

---

4. See for example Gross and Muck, *Christians Talk about Buddhist Meditation, Buddhists Talk about Christian Prayer*; and Petchsongkram, *Talk in the Shade of the Bo Tree*, 38–51; Ukosakul, *A Turn from the Wheel to the Cross*.

5. While "Christian spirituality" is differently defined by different Christian traditions, it can be generally described as "the way in which the Christian life is understood and the explicit y devotional practices which have been developed to foster and sustain that relationship with Christ" and "the way in which Christian individuals or groups aim to deepen their experience

other words, Buddhists practice meditation to empty their minds so they will be freed from all attachments, but Christians engage in the various activities of Christian spirituality to empty themselves so they will be filled with the fullness of Christ.[6]

While meditation is greatly emphasized by Buddhists, it is sad that within Christian spirituality this practice is often neglected by many Protestant Christians at the present time. Focusing so much on salvation by faith alone, the importance of works, which confirm an authentic faith, is often overlooked (cf. Jas 2). Relatively, faith in God has become a matter of inner belief rather than the commitment of individuals who truly have crucified minds – to deny themselves, take up their crosses, and follow Christ. Consequently, it is not unusual that some Christians cannot maintain their faith when they face hardship, not to mention when they willingly suffer for Christ and others.

In the light of the Buddhist emphasis on meditation, Thai Christians – fully aware that humankind is saved by faith, not by works – should give more attention to the crucial role of spiritual disciplines in nurturing their faith and cultivating a closer relationship with God. While Buddhist meditation is usually compared with Christian prayer, I would suggest that it can also be compared with other Christian devotional practices, both personal and communal, such as meditation, solitude, fasting, study, worship, fellowship, and confession.[7] In addition, I would propose that Thai Christians should learn from Buddhist meditation, particularly the notion of bringing one's consciousness to a single point in meditation, in order to develop more meaningful and profound Christian meditation. For example, take meditation upon Scripture. Thai Christians should begin by learning an appropriate way to interpret the Bible, seeking a suitable place for meditation, and quieting their hearts and minds. Then, they must choose a biblical passage or verse to meditate on rather than reading through many passages superficially. Finally, they must really concentrate on that particular passage so that the written Word will become a living word addressed to them, and the meditation upon

---

of God, or to 'practise the presence of God,' to use a phrase especially associated with Brother Lawrence (*c*.1614–91)." McGrath, *Christian Spirituality*, 2–3.

6. See Ukosakul, *A Turn from the Wheel to the Cross*.

7. For more information on spiritual disciplines, see Foster, *Celebration of Discipline*; and Willard, *The Spirit of the Disciplines*.

Scripture will truly become a way to listen to God, communicate with the Creator, and experience the eternal Lover of the world.[8]

In the realm of Christian meditation, David F. Ford has several helpful suggestions. In *Christian Wisdom: Desiring God and Learning in Love*, he proposes ten principles of reading Scripture that enable Christians to receive the wisdom of God. First, Christians should read and reread Scripture for the sake of God and God's purposes. They must listen to the voice of God, and respond to it with love for God and for the world God loves. Second, Christians should read Scripture in the light of the wisdom of the church's tradition. Third, Christians should read the Old and New Testament together in the Spirit of the risen Christ. Fourth, Christians should attempt to understand a biblical passage in its original sense, yet they must be open to other senses. Fifth, Christians should pay attention to biblical witnesses to Jesus Christ. Sixth, Christians should read Scripture as part of the church, and they must also read it in the light of the realities and cries of the world. Seventh, Christians should become apprentices of past and present wise readers of Scripture. Eighth, Christians should read Scripture in dialogue with diverse others outside the church. Ninth, Christians should read the Bible in light of the Holy Spirit's ongoing work in the world. Tenth, Christians should read Scripture in love for God and neighbor.[9]

It seems at first glance that Ford's proposal is in contrast to the Buddhist notion of a single point in meditation because it includes many different principles. A closer look at these principles, however, indicates that they revolve around the centrality of God. Ford says:

> The specifically theological character of the rereading lies in it being done before God, in relationship with God, seeking in the Spirit to follow the purposes of God in the world and finding in scriptures inspired testimony to what all of that involves. If "the fear of the Lord is the beginning of wisdom" then wisdom interpretation of scripture is done primarily with respect to and for God.[10]

---

8. Foster, *Celebration of Discipline*, 33.
9. Ford, *Christian Wisdom*, 79–89.
10. Ford, 68.

Therefore, it can be said that Ford's proposal is actually in harmony with the basic Buddhist concept of meditation. It promotes meditation upon Scripture that truly focuses on God. In fact, the emphasis on God should be the heart of all exercises in Christian spirituality because it will help Christians move beyond superficially practicing spiritual disciplines to focusing on God, hearing his voice, and experiencing his presence. In so doing, Christians can develop a closer relationship with God that will enable them to sustain their faith in the midst of suffering.

The second appropriate response to suffering, especially suffering caused by oppression and injustice, is to be in solidarity with the oppressed and the poor. The painful situations of others call for Thai Christians' solidarity with the afflicted in Thai society. This response is the heart of liberation theology, and it corresponds with the second aspect of the crucified mind, "suffering presence." Thai Christians who have the mind of Christ will be sensitive to the needs of other people, and they will participate in the suffering of others in their actions. This response is not just the imitation of Christ's ministry in the past, but it is the continuation of his ministry in this world. It is not asking the question, "What would Jesus do in this situation?," which implies his absence from our present situation, but it is to ask, "What is Jesus *doing* in this situation and what am I to do as a Christian?"[11] After his resurrection, Jesus promised the coming of the Holy Spirit upon his followers as a continuation of his ministry on earth. Therefore, Christ's redemptive work still continues in the present situations through the ministry of the Holy Spirit in the lives of believers.[12]

More specifically, Thai Christians are called to participate in the ministry of an advocate or *paraclesis*. The word "advocate" comes from the Greek word "*paraclete*" which literally means "called to the side." This word signifies "a role of comforting, exhorting and encouraging."[13] In his earthly ministry, Christ's role as an advocate is apparent, and he continues his role as our advocate in our contemporary concrete circumstances through the presence and work of the Holy Spirit. To participate in the suffering of others, consequently, is to

---

11. Anderson, *The Shape of Practical Theology*, 56.
12. Anderson, 44.
13. Anderson, 195.

be their advocate and to enable them to experience the presence and power of Christ alongside them in their needs and struggles.[14]

Finally, suffering can be the result of sin that demands repentance and submission to God. The lengthy allusion to retribution by Job's friends is not without any merit. Retribution was wrong in Job's case, but it may be right in some circumstances in our lives. Therefore, when we face hardship we should humbly and carefully examine if it is the result of our sins. Then, we must repent. It is interesting that passages which support retribution also include the call for repentance (e.g. Deut 30:15–20). In 1 and 2 Kings, the prophets called God's people to repent in order to avoid the national disaster which was to come. The call for repentance continues in the prophetic books and in the New Testament, where the main focus of the call goes beyond earthly suffering to eternal suffering. This response to suffering is also applicable for those who have not reconciled to God through Christ. People may be far from physical suffering, yet they constantly undergo spiritual suffering. This kind of suffering will ultimately lead them to God, the only person who can free them from the suffering that greatly afflicts their soul. It is precisely in this context that Luther proclaims that suffering, "in so far as it takes everything away from us, leaves us nothing but God: it cannot take God away from us, and actually brings him closer to us."[15]

As mentioned in the beginning, this dissertation is not a complete theological discussion of suffering, but it is a discussion of the Christian teachings on suffering in relationship to the Buddhist teachings on this topic. It is also not intended to be a comprehensive comparative study between the Buddhist and Christian concept of suffering. This study is simply an exercise in a trinitarian comparative theology of religions that compares and contrasts *the basic* Buddhalogy and Christian theology of suffering in order to formulate a Christian theology of suffering that is more relevant to the context of Theravada Buddhism in Thailand. While some of the questions about the subject matter of suffering have been answered, many questions still await Thai theologians who want to fulfill their calling in the Kingdom of Thailand. More careful studies need to be done, and more authentic Buddhist-Christian dialogue is needed. Nevertheless, I hope that this study will achieve

---

14. Anderson, *The Soul of Ministry*, 179.
15. WA 5.165.39–166.1.

its goal, even in a small step, of helping the Thai people, both Buddhists and Christians, better understand and experience the way to overcome the misery of life that we all share.

Bibliography

Andersen, Francis I. *Job: An Introduction and Commentary*. Tyndale Old Testament Commentaries, vol. 13. Downers Grove, IL: InterVarsity Press, 1976.

Anderson, Ray S. *The Shape of Practical Theology: Empowering Ministry with Theological Praxis*. Downers Grove, IL: InterVarsity Press, 2001.

———. *The Soul of Ministry: Forming Leader's for God's People*. Louisville, KY: Westminster John Knox Press, 1997.

———. *Theology, Death and Dying*. New York, NY: Basil Blackwell, 1986.

Anderson, Norman. *Christianity and World Religions: The Challenge of Pluralism*. Downers Grove, IL: InterVarsity Press, 1984.

Augustine. *The City of God*. Translated by Marcus Dods. New York: Modern Library, 1950.

Barth, Karl. *Church Dogmatics*. Translated by G. W. Bromiley and R. J. Ehrlich. Vol. 3. Edinburgh: T&T Clark, 1960.

Beker, Johan Christiaan. *Suffering and Hope: The Biblical Vision and the Human Predicament*. Philadelphia: Fortress Press, 1987.

Bhikkhu, Phra Buddhadāsa. *Idappaccayatā* [Conditionality]. Bangkok: Mental Health, 2001.

———. *Koomeu Manut* [Handbook of Human]. Bangkok: Buddhadhamma Foundation, 2006.

Billman, Kathleen D., and Daniel L. Migliore. *Rachel's Cry: Prayer of Lament and Rebirth of Hope*. Cleveland: United Church Press, 1999.

Bodhi, Bhikkhu. *The Noble Eightfold Path: The Way to the End of Suffering*. Kandy, Sri Lanka: Buddhist Publication Society, 1998.

Boonyakiat, Satanun. "The Divine Comedy." In *Global Dictionary of Theology: A Resource for the Worldwide Church*, edited by William A. Dyrness and Veli-Matti Kärkkäinen, 237–239. Downers Grove, IL: IVP Academic, 2008.

Browning, Don S. *A Fundamental Practical Theology: Descriptive and Strategic Proposals*. Minneapolis, MN: Fortress Press, 1991.

Brunner, Emil. *The Christian Doctrine of God*. Philadelphia: Westminster, 1950.

Burnett, David. *The Spirit of Buddhism*. Rev. edition. Grand Rapids, MI: Monarch Books, 2003.

Butr-Indr, Siddhi. *The Social Philosophy of Buddhism*. 6th edition. Bangkok: Mahamakut Buddhist University, 1999.

Calvin, John. *Genesis*. 1554. Edinburgh: Banner of Truth. 1984.

———. *Institutes of the Christian Religion*. Translated by John Allen. Vol. 1. 4th American edition. Philadelphia: Presbyterian Board of Publication, 1943.

Carson, D. A. *How Long, O Lord? Reflections on Suffering and Evil*. Grand Rapids, MI: Baker Book House, 1990.

Chandngarm, Saeng. *Arriyasatsee* [The Four Noble Truths]. Bangkok: Sangsan Books, 2001.

Chapman, Stephen B. "Reading the Bible as Witness: Divine Retribution in the Old Testament." *Perspectives in Religious Studies* 31, no. 2 (Summer 2004): 171–190.

Commission on Theological Concerns of the Christian Conference of Asia, eds. *Minjung Theology: People as the Subjects of History*. Rev. edition. Maryknoll, NY: Orbis Books, 1983.

The Church in the Present-Day: Transformation of Latin America in the Light of the Council. Second General Conference of Latin American Bishops. 2nd edition. Washington, DC: USCCM, 1973.

Clines, David J. A. "Job." In *New Bible Commentary: 21st Century Edition*, edited by D. A. Carson, R. T. France, J. A. Motyer and G. J. Wenham. Downers Grove, IL: InterVarsity Press, 1994.

———. *Job 1–20*. Waco, TX: Word Books, 1989.

———. *Job 21–37*. Waco, TX: Word Books, 2006.

Clooney, Francis X. "Comparative Theology: A Review of Recent Books (1989–1995)." *Theological Studies* 56, no. 3 (1995): 521–550.

———. *Hindu God, Christian God*. New York, NY: Oxford University Press, 2001.

———. *Theology after Vedānta: An Experiment in Comparative Theology*. Albany, NY: State University of New York Press, 1993.

Cobb, John B., and David Ray Griffin. *Process Theology: An Introductory Exposition*. Philadelphia, PA: Westminster Press, 1976.

Cone, James H. *A Black Theology of Liberation*. 20th anniversary edition. Maryknoll, NY: Orbis Books, 1990.

———. *God of the Oppressed*. New York, NY: Seabury Press, 1975.

Coomaraswamy, Ananda K. *Buddha and the Gospel of Buddhism*. New York: Harper & Row, 1964.

Copeland, E. Luther. "Christian Theology and World Religions." *Review and Expositor* 94 (1997): 423–435.

Corduan, Winfried. *A Tapestry of Faiths: The Common Threads between Christianity & World Religions*. Downers Grove, IL: InterVarsity Press, 2002.

Cove, Philip B., ed. *Webster's Third New International Dictionary of the English Language Unabridged*. Springfield, MA: Merriam-Webster, 1993.
Davis, John R. *Poles Apart? Contextualizing the Gospel*. Bangkok: Kanok Bannasan, 1993.
D'Costa, Gavin. *The Meeting of Religions and the Trinity*. Maryknoll, NY: Orbis, 2000.
Dhammanada, K. *What Buddhists Believe*. 4th edition. Kuala Lumpur, Malaysia: Buddhist Missionary Society, 2002.
Dhammapitaka, Phra (P. A. Payutto). *Arriyasat* [The Four Noble Truths]. Bangkok: Buddhadhamma Foundation, 2000.
———. *Buddhadhamma*. Bangkok: Mahachulalongkornrajavidyalaya University, 2003.
———. *Dictionary of Buddhism*. Bangkok: Mahachulalongkornrajavidyalaya University, 2003.
———. *Tri-Luk* [Three Characteristics of Existence]. Bangkok: Buddhadhamma Foundation, 2004.
Dillard, Raymond B. "Reward and Punishment in Chronicles: The Theology of Immediate Retribution." *Westminster Theological Journal* 46, no. 1 (Spring 1984): 164–172.
Dillard, Raymond B., and Tremper Longman III. *An Introduction to the Old Testament*. Grand Rapids, MI: Zondervan, 1994.
Duffy, Stephen J. "A Theology of Religions and/or Comparative Theology?" *Horizons* 26, no. 1 (1999): 105–115.
Dunn, James D. G. *Romans*. Dallas, TX: Word Books, 1988.
Dupuis, Jacques. *Toward a Christian Theology of Religious Pluralism*. Maryknoll, NY: Orbis Books, 1997.
Eichrodt, Walther. *Theology of the Old Testament*. Translated by John A. Baker. 2 vols. Philadelphia: Westminster Press, 1961.
Erickson, Millard J. *Christian Theology*. 2nd edition. Grand Rapids, MI: Baker, 1998.
Farley, Wendy. *Tragic Vision and Divine Compassion: A Contemporary Theodicy*. Louisville, KY: Westminster John Knox Press, 1990.
Flannery, Austin, ed. *Vatican Council II: The Conciliar and Post Conciliar Documents*. Grand Rapids, MI: Eerdmans, 1992.
Ford, David F. *Christian Wisdom: Desiring God and Learning in Love*. Cambridge: Cambridge University Press, 2007.
Foster, Richard J. *Celebration of Discipline: The Path to Spiritual Growth*. Rev. edition. San Francisco: Harper & Row, 1989.
Fox, Michael V. "The Meaning of Hebel for Qohelet." *JBL* 105, no. 3 (1986): 409–427.
Fredericks, James L. *Faith among Faiths: Christian Theology and Non-Christian Religions*. New York, NY: Paulist Press, 1999.

———. "A Universal Religious Experience? Comparative Theology as an Alternative to a Theology of Religions." *Horizons* 22 (1995): 67–87.

Fretheim, Terence E. "Genesis." In *The New Interpreter's Bible*, vol. 1, edited by Leander E. Keck, 321–674. Nashville, TN: Abingdon, 1994.

———. "כאב." In *New International Dictionary of Old Testament Theology & Exegesis*, vol. 2, edited by Willem VanGemeren. Grand Rapids, MI: Zondervan, 1997.

Gartner, Burkhard. "Suffer." In *New International Dictionary of New Testament Theology*, vol. 3, edited by Colin Brown. Grand Rapids, MI: Zondervan, 1986.

Gerstenberger, Erhard, and Wolfgang Schrage. *Suffering*. Nashville, TN: Abingdon, 1980.

Glatzer, Nahum N. *The Dimensions of Job: A Study and Selected Readings*. New York: Schocken Books, 1969.

Gordis, Robert. *The Book of God and Man: A Study of Job*. Chicago: University of Chicago Press, 1965.

Grenz, Stanley J. *Theology for the Community of God*. Grand Rapids, MI: Eerdmans, 2000.

Grenz, Stanley J., and John R. Franke. *Beyond Foundationalism: Shaping Theology in a Postmodern Context*. Louisville, KY: Westminster John Knox Press, 2001.

Grenz, Stanley J., and Roger E. Olson. *20th-Century Theology: God and the World in a Transitional Age*. Downers Grove, IL: InterVarsity Press, 1997.

Grimm, George. *The Doctrine of the Buddha: The Religion of Reason and Meditation*. Berlin: Akademie-Verlag, 1958.

Gross, Rita M., and Terry C. Muck, eds. *Christians Talk about Buddhist Meditation, Buddhists Talk about Christian Prayer*. New York: Continuum, 2003.

Gunton, Colin E. *The Triune Creator: A Historical and Systematic Study*. Grand Rapids, MI: Eerdmans, 1998.

Gutiérrez, Gustavo. *On Job: God-Talk and the Suffering of the Innocent*. Maryknoll, NY: Orbis Books, 1987.

———. *A Theology of Liberation: History, Politics, and Salvation*. Rev. edition. Maryknoll, NY: Orbis Books, 1988.

Hall, Douglas John. *God and Human Suffering: An Exercise in the Theology of the Cross*. Minneapolis, MN: Augsburg, 1986.

Hamilton, Victor P. *The Book of Genesis: Chapter 1–17*. Grand Rapids, MI: Eerdmans, 1995.

Hartley, John E. *The Book of Job*. Grand Rapids, MI: Eerdmans, 1988.

Hick, John. *A Christian Theology of Religions: The Rainbow of Faiths*. Louisville, KY: Westminster John Knox Press, 1995.

———. *Evil and the God of Love*. New York: Harper & Row, 1966.

———. *The Second Christianity*. London: SCM Press, 1983.

Hubbard, David Allan. *Proverbs*. Dallas, TX: Word Books, 1989.

Humphreys, Christmas. *Buddhism*. 3rd edition. London: Penguin Books, 1990.
Inbody, Tyron. *The Transforming God: An Interpretation of Suffering and Evil*. Louisville, KY: Westminster John Knox Press, 1997.
Irvin, Dale T., and Akintunde E. Akinade, eds. *The Agitated Mind of God: The Theology of Kosuke Koyama*. Maryknoll, NY: Orbis Books, 1996.
Johnson, Dale A. *Christ Mind, Buddha Heart*. Morrisville, NC: Lulu Press, 2005.
Kärkkäinen, Veli-Matti. *Christ and Reconciliation: A Constructive Christian Theology for the Pluralistic World, Volume 1*. Grand Rapids, MI: Eerdmans, 2013.
———. *Creation and Humanity: A Constructive Christian Theology for the Pluralistic World, Volume 3*. Grand Rapids, MI: Eerdmans, 2015.
———. *The Doctrine of God: A Global Introduction*. Grand Rapids, MI: Baker Academic, 2004.
———. *Doing the Work of Comparative Theology: A Primer for Christians*. Grand Rapids, MI: Eerdmans, 2020.
———. "'Evil, Love and the Left Hand of God': The Contribution of Luther's Theology of the Cross to an Evangelical Theology of Evil." *Evangelical Quarterly* 74, no. 3 (2002): 215–234.
———. *Hope and Community: A Constructive Christian Theology for the Pluralistic World, Volume 2*. Grand Rapids, MI: Eerdmans, 2017.
———. "How to Speak of the Spirit among Religions: Trinitarian 'Rules' for a Pneumatological Theology of Religions." *International Bulletin of Missionary Research* 30, no. 3 (July 2006): 121–127.
———. *An Introduction to the Theology of Religions: Biblical, Historical, and Contemporary Perspectives*. Downers Grove, IL: InterVarsity Press, 2003.
———. *Spirit and Salvation: A Constructive Christian Theology for the Pluralistic World, Volume 4*. Grand Rapids, MI: Eerdmans, 2016.
———. *Trinity and Religious Pluralism: The Doctrine of the Trinity in Christian Theology of Religions*. Aldershot, UK: Ashgate, 2004.
———. *Trinity and Revelation: A Constructive Christian Theology for the Pluralistic World, Volume 2*. Grand Rapids, MI: Eerdmans, 2014.
———. *The Trinity: Global Perspectives*. Louisville, KY: Westminster John Knox Press, 2007.
King, Winston L. *Buddhism and Christianity: Some Bridges of Understanding*. Philadelphia: Westminster Press, 1962.
Kitamori, Kazoh. "The Problem of Pain in Christology." In *Christ and the Younger Churches: Theological Contributions from Asia, Africa and Latin America*, edited by Georg F. Vicedom, 83–90. London: SPCK, 1972.
———. *Theology of the Pain of God*. Richmond, VA: John Knox Press, 1965.
Knitter, Paul F. *Introducing Theologies of Religions*. Maryknoll, NY: Orbis Books, 2002.

———. *Jesus and the Other Names: Christian Mission and Global Responsibility.* Maryknoll, NY: Orbis Books, 1996.

———. *No Other Name? A Critical Survey of Christian Attitudes toward the World Religions.* Maryknoll, NY: Orbis Books, 1985.

———. *One Earth, Many Religions: Multifaith Dialogue and Global Responsibility.* Maryknoll, NY: Orbis Books, 1995.

Koch, Klaus. "Is There a Doctrine of Retribution in the Old Testament?" In *Theodicy in the Old Testament*, edited by James L. Crenshaw, 57–87. Philadelphia: Fortress Press, 1983.

Koyama, Kosuke. *No Handle on the Cross: An Asian Meditation on the Crucified Mind.* Maryknoll, NY: Orbis Books, 1977.

———. *Three Mile an Hour God: Biblical Reflections.* Maryknoll, NY: Orbis Books, 1980.

———. *Water Buffalo Theology.* 25th anniversary revised edition. Maryknoll, NY: Orbis Books, 1999.

Kusalasaya, Karuna, ed. *Buddhism in Thailand: Its Past and Its Present.* Kandy, Sri Lanka: Buddhist Publication Society, 2005.

Kushner, Harold S. *When Bad Things Happen to Good People.* New York, NY: Avon Books, 1983.

Lewis, C. S. *The Problem of Pain.* New York, NY: Macmillan, 1962.

Loewenich, Walther von. *Luther's Theology of the Cross.* Minneapolis: Augsburg, 1976.

Longman, Tremper. *The Book of Ecclesiastes.* Grand Rapids, MI: Eerdmans, 1998.

Lorgunpai, Seree. "World Lover, World Leaver: The Book of Ecclesiastes and Thai Buddhism." PhD diss., New College, University of Edinburgh, 1995.

Luther, Martin. *D. Martin Luthers Werke. Kritische Gesamtausgabe. Schriften.* 68 vols. Weimar: Herman Böhlaus Nachofolger, 1883–1999.

———. *Luther's Works.* Edited by Jaroslav Jan Pelikan, Hilton C. Oswald, and Helmut T. Lehmann. American Edition. 56 vols. Saint Louis: Concordia, 1955.

McDermott, Gerald R. *Can Evangelicals Learn from World Religions? Jesus, Revelation, and Religious Traditions.* Downers Grove, IL: InterVarsity Press, 2000.

McDermott, Gerald R., and Harold A. Netland. *A Trinitarian Theology of Religions: An Evangelical Proposal.* New York: Oxford University Press, 2014.

McGrath, Alister E. *Christian Spirituality.* Malden, MA: Blackwell, 1999.

———. *Luther's Theology of the Cross: Martin Luther's Theological Breakthrough.* Grand Rapids, MI: Baker, 1994.

McKeating, Henry. "The Central Issue of the Book of Job." *Expository Times* 82 (May 1971): 244–247.

Michaelis, Wilhelm. "Πασχω." In *Theological Dictionary of the New Testament*, edited by Gerhard Kittel, Gerhard Friedrich, and Geoffrey William Bromiley. Grand Rapids, MI: Eerdmans, 1985.

Míguez Bonino, José. *Doing Theology in a Revolutionary Situation*. Confrontation Books. Philadelphia: Fortress Press, 1975.

Moltmann, Jürgen. "Crucified God." *Theology Today* 31 (1974): 6–18.

———. *The Crucified God: The Cross of Christ as the Foundation and Criticism of Christian Theology*. Translated by R. A. Wilson and John Bowden. Minneapolis, MN: Fortress Press, 1993.

———. *The Spirit of Life: A Universal Affirmation*. Translated by Margaret Kohl. Minneapolis, MN: Fortress Press, 2001.

———. *The Trinity and the Kingdom: The Doctrine of God*. Translated by Margaret Kohl. Minneapolis, MN: Fortress Press, 1993.

Moo, Douglas J. *The Epistle to the Romans*. Grand Rapids, MI: Eerdmans, 1996.

Muck, Terry C. "Theology of Religions after Knitter and Hick: Beyond the Paradigm." *Interpretation* 61, no. 1 (January 2007): 7–22.

Murphy, Roland E. *The Tree of Life: An Exploration of Biblical Wisdom Literature*. 3rd edition. Grand Rapids, MI: Eerdmans, 2002.

Muthukan, Pin. *Buddha-Sart* [Buddhalogy]. Vol. 3. Bangkok: Mahamakut Buddhist University Press, 1992.

———. *Buddha-Sart* [Buddhalogy]. Vol. 2. Bangkok: Mahamakut Buddhist University Press, 1992.

———. *Golwitee Gae Tuk* [Suffering Solving Strategies]. Bangkok: Sangsun Book, 1998.

National Statistical Office. *Statistical Yearbook of Thailand 2006*. Bangkok: National Statistical Office, 2006.

Netland, Harold A. *Encountering Religious Pluralism: The Challenge to Christian Faith & Mission*. Downers Grove, IL: InterVarsity Press, 2001.

Newbigin, Lesslie. *The Gospel in a Pluralist Society*. Grand Rapids, MI: Eerdmans, 1989.

Newsom, Carol A. "The Book of Job." In *The New Interpreter's Bible*. Vol. 4, 317–637. Nashville, TN: Abingdon, 1996.

Nowell, Robert. *What a Modern Catholic Believes about Death*. Chicago, IL: Thomas Moore Press, 1972.

Nyanatiloka, ed. *Buddhist Dictionary: Manual of Buddhist Terms and Doctrines*. Kandy, Sri Lanka: Buddhist Publication Society, 1980.

Okholm, Dennis L., and Timothy R. Phillips. *Christians and Religious Pluralism*. London: SCM Press, 1983.

Oldenberg, Hermann. *Buddha: His Life, His Doctrine, His Order*. Translated by William Hoey. New Delhi: Lancer International, 1992.

Orchard, Ronald K. *Witness in Six Continents: Records of the Meeting of the Commission on World Mission and Evangelism of the World Council of Churches Held in Mexico City, December 8th to 19th, 1963.* London: Edinburgh House Press, 1964.

Panikkar, Raimundo. *The Unknown Christ of Hinduism: Towards an Ecumenical Christophany.* Revised edition. Maryknoll, NY: Orbis Books, 1981.

Pannenberg, Wolfhart. *Systematic Theology.* 3 vols. Grand Rapids, MI: Eerdmans, 1991–1998.

Petchsongkram, Wan. *Talk in the Shade of the Bo Tree: Some Observations on Communicating the Christian Faith in Thailand.* Translated by Frances E. Hudgins. Bangkok: Thai Gospel Press, 1975.

Pieris, Aloysius. *An Asian Theology of Liberation.* Maryknoll, NY: Orbis Books, 1988.

Pinnock, Clark H. *A Wideness in God's Mercy: The Finality of Jesus Christ in a World of Religions.* Grand Rapids, MI: Zondervan, 1992.

Plantinga, Alvin. *God, Freedom, and Evil.* New York, NY: Harper & Row, 1974.

Preuss, Horst Dietrich. *Old Testament Theology.* Louisville, KY: Westminster John Knox Press, 1995.

Rad, Gerhard von. *Genesis: A Commentary.* Rev. ed. Old Testament Library. Philadelphia: Westminster Press, 1972.

———. *Old Testament Theology.* 2 vols. London: SCM Press, 1975.

Rahula, Walpola. "Bodhisattva Ideal in Buddhism." In *Gems of Buddhist Wisdom*, 461–471. Kuala Lumpur, Malaysia: Buddhist Missionary Society, 1996.

———. "Theravada – Mahayana Buddhism." In *Gems of Buddhist Wisdom.* Kuala Lumpur, Malaysia: Buddhist Missionary Society, 1996.

———. *What the Buddha Taught.* Revised edition. Bangkok: Haw Trai Foundation, 2006.

Richard, Lucien. *What Are They Saying about the Theology of Suffering?* New York, NY: Paulist Press, 1992.

Rowley, H. H. "The Intellectual Versus the Spiritual Solution." In *The Dimensions of Job: A Study and Selected Readings*, edited by Nahum N. Glatzer, 123–128. New York: Schocken Books, 1969.

Samartha, S. J. *One Christ, Many Religions: Toward a Revised Christology.* Maryknoll, NY: Orbis Books, 1991.

Schebera, Richard. "Comparative Theology: A New Method of Interreligious Dialogue." *Dialogue and Alliance* 17, no. 1 (Spring/Summer 2003): 7–18.

Schreiner, Thomas R. *Romans.* Grand Rapids, MI: Baker Books, 1998.

Segundo, Juan Luis. *The Liberation of Theology.* Maryknoll, NY: Orbis Books, 1976.

Simundson, Daniel J. "Suffering." In *Anchor Bible Dictionary*, edited by David Noel Freedman. Vol. 6. New York, NY: Doubleday, 1992.

Skinner, John. *A Critical and Exegetical Commentary on Genesis*. 2nd edition. Edinburgh: T&T Clark, 1930.

Sölle, Dorothee. *Suffering*. Philadelphia, PA: Fortress Press, 1975.

Song, Choan-Seng. *Third-Eye Theology: Theology in Formation in Asian Settings*. Revised edition. Maryknoll, NY: Orbis Books, 1991.

Surin, Kenneth. *Theology and the Problem of Evil*. New York, NY: Blackwell, 1986.

Swart, I., and Robin Wakely. "צוק." In *New International Dictionary of Old Testament Theology & Exegesis*, vol. 3, edited by Willem VanGemeren. Grand Rapids, MI: Zondervan, 1997.

Tennent, Timothy C. *Christianity at the Religious Roundtable: Evangelicalism in Conversation with Hinduism, Buddhism, and Islam*. Grand Rapids, MI: Baker Academic, 2002.

Thomas, M. M. "Christology and Pluralistic Consciousness." *International Bulletin of Missionary Research* 10, no. 3 (1986): 390–391.

Thompson, David. "עמל." In *New International Dictionary of Old Testament Theology & Exegesis*, vol. 3, edited by Willem VanGemeren. Grand Rapids, MI: Zondervan, 1997.

Tillich, Paul. *Christianity and the Encounter of World Religions*. Minneapolis: Fortress Press, 1994.

———. *Systematic Theology*. Vol. 2. Chicago: University of Chicago Press, 1957.

Tracy, David. *The Analogical Imagination: Christian Theology and the Culture of Pluralism*. New York, NY: Crossroad, 1981.

———. "Comparative Theology." In *The Encyclopedia of Religion*, vol. 14, edited by Mircea Eliade and Charles J. Adams, 446–455. New York, NY: Macmillan, 1987.

Travis, Stephen. *Christ and the Judgment of God: Divine Retribution in the New Testament*. Basingstoke, UK: Marshall Pickering, 1986.

Ukosakul, Chaiyun. *A Turn from the Wheel to the Cross: Crucial Considerations for Discipling New Thai Christians* (forthcoming).

The United Nations Development Program. *Human Development Report 2007/2008*. New York, NY: United Nations Development Program, 2007.

Vajirananavarorasa, Somdet Phra Maha Samana Chao Krom Phraya. *Dhammawijarn* [Dhamma Analysis]. Bangkok: Mahamakut Buddhist University Press, 1920.

Vawter, Bruce. *On Genesis: A New Reading*. Garden City, NY: Doubleday, 1977.

Volf, Miroslav. *The End of Memory: Remembering Rightly in a Violent World*. Grand Rapids, MI: Eerdmans, 2006.

Ward, Keith. *Religion and Community*. Oxford: Clarendon Press, 2000.

———. *Religion and Creation*. Oxford: Clarendon Press, 1996.

———. *Religion and Human Nature*. Oxford: Clarendon Press, 1998.

———. *Religion and Revelation: A Theology of Revelation in the World's Religions*. Oxford: Clarendon Press, 1994.

Waters, Larry J. "Reflections on Suffering from the Book of Job." *Bibliotheca Sacra* 154 (1997): 436–451.

Webster, Douglas D. "Liberation Theology." In *Evangelical Dictionary of Theology*, edited by Walter A. Elwell. Grand Rapids, MI: Baker Books, 1984.

Wehmeier, Sally, ed. *Oxford Advanced Learner's Dictionary of Current English*. Oxford: Oxford University Press, 2000.

Wenham, Gordon J. *Genesis 1–15*. Waco, TX: Word Books, 1987.

Westermann, Claus. *Creation*. Translated by J. J. Scullion. Philadelphia: Fortress Press, 1974.

———. *Genesis 1–11: A Commentary*. Translated by John Scullion. Minneapolis, MN: Augsburg, 1984.

Whitney, Barry L. *What Are They Saying about God and Evil?* New York, NY: Paulist Press, 1989.

Willard, Dallas. *The Spirit of the Disciplines: Understanding How God Changes Lives*. San Francisco: Harper & Row, 1988.

Wood, James. *Job and the Human Situation*. London: Geoffrey Bles, 1966.

Yong, Amos. *Beyond the Impasse: Toward a Pneumatological Theology of Religions*. Grand Rapids, MI: Baker Academic, 2003.

———. *Discerning the Spirit(s): A Pentecostal-Charismatic Contribution to Christian Theology of Religions*. Sheffield: Sheffield Academic Press, 2000.

Langham Literature, with its publishing work, is a ministry of Langham Partnership.

Langham Partnership is a global fellowship working in pursuit of the vision God entrusted to its founder John Stott –

> *to facilitate the growth of the church in maturity and Christ-likeness through raising the standards of biblical preaching and teaching.*

Our vision is to see churches in the Majority World equipped for mission and growing to maturity in Christ through the ministry of pastors and leaders who believe, teach and live by the word of God.

Our mission is to strengthen the ministry of the word of God through:
- nurturing national movements for biblical preaching
- fostering the creation and distribution of evangelical literature
- enhancing evangelical theological education

especially in countries where churches are under-resourced.

Our ministry

Langham Preaching partners with national leaders to nurture indigenous biblical preaching movements for pastors and lay preachers all around the world. With the support of a team of trainers from many countries, a multi-level programme of seminars provides practical training, and is followed by a programme for training local facilitators. Local preachers' groups and national and regional networks ensure continuity and ongoing development, seeking to build vigorous movements committed to Bible exposition.

Langham Literature provides Majority World preachers, scholars and seminary libraries with evangelical books and electronic resources through publishing and distribution, grants and discounts. The programme also fosters the creation of indigenous evangelical books in many languages, through writer's grants, strengthening local evangelical publishing houses, and investment in major regional literature projects, such as one volume Bible commentaries like the *Africa Bible Commentary* and the *South Asia Bible Commentary*.

Langham Scholars provides financial support for evangelical doctoral students from the Majority World so that, when they return home, they may train pastors and other Christian leaders with sound, biblical and theological teaching. This programme equips those who equip others. Langham Scholars also works in partnership with Majority World seminaries in strengthening evangelical theological education. A growing number of Langham Scholars study in high quality doctoral programmes in the Majority World itself. As well as teaching the next generation of pastors, graduated Langham Scholars exercise significant influence through their writing and leadership.

To learn more about Langham Partnership and the work we do visit **langham.org**

www.ingramcontent.com/pod-product-compliance
Lightning Source LLC
Chambersburg PA
CBHW070806230426
43665CB00017B/2507